THE ABC's of 1-2-3

Lotus

Spreadsheet
DATA BASE
Graphics

worksheet
Global
Column

File
Retrieve
Esc
Patch.DSS

THE ABC's of 1-2-3®

Second Edition

Chris Gilbert and Laurie Williams

Cover design by Thomas Ingalls + Associates
Cover illustration by Patrice Larue
Book design by Nina Hoecker

Library of Congress Card Number: 86-61485
ISBN 0-89588-355-4
Manufactured in the United States of America
10 9 8

To R.J.L.

—L.W.

To Mom for the computer.

—C.G.

ACKNOWLEDGEMENTS

Without Janos Gereben, *The ABC's of 1-2-3* only would have been another "good idea." Thanks also to the people at SYBEX: Jim Hill for his patience during the book's growing pains, Laurel Ornitz for her dogged attention to detail, and Joel Kreisman for his technical expertise. Finally, many thanks to Rick Nielsen whose timely appearance and positive thinking were crucial.

For this revised edition, I would like to thank Fred Friedman for his valuable suggestions. Thanks too to the people at SYBEX who helped with this edition: David Kolodney, editor; Ray Keefer, technical support; Olivia Shinomoto, word processing; Donna Scanlon, typesetting; and Jon Strickland, proofreading. And thanks to Nancy Mulvany for doing the index.

CONTENTS

CHAPTER THREE 134

Graphing the Worksheet

CHAPTER FOUR 172

Data-base Management

PREFACE

If you've never used Lotus 1-2-3 before and want to learn how, this book is for you. Written in nontechnical, everyday English, it is a series of lessons that introduce 1-2-3, simply and practically. As the product of two authors—one with the technical background to teach corporate users, the other a novice who never before used the program—the book is a readable, easy-to-follow set of explanations and instructions that anyone can follow, including those who have never operated a computer.

This book is written for use with IBM and IBM-compatible personal computers. This includes the IBM PC, the IBM PC/XT, the IBM PC/AT, the Compaq Desktop and Portable Computers, and other compatible computers. If you are using another computer that is compatible with the IBM, your keyboard may differ slightly. For example, depending on the computer, the key that instructs 1-2-3 to perform an operation may be labeled with a symbol, such as an arrow, or by a word, such as Return or Enter. If you don't know which keys on your keyboard correspond to the keys in the book's instructions, refer to your computer manual.

This book is written especially for use with Version 2, the upgraded version of 1-2-3. If you have the earlier version of the program, bypass the installation procedure in Chapter 1, and begin with the lessons in Chapter 2. You will notice some discrepancies; however, they are minor. (For a detailed list of the differences between the two versions, refer to your 1-2-3 *Getting Started* pamphlet.)

The book is designed so that you can begin working immediately. The first chapter, "Getting Started," consists of four sections. If you just purchased 1-2-3 and have never used it on your computer, follow the instructions that fit your computer's disk system, floppy or hard. This will take approximately one-half to one hour, and it is recommended that it be done in one sitting.

If 1-2-3 has already been set up to operate on your computer, but you do not have an extra, specially prepared disk on which to save your work, read the introductory explanations for each of the four sections and follow only the instructions in Section 1 under the subheading, "How to Format a Diskette."

If 1-2-3 is set up to work on your computer and you have disks already prepared on which to store your work, skim the first four sections, without completing the instructions, then begin with Section 5, "Bringing Up the Worksheet on Your Screen."

The introduction of new ingredients, such as various keys and commands, is staggered throughout the book. Every time a new ingredient is introduced, it is noted after the section title, right before the text.

INTRODUCTION

Does the following sound familiar?

You're working on a report, and you need to compile a lot of numbers. Your employer just purchased the Lotus 1-2-3 software program, and you can't wait to start calculating your figures, forecasting profits, and creating fancy graphs. You've never operated a computer and, although they do sound familiar, you have to admit you don't know what disks, drives, and data-base management really are.

"No problem," you tell yourself, "with the manual, I'll be able to do it in no time."

Two hours later, you're still trying to figure out how to get the program to run.

"And I thought all I had to do was slip in the program, turn on the machine, and start entering . . . ," you mumble under your breath.

If this sounds familiar, you're not alone. You're in the company of other somewhat confused first-time computer users, among whom are small business owners who need to keep track of inventory, college administrators who need an effective means of presenting budgets to the board, division sales managers who need to forecast sales over the next six months, shop owners who want to determine which items are most profitable, teachers who want to analyze test scores to evaluate innovative programs, accounts-receivable clerks who need to mail hundreds of bills every month, and the entrepreneur who wants to open a chain of stores but first must gather information about particular neighborhoods. In fact, anyone who is even vaguely aware of what 1-2-3 can do will be anxious to see immediate results.

What can 1-2-3 do?

On its own, nothing. But with your data input and instructions, you have at your fingertips a powerful, integrated program that combines three programs in one: a spreadsheet (or worksheet) program, a graphics program, and a data-base management program. A closer look at each component best illustrates how you can conveniently put several capabilities to work without having to use a new program or a new set of instructions.

The first and most sophisticated of the three, the *spreadsheet,* electronically duplicates an accountant's or bookkeeper's tools: a ledger pad, a pencil, an eraser, and a calculator. With the spreadsheet, however, you enter and correct figures by typing on a keyboard, rather than writing with a pencil, and you view the figures on a computer screen, or monitor, rather than read a ledger pad.

Once you enter data on the spreadsheet, you can apply a variety of calculations—from simple addition, subtraction, multiplication, and division to trigonometric, statistical, and business calculations. With the spreadsheet you can prepare such things as:

- Budgets
- Annual Reports
- Portfolio Analyses
- Accounts Payable and Receivable
- Production Schedules
- Invoices
- Income Statements
- Loan Analyses
- Tax Statements

In addition to entering and calculating numbers, the spreadsheet responds to "what if" scenarios. For example, let's assume you own a retail business and you want to know how a holiday sale will affect your profit. You start by entering the current prices of the items you are selling, the number of items for sale, and the cost of each item. After entering a formula to calculate your projected profit without the sale, you can recalculate to answer the question: If I put several items on sale for 30 percent less, how will this affect profit? As you enter each new figure, 1-2-3 automatically recalculates profit and displays the answer on the screen.

But that's only the beginning. By expanding this particular worksheet to include overhead and salaries, you can ask more questions, such as: How will a drop in overhead or an increase in salaries affect profit? And, if you want to discuss the possibilities with others in the office, you can print copies of each version of the worksheet.

The second component, *graphics,* enables you to create various kinds of graphs, such as a bar or line graph, from the information on the worksheet. Therefore, continuing with the previous example, the retail profits before and after the sale can be viewed on a bar graph where they can be compared visually. The visual impact of the graph makes it an effective communication tool since it is simpler to interpret a graph than it is to interpret columns of numbers—and not so boring.

Although you may not realize it, you probably have in your possession several examples of *data-base management,* 1-2-3's third component. Do you keep an address book in your briefcase? What about a notebook where you tally up your work-related car mileage and bridge tolls? Do you keep your paycheck stubs in order? Each is a source of information, as well as a means of managing it; hence, each is a data base. Other examples are personnel files, inventory lists, customer records, and "to do" lists. The major difference between managing any of these examples and using data-base management to do it for you is that 1-2-3 can instantly retrieve and reorganize all the information without consuming time by turning pages or searching through files.

Another advantage of 1-2-3's data-base management is that it can retrieve and organize by using any one piece of the data base. For example, consider a traditional phone book as a data base. You can find the phone number of a friend only if you know your friend's last name. With 1-2-3, however, you could find his phone number by entering his address or the first three numbers of his phone number. 1-2-3 can index every category of information: first name, last name, address, and phone number. Plugging in any one piece brings up the entire entry.

In addition to the three main components, 1-2-3 offers a fourth, more complex feature: *keyboard macros,* which simplify tasks that you find yourself doing over and over again, such as typing the twelve months of the year across the top of every budget you prepare. Rather than retype the headings each time, you can program your computer to do this for you automatically with two keystrokes. The set of instructions included in the keystrokes is called a macro. Keyboard macros are especially helpful on forms such as invoices that require you to type the same information hundreds or thousands of times.

A note of warning, though. Macros are considered an advanced use of 1-2-3. While there are some simple macros that a beginner can quickly put to use, it helps to be familiar with programming procedures.

Now, let's take a closer look at how the four features interact with each other. To do so, assume you are an accountant for a firm that manufactures industrial equipment for fertilizer plants. It's October, and you are conscientiously preparing some figures for your annual report, which you will present at the January board meeting. An early draft should save time, you think to yourself.

You start by finding the dollar values of your assets and liabilities. 1-2-3 calculates your total inventory value from a list in the data base, which includes the number of items on hand and their value at cost. From several other worksheets, you transfer more figures, such as cash on hand, accounts payable and receivable, fixed assets, and outstanding loans. Once you've calculated net worth, you want to see what percentage of total assets is represented by inventory. With a few keystrokes, a pie chart represents the unsold inventory as a large part of assets. (So far, everything you've done has required only a few keystrokes since you've speeded up this annual task by using macros.)

But it's only October. What will happen to net worth if half of the inventory is shipped C.O.D. before the end of the year? 1-2-3 recalculates the figures, and you view the graph again. The results are more positive. But how do the results compare to figures for the past five years? From previous years' budgets, you transfer the end-of-year figures for all five years to a line graph, and again the results are impressive. After adding some last-minute labels, you print several copies and show them to the sales-department managers to see if they agree with your projections.

What can this book do for you?

Because 1-2-3 is a powerful business tool, it can be complex. If you've never used a computer before, just learning how to get started will take time. The program manual and its accompanying on-screen lessons are excellent reference tools, but each requires several hours of reading before you can begin to take advantage of 1-2-3's capabilities. The manual does not help the novice make use of the program from the very start, and the on-screen lessons do not leave room for experimentation. Each explains how to operate the program, but not how to apply it.

This book does both. In a sense, this book, like the program, is integrated. It provides step-by-step instructions that get you started immediately while it explains each step. As a hands-on introduction for the novice, it is meant to be read while you operate the computer. You will produce results while you learn and, since you will learn how as well as why, you will be able to apply what you learn to your own work.

Since each step builds on preceding steps, it is necessary to follow them in order. However, after you complete the lessons once, you can use this book as a reference guide. By the time you finish reading it, you will have built a worksheet, displayed the worksheet as a graph, built a data base, and simplified several operations using some simple macros. Along the way, you will accomplish many more related tasks, such as calculating data within the worksheet and printing reports.

Never Used a Computer Before?

No problem. Everything is explained, step-by-step, throughout the book. A quick overview of how your computer works, though, will set you straight from the very start.

What is normally referred to as a computer is actually a computer system which consists of microprocessors (which include the brains and memory), a display screen, a printer, a keyboard, and storage devices such as disks. These, and any other pieces of equipment you might add to your system, are called *hardware.*

In order for the entire system to operate, it needs instructions, or *software programs.* The basic set of instructions needed to run the computer is referred to as *DOS,* for disk operating system. Another example of a software program is 1-2-3 itself.

Programs are generally stored on floppy disks (also called diskettes) or hard disks. 1-2-3 can be used on both floppy-disk and hard-disk systems. Floppy disks are thin, circular sheets of plastic like the ones your 1-2-3 program came on. Looking like undersized 45 rpm records, they are enclosed in square jackets to protect them from damage. The plastic is coated with a substance that the computer encodes with magnetic impulses, much as a stereo tape deck encodes music on a tape cassette. Hard disks operate similarly, but instead of being thin and soft, they are rigid.

A floppy disk may be single-sided or double-sided; with a double-sided disk, you can store information on both sides. 1-2-3 comes on double-sided diskettes, each of which can store about 180 pages of double-spaced text. In contrast, a hard disk can store about 5,000 pages of text.

Unless your computer can find its DOS operating instructions on a floppy or hard disk and place them in its memory (or RAM, for *random access memory*), the computer is useless for programs such as 1-2-3. One of the disk drives must *read* a disk on which DOS resides. Depending on the kind of disk drives you have, DOS may be stored on a floppy disk that you insert in one of the two floppy-disk drives or it may be stored on a hard disk that is permanently sealed in a hard-disk drive.

Computers that use 1-2-3 have either one or two floppy-disk drives or a floppy drive paired with a hard-disk drive. Each drive has a one-letter name to identify it. The floppy-disk drives are called drive A and drive B. The hard-disk drive is drive C.

Because the computer's memory is short-term; it forgets everything as soon as you turn it off, including how to operate. Therefore, DOS must be read from disk to memory every time you want to operate your computer. This is commonly referred to as *bootstrapping* or *booting* the computer because, the machine pulls itself up by its bootstraps.

123

Chapter One

GETTING STARTED

1

Preparing Blank Disks and Making Backup Copies of 1-2-3: For Floppy-Disk Systems Only

FEATURING:

disk formatting, the Enter, Backspace, and Shift keys

Imagine how frustrated you would feel if you had just spilled a cup of hot tea on the 1-2-3 Install or PrintGraph disk, or both. To be sure that you don't risk losing them and your investment, it is always advisable to make copies of the original 1-2-3 disks. Then, if you destroy or lose one of your copies, you will still have the original.

1-2-3 allows you to make copies of all of the disks except the System disk and its backup copy. There is a small portion on each of these two disks that cannot be copied. If you could copy them, it would be possible to copy the entire program without having to purchase it.

Before you copy the program disks, you will first prepare all five diskettes. In order to copy files onto a new floppy disk, it must be prepared or *formatted.* This needs to be done only once to each new diskette. Never format a disk that contains valuable data; it will all be erased.

When a disk is formatted, it is divided into sectors, much like slices of a pie, and tracks, which are like grooves in a record. These sectors and tracks store information in *files.* A *directory* of file names is created from all the files stored on a particular disk.

Have five blank diskettes on hand before you begin.

If you have a hard-drive computer skip to the next section.

How to Format a Diskette

To format disks and make backup copies of the originals, you will use three keys in addition to letters and numbers: Enter, Backspace, and Shift, shown in Figure 1.1. When you press Enter, 1-2-3 is instructed to perform any instructions you have typed and to proceed to the next step. When you press Backspace, you erase what you have just typed, one character at a time to the left. The Shift key, pressed in conjunction with another key, types uppercase letters and makes available all the punctuation and symbols on the top halves of the keys.

Do not use the 1-2-3 Program disks for the next steps on formatting disks.

1. Place the operating system (DOS) disk for your computer in drive A, the one on the left if the drives are side by side, or the one on top if the drives are one above the other. To ensure that you don't erase the DOS disk, use a copy if you have one. Do not touch any of the disk's exposed areas and be sure that the long, oval slot is towards the back of the computer. The label should face up if the disk is inserted horizontally or to the left if the disk is inserted vertically.
2. Close the drive door.

***Figure 1.1:** The Enter, Backspace, and Shift keys*

3. Turn on the computer. Wait a few moments. A whirring sound is emitted from the drive as the DOS programs are read into the computer.
4. Enter the date and time if necessary. (Some computers automatically display the date and time since they contain internal clocks. If your computer does this, you do not need to type them in.) Although various ways of typing the date are acceptable, one is recommended for simplicity's sake. If it were July 3, 1987, you would enter:

   7-3-87

   If you make a mistake, use the Backspace key to correct it.
5. Press Enter. If the word **Invalid** appears, you've made an error. Repeat step four and press Enter.
6. Type in the current time. Again, one way is recommended. If it were 8:20 in the morning, you would enter:

   8:20

   If you prefer, you can add seconds after another colon; however, seconds, as well as minutes, are optional. When it is after 12 noon, hours are entered the way they are referred to in the military: 1:00 PM is 13:00, 4:15 PM is 16:15, and so on.
7. Press Enter. The **A>** prompt will appear on the screen. It means you are using drive A.
8. If you have two floppy-disk drives, after the **A>**, type:

   FORMAT B:

   If you have one floppy-disk drive, after the **A>**, type:

   FORMAT

   (You may type using uppercase or lowercase letters.)
9. Press Enter.
10. If you have two floppy-disk drives, place a new disk in drive B. If you have a single floppy-disk drive, replace the DOS diskette in drive A with a new diskette.
11. Press any key. When the red light(s) on the disk drive(s) goes off, indicating that formatting has finished, remove the newly formatted diskette and set it aside.
12. After the **Format another (Y,N)?** prompt appears, type:

    Y

13. Insert a second new diskette in the appropriate drive and repeat the same process until the remaining blank diskettes are all formatted.
14. When you have finished formatting and the **Format another (Y,N)?** message appears, type:

    N

    The A> appears on the screen.
15. Put blank labels on the diskettes and proceed to back up the program diskettes.

How to Back Up Your 1-2-3 Program Disks

After removing the six floppy disks that come with 1-2-3 from their sealed envelope, set aside four: the Utility disk, the Install Library disk, A View of 1-2-3, and the PrintGraph disk. (As explained, you can't back up the System disk since it is copy-protected. Instead, you receive a backup with the 1-2-3 package.)

1. Have on hand the Utility disk, Install Library disk, PrintGraph disk, and A view of 1-2-3 disk. We recommend that you place a gummed write-protect tab over the small rectangular slot cut in on the right side of each diskette. This tab protects the disk from being erased accidentally, but it allows you to copy information from the diskette. To store new information on the diskette, you would have to remove the tab. Write-protect tabs come with your 1-2-3 disks and are included in boxes of new blank diskettes.
2. Place any of the four 1-2-3 program diskettes listed above in drive A.
3. Place a formatted diskette in drive B.
4. Whether you have one or two floppy drives, after the A>, type:

    COPY A:*.* B:

    If you have a single floppy drive, your computer treats drive A as if it were both drives A and B. You simply need to swap the disks in the drive as you are prompted.
5. Press Enter. This command tells your computer to copy all of the files on the diskette in drive A to the diskette in drive B. As the files are copied, their names appear on the screen.

6. When the screen tells you copying is complete, remove both disks. Write the name of the disk on the label, being sure not to use a metal-tipped writing tool, such as a ball-point pen. This can harm the diskette.
7. Repeat steps 2 through 6 until all four program diskettes have been copied.
8. Place the DOS diskette in drive A. Place the System diskette in drive B.
9. Whether you have one or two floppy drives, after the **A>**, type:

   COPY A:COMMAND.COM B:

10. Press Enter. This command copies the command.com file from the DOS disk to the program disk. This will enable you to perform DOS-level tasks, such as erasing and renaming files, from within 1-2-3, rather than having to exit to the operating system.
11. Repeat the previous three steps for the backup System disk, and the copies of the PrintGraph and Utility disks, and A View of 1-2-3. When you are finished, the **A>** appears on the screen.

2
Storing 1-2-3 on a Hard-Disk Drive

The fastest way to run 1-2-3 is from a hard-disk drive. Once the steps in this section are completed, you will be able to run 1-2-3 from your hard disk, though you will still need to place the System disk in drive A in order to start using 1-2-3. However, after completing section four, you will be able to run 1-2-3 from the hard-disk drive alone.

If you have a hard-disk system and you anticipate wanting to copy information from your hard disk onto a diskette for use on another computer, you will need a formatted diskette. To format a diskette, complete the instructions in Section 1 under "How to Format a Diskette." Where indicated, follow the instructions for single-drive systems.

How to Store 1-2-3 on a Hard-Disk Drive

1. With drive A empty, turn your computer on. In order to proceed, your hard disk must have DOS on it already. You will know that it does if the date or **C>** prompt appears on the screen when you turn the computer on. If it doesn't, you need to place DOS on the hard disk. To do so, consult the manual for DOS.

2. Enter the date and time if applicable. (See Section 1, steps 4 through 6 for floppy-disk systems.)

3. Press Enter. The **C>** prompt appears on the screen.

4. Place the 1-2-3 System disk in Drive A, the floppy drive. In the following steps, you will be placing 1-2-3 on your hard disk. You now have the option of putting 1-2-3 in a separate area of the disk in order to organize the disk more efficiently. This area is called a *subdirectory.*

You should consider doing this if, for example, you plan to store another software program, such as a word-processing program, on the disk. (For additional information about subdirectories, refer to the appendix "Using 1-2-3 on Hard-Disk Systems.")

5. To make a directory named 123, after the C>, type:

   MD \123

6. Press Enter.
7. To change to the new directory, type:

   CD \123

8. Press Enter.
9. After the C>, type:

   COPY A:*.*

10. Press Enter. This command copies all the files on the floppy disk onto the hard disk.
11. Once the copy is complete, replace the System disk with any of the four remaining disks and repeat steps 9 and 10. (Do not bother to copy the backup System disk since it's a duplicate of the System disk.) Because 1-2-3 is "copy-protected," not all of it can be copied onto the hard disk. This means that, even though you have just placed 1-2-3 on the hard disk, you will still need to place the System floppy disk in Drive A each time you begin to work with the program. By completing the steps in Section 4, however, you will be able to run 1-2-3 from the hard-disk drive alone.
12. Leave your computer on and proceed to the next section, "Installing 1-2-3."

3 Installing 1-2-3 on Floppy-Disk and Hard-Disk Systems

FEATURING:

The arrow, Escape, F1 (Help), F9, and F10 keys

Assume that you are about to ride a bicycle blindfolded and you do not know what kind of bicycle it is. Knowing whether it is a three-speed, a ten-speed, or a unicycle would probably influence how you attempt to ride it.

1-2-3 is also influenced by the kind of equipment on which it operates but, unlike the blindfolded bicyclist, it cannot depend on trial and error. 1-2-3 must have the information in advance. For example, 1-2-3 needs to know what kind of display screen or *monitor* you are using. Are you operating a black-and-white (monochrome) or a color display monitor?

To tell 1-2-3 about your equipment, small programs called *drivers* are stored on the Utility Disk. Each driver identifies some aspect of your equipment. The installation procedure prompts you to identify exactly what kind of equipment you are using. After you specify each driver, the set of drivers is saved in a file named 123.SET on the System disk. If you like, you can use different file names for different sets of drivers.

How to Install 1-2-3

Proceed by following all the instructions that fit your computer's disk system: floppy or hard. If you have a floppy disk system, be sure the **A>** prompt is displayed. If you have a hard disk system, be sure the **C>** is displayed.

Though you can install 1-2-3 from both DOS and the Access System menu, the following instructions direct you from the Access System.

If you have a floppy-disk system

1. Be sure the **A>** is displayed.
2. Insert the copy of the Utility disk in drive A.
3. Type:

   LOTUS

   Proceed to the instructions outlined below under "Whether you have a floppy-disk or hard-disk system."

If you have a hard-disk system

1. Be sure the **C>** is displayed. Also, if you created a subdirectory, be sure you are in the correct subdirectory. (To change subdirectories, type **CD** followed by a blank space and the subdirectory name—CD \123, for example—and then press Enter.)
2. Type:

   LOTUS

   Proceed to the instructions outlined next under "Whether you have a floppy-disk or hard-disk system."

Whether you have a floppy-disk or hard-disk system

4. Press Enter. The Access System menu appears (see Figure 3.1). The Access menu is the first menu that appears when you enter 1-2-3. A

menu is a list of options from which you can choose. You will use this particular menu now to install 1-2-3. You can also use it to enter 1-2-3, print graphs, use files from other programs such as dBASE III or Visi-Calc, run A View of 1-2-3 (the on-screen lessons), or exit to the operating system (DOS).

5. Using the Right-Arrow key, move the highlighted rectangle across until it appears over the word **Install**.
6. Press Enter. When the Install program begins, you will be prompted to read screens of information, change disks, and follow other instructions. 1-2-3 prompts you with clear questions, background information, and directions.

   You have three options: first-time installation, change selected equipment, and advanced options.

   - If you are installing 1-2-3 for the first time or you want to create a completely new—and perhaps additional—driver set, select first-time installation on the main menu.
   - If you want to change some of the information that has been stored already, use the second option on the main Install menu.
   - If you want to make one of several driver sets current and change that driver set, or if you want to create a library for drivers

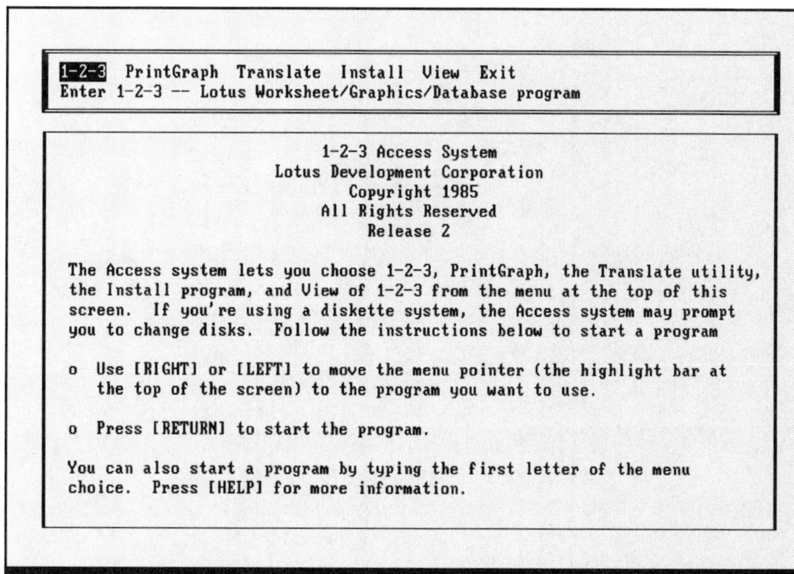

Figure 3.1: *The Access Menu*

not included in the Install Library and you want to add them to the Install menu, use the third menu option.

7. Proceed through the installation as you are prompted on the screen. Specific keys perform certain functions:

    - The arrow (or *pointer*) keys move the cursor.
    - The Escape key returns you to the previous screen.
    - The F1 (Help) key displays additional explanations of the screen options. (Be sure not to type F and then 1; there is a single key on the left marked F1.)
    - The F9 key returns you to the main installation menu.
    - The F10 displays the current driver selections.

    When you finish, the Access menu returns. If you have a floppy-drive system, proceed to Chapter 2. If you have a hard-disk system, proceed to the next section.

4

Running 1-2-3 Directly from a Hard-Disk Drive

FEATURING:

the COPYON and COPYOFF programs

You use a computer to save time, right? Completing these final steps will make start-up even faster since you won't have to insert the System disk in order to run 1-2-3. Instead, you will be able to run 1-2-3 directly from your hard-disk drive.

COPYON and COPYOFF are two optional programs included with 1-2-3 that are designed to accomplish this task. COPYON copies protected information from the System disk to the hard disk, including the unique serial number of your 1-2-3 package. You can only keep the protected information on one hard disk at a time. If you change computers and you want to run 1-2-3 from another hard-disk drive, you must first remove the protected information from the first hard-disk drive using the COPYOFF program. This protects 1-2-3 from being copied to many machines for use by multiple users. You would also have to use COPYOFF first if you accidentally erased the 1-2-3 program files and needed to copy all the files to the hard disk again.

The COPYON program, like the installation program, provides on-screen directions. There are also several opportunities to change your mind and quit before completing the COPYON program.

How to Set Up Your Hard Disk to Run 1-2-3 Automatically

Note: If you have an IBM PC/AT or are the server in a local area network, refer to your 1-2-3 manuals. Do not complete the following instructions.

1. Be sure the **C>** is displayed. (If the Access menu is displayed, press the Right-Arrow key until **Exit** is highlighted, then press Enter.)
2. Be sure that you are in the subdirectory in which you stored 1-2-3. (Typing **CD** and pressing Enter displays the current subdirectory. Typing **CD \123** and pressing Enter again will switch you to the 123 subdirectory.)
3. Be sure that the System and PrintGraph disks do not have write-protect tabs on them.
4. Place the PrintGraph disk in drive A.
5. Type:

   A:
6. Press Enter. The current drive is changed from C to A.
7. Type:

   COPYON
8. Press Enter. The COPYON program begins.
9. Press any key to continue, or press Ctrl-C to stop. (The Control key is used in conjunction with other keys to perform specific tasks. It is always identified as *Ctrl-* followed by the name of another key.)
10. When prompted, replace the PrintGraph disk in drive A with the System disk.
11. Press Enter.
12. Again, you have the option of continuing. To continue, type:

    Y

    To stop, type **N**.

13. Press Enter. The COPYON program displays several messages, but you don't have to do anything further. When it is finished, the C> returns.

14. Type:

    LOTUS

15. Press Enter. The Access System menu is displayed.
    Remove the System disk from drive A. Put the write-protect tabs back on the two disks and store them away. You can now run 1-2-3 from the hard-disk drive without first inserting the System disk in drive A. Proceed to Chapter 2.

How to Remove the Copy-Protected Information from Your Hard Disk Drive: COPYOFF

1. Repeat all of the steps above, except step 7. Instead of typing COPYON, type:

    COPYOFF

    When the COPYOFF program is finished, you will no longer be able to run 1-2-3 from the hard-disk drive alone. You will have to place the System disk in drive A.

Chapter Two

BUILDING A WORKSHEET

5 Bringing Up the Worksheet on Your Screen

You are ready to begin building a worksheet. How you bring up the worksheet on your screen depends upon whether you have a hard- or floppy-disk computer and whether your machine is on or off. If your machine is off and you have a floppy-disk system, you must always place the 1-2-3 System disk in drive A, then turn on the computer. If your machine is off and you have a hard-disk system, and if you have installed 1-2-3 on the hard disk with the COPYON program, you do not need to have the System disk in Drive A. If you have not used COPYON, place the System disk in A. If your computer is on, go directly to step 4 below.

Before any more explanation, let's take a look at the blank worksheet.

How to Bring Up the Worksheet

Follow the instructions that fit your computer system, floppy or hard.

If your computer is off

1. If you have a floppy-disk system, place the 1-2-3 System disk in drive A, then place a formatted or prepared disk in drive B. If you have a hard-disk system, drive A must be empty.
2. Whether you have a floppy- or hard-disk system, if your computer is off, turn it on.
3. Enter the date and time if necessary. See Section 1, steps 4 through 6 for floppy-disk systems. After pressing Enter, the Lotus Access System menu, shown in Figure 5.1, appears.
4. If you have a floppy-disk system, since the pointer is on 1-2-3, press Enter to bring up the 1-2-3 worksheet. If you have a hard-disk system, and you have not used the COPYON programs, place the 1-2-3 System

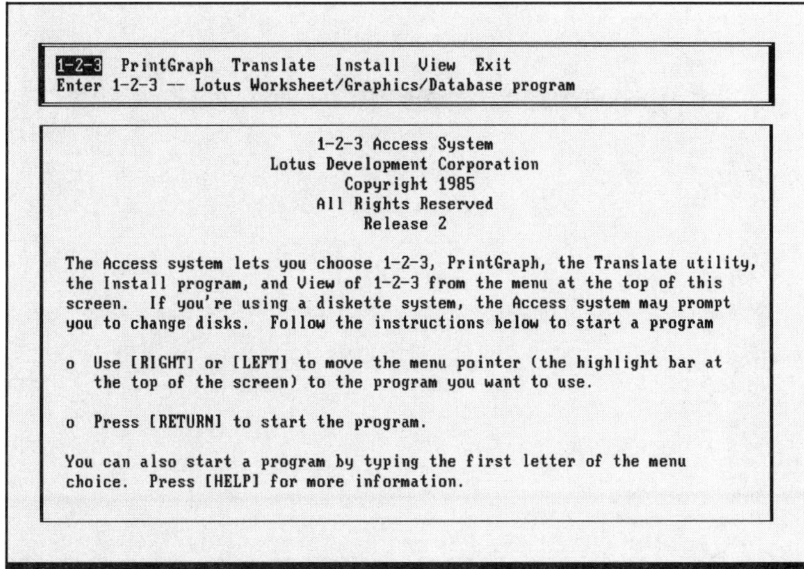

Figure 5.1: *The Access Menu*

disk in drive A, close the drive door, and press Enter. Otherwise press Enter without the System disk in drive A.

5. The Lotus 1-2-3 logo, the serial number for your copy of 1-2-3, and copyright information appear on the screen. In a moment, the worksheet will appear. If you have a hard-disk system you may get the following message: **Insert a disk in Drive B:, press any key to continue.** If so, press the Escape key on the left side of the keyboard to continue. This will be corrected later.

If your computer is on

If you are continuing from the previous chapter, the Access menu is displayed. With the pointer on **1-2-3**, press the Enter key.

What you see in Figure 5.2 is a blank grid with numbers down the left side that identify *rows,* and letters along the top that identify *columns.* Typically, once the worksheet is put to use, the top row or rows and the left column are filled with titles and headings to identify the content of all the cells on the worksheet.

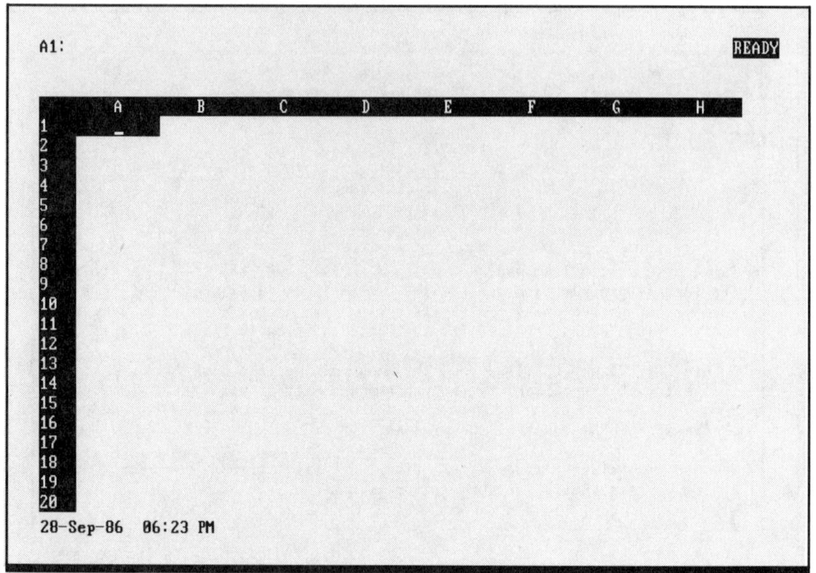

Figure 5.2: *Blank Worksheet*

Suppose you want to keep a daily record of your out-of-pocket business expenses. You could start by entering the days of the week along row 1, beginning at column B. In column A, you would type the dates for every week of the year next to the numbers. Your worksheet would look like the one in Figure 5.3. Your first dollar entry for the first Monday of the new year would be entered where column B (Monday) and row 2 (Week 1) intersect. This place is called a *cell,* and B2 would be the *cell address* for your first entry. Your worksheet would now look like the one in Figure 5.4.

The *control panel* is the area above the worksheet. On the left side of the control panel, above the blank worksheet, **A1**: appears. This is the cell address of the *pointer,* the highlighted rectangle that is in cell **A1**. Since the pointer is in **A1**, you can't see the rectangle's top and left borders. In the next section, you will be using the pointer to move around the worksheet.

The *mode indicator* is on the right side of the control panel. It announces what 1-2-3 is doing. For example, when it indicates **READY** and the worksheet is blank, 1-2-3 is waiting for you to enter information. The date and time are displayed at the bottom left of the screen.

If the CapsLock or NumLock keys are on, **CAPS** or **NUM** is displayed at the bottom right of the screen.

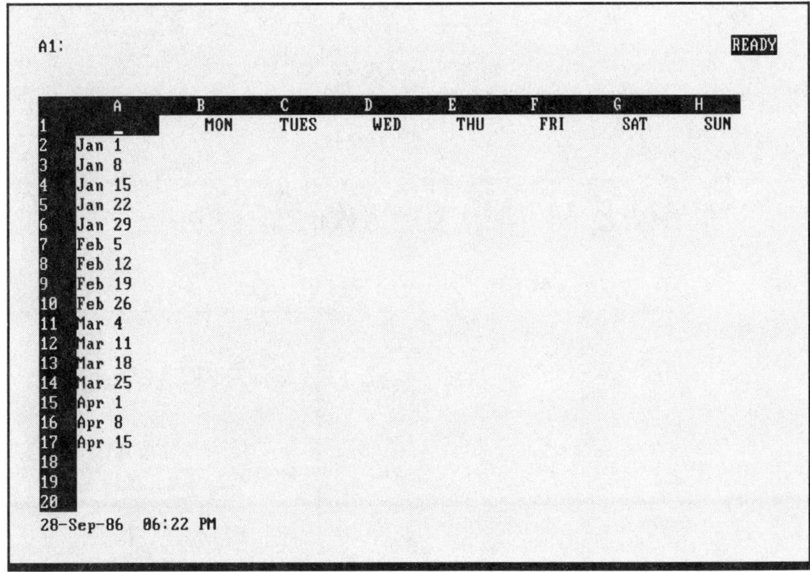

Figure 5.3: *Sample Worksheet*

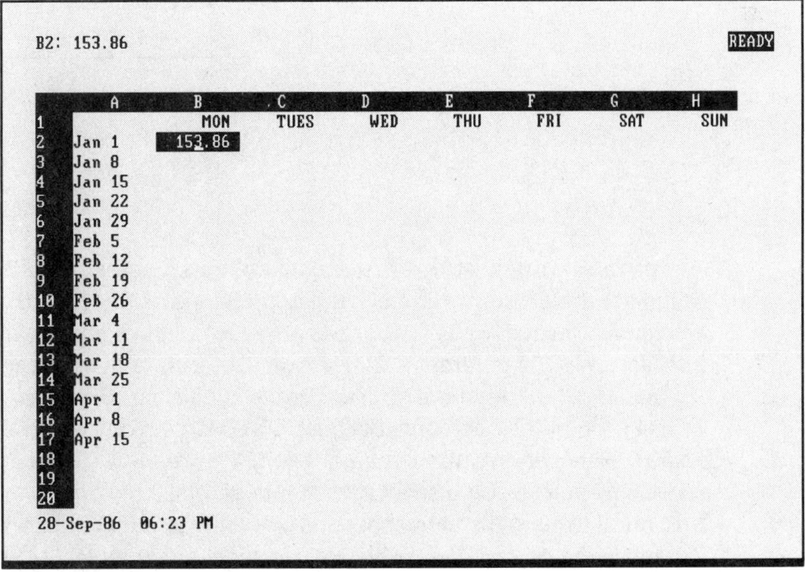

Figure 5.4: *Worksheet with the Dollar Entry*

6
Moving Within the Worksheet

FEATURING:

the Arrow, Tab, PgUp, PgDn Home, End, Scroll Lock, and Num(eric) Lock keys, and the F5 (GoTo) function key

The blank worksheet that first appears on your screen is only a small portion of the entire worksheet. Although it appears to have 20 rows and 8 columns, it actually has 8,192 rows and 256 columns totaling more than 2 million cells. (In contrast, 1-2-3 version 1A has one quarter the number of rows, 2,048.) The entire spreadsheet is equivalent to a piece of paper 21 feet wide by 130 feet long. Because it is so large, you can never see the entire worksheet on your screen at once. Viewing it is similar to using a zoom lens to focus on a small part of a huge piece of paper.

To move around the worksheet and view the area that's not visible, you can move the pointer, the highlighted rectangle now in cell A1. One way to do this is to press the *arrow keys* on the right side of the keyboard.

These keys, shown in Figure 6.1, move the pointer one cell at a time in a specific direction—up, down, left, or right.

Other keys, shown in Figure 6.2, move the pointer more than one cell at a time. These keys and the arrow keys are called *pointer-movement keys* and are summarized in the list that follows.

↑	Moves the pointer up one cell at a time.
↓	Moves the pointer down one cell at a time.
→	Moves the pointer to the right one cell at a time.
←	Moves the pointer to the left one cell at a time.
PgUp	Moves the pointer up one full "page" or 20 lines at a time.
PgDn	Moves the pointer down one full "page" or 20 lines.

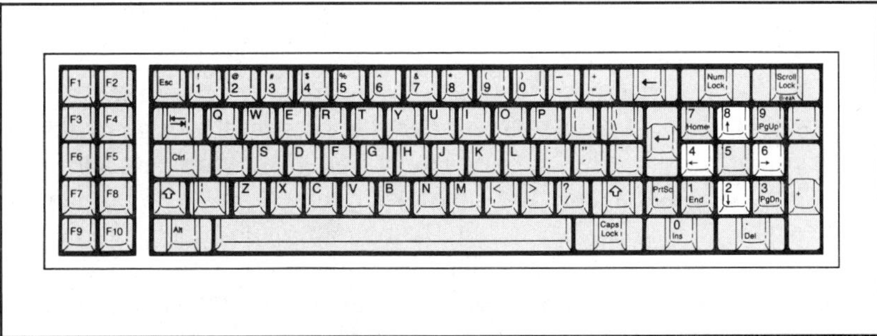

Figure 6.1: *Arrow Keys*

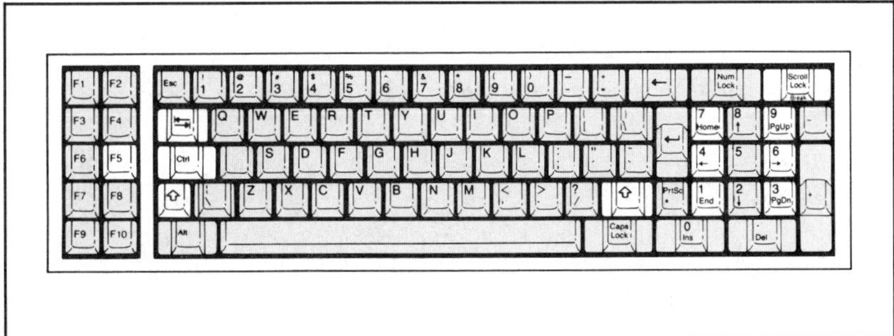

Figure 6.2: *Remaining Pointer-Movement Keys*

⭾ or Ctrl→	Moves the pointer to the right one full screen. Holding down the Control key and tapping the Right-Arrow key does the same.
⇧ ⭾ or Ctrl←	Moves the pointer left one full screen. Holding down the Control key and tapping the Left-Arrow key does the same.
Home	Moves the pointer to cell A1.
End	In conjunction with the arrow keys, it moves the pointer in a specific direction to the nearest entry.
F5 (Goto) function key	Allows you to type the address of the cell where you want to move the pointer. After typing, you must press Enter.
Scroll Lock	In conjunction with the arrow keys, it moves the worksheet in a specific direction as it pulls the pointer to the edge of the worksheet.

Although it is not a pointer-movement key, you should be aware of the *Num(eric) Lock* key because it changes the pointer-movement keys to number keys. If, when using the pointer-movement keys, numbers appear on the control panel, you have accidentally pressed the Num Lock key. If this happens, press the Backspace key to erase the numbers and press the Num Lock key again. The pointer-movement keys will move the pointer when **NUM** disappears from the bottom right of the screen.

As you read through the following directions, you may notice that they are extremely explicit. In the beginning, nothing will be left unexplained; however, as you become more proficient, you will be asked to perform tasks without being told how, if you have already performed the task once.

How to Move Within the Worksheet

1. Using the Right-Arrow key, move the cell pointer to and then beyond column H. Notice that, as you move across the worksheet to the right, columns on the left disappear. Notice also that the cell address on the control panel changes to reflect the cell address of the pointer as it moves across the screen.
2. Using the Left-Arrow key, return to cell A1. Hold the key down rather

than tap it. The pointer will move more rapidly. 1-2-3 will beep at you when the pointer reaches the left side of the worksheet.

3. With the Down-Arrow key, move the pointer to and then beyond row 20. Continue moving the pointer to row 40. This time, notice that rows disappear off the top as you move down the worksheet.
4. Press the key marked PgUp (for page up). Notice that the pointer is now on row 20. The PgUp key always moves the pointer up one full screen—or 20 lines—each time you press it.
5. Press the key marked PgDn (for page down). The pointer returns to row 40. The PgDn key always moves the pointer down a full screen—or 20 lines.
6. Press the Home key. The pointer is back in cell A1.
7. Press the End key. The word **END** appears in the lower right corner of the screen. The End key is a *toggle* key. This means that you can disengage it by pressing it a second time. The End key, on its own, does nothing; it only operates in conjunction with arrow keys as illustrated in the next step.
8. With the End key on (the **END** message is displayed in the bottom right of the screen), press the Down-Arrow key. The pointer is now in row 8192—the last row of the worksheet. This is because the End key, followed by an arrow key, moves the pointer in a specific direction to the first entry on the screen. Since there are no entries yet, the pointer goes directly to the last cell in the column. The word **END** disappears from the screen.
9. Press the Home key again.
10. Press the key marked F5 on the left side of your keyboard. Do not type the letter F and the number 5; there is a single key marked F5. This key is called the Goto key because you use it to tell 1-2-3 where you want the pointer to *go to* by typing a cell address. The prompt **Enter address to go to:** appears on the screen. 1-2-3 suggests the current position of the pointer.
11. Type **G10**. If you typed incorrectly, use the Backspace key to erase. (See Figure 1.1.)
12. Press Enter. The pointer moves to the cell you specify; in this case, it is G10.
13. Press the key marked Scroll Lock in the upper right corner of your keyboard. The word **SCROLL** is highlighted on the screen. The Scroll

Lock key is also a toggle key. It operates with the pointer-movement keys to move the screen as it pulls the pointer to the edge of the worksheet. (Moving through rows or columns is also called *scrolling.*)

14. Press the Right-Arrow key until several columns scroll off to the left and the pointer is pulled to the left edge of the worksheet.
15. Press the Down-Arrow key until several rows scroll off the top of the worksheet and the pointer is pulled to the top edge.
16. Press Home.
17. Press the Scroll Lock key again to release it.
18. Press the Tab key. The pointer moves one full screen to the right.
19. Hold down the Shift key, and press the Tab key. The pointer returns Home—or moves one full screen to the left.
20. An alternative way to move one screen at a time is to hold down the Control key, and tap the Right-Arrow key. The pointer moves a full screen to the right again.
21. Hold down the Control key, and tap the Left-Arrow key. The pointer returns Home—or moves one full screen to the left.

7 Labeling the Worksheet

FEATURING:

the Escape and Caps Lock keys and Label-Prefix Characters

There are endless variations of what might go onto a blank worksheet. However, since the worksheet is often used for a budget in one form or another, the following instructions show you how to set up a budget. If you want to customize your own budget later on, the budget you will build in this book, shown in Figure 7.1, will give you the skills and confidence to do so. (This is the finished worksheet. Do not enter it yet.)

But first things first. A worksheet needs labels or it won't be much help to you. To make sense of the figures you enter on the worksheet, you need to label your rows and columns. Your readers need to know, for example, that the four columns of figures you're presenting to them represent the year's four quarters and the numbers along the bottom row represent profits, not expenses.

Depending on how you want your worksheet to look, you can align on the left or the right, center, or repeat a label within a column, as shown in Figure 7.2. A repeating label creates a row of characters, such as dashes or asterisks.

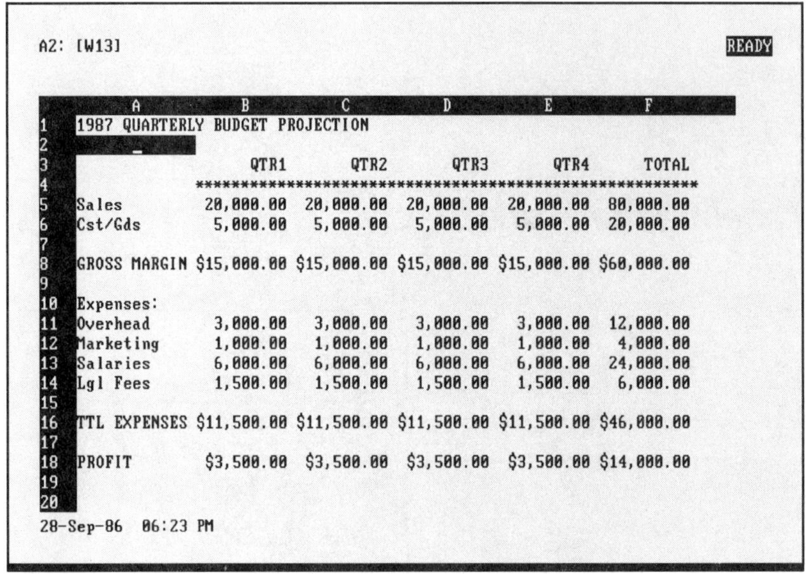

A2: [W13] READY

	A	B	C	D	E	F
1	1987 QUARTERLY BUDGET PROJECTION					
2						
3		QTR1	QTR2	QTR3	QTR4	TOTAL
4		***********	***********	***********	***********	***********
5	Sales	20,000.00	20,000.00	20,000.00	20,000.00	80,000.00
6	Cst/Gds	5,000.00	5,000.00	5,000.00	5,000.00	20,000.00
7						
8	GROSS MARGIN	$15,000.00	$15,000.00	$15,000.00	$15,000.00	$60,000.00
9						
10	Expenses:					
11	Overhead	3,000.00	3,000.00	3,000.00	3,000.00	12,000.00
12	Marketing	1,000.00	1,000.00	1,000.00	1,000.00	4,000.00
13	Salaries	6,000.00	6,000.00	6,000.00	6,000.00	24,000.00
14	Lgl Fees	1,500.00	1,500.00	1,500.00	1,500.00	6,000.00
15						
16	TTL EXPENSES	$11,500.00	$11,500.00	$11,500.00	$11,500.00	$46,000.00
17						
18	PROFIT	$3,500.00	$3,500.00	$3,500.00	$3,500.00	$14,000.00
19						
20						

28-Sep-86 06:23 PM

Figure 7.1: *Quarterly Budget*

To tell 1-2-3 where you want to place your label within the column, you precede the label with a *label-prefix character.* You have four choices:

'	(apostrophe)	for a left-aligned label
"	(quotation mark)	for right-aligned label
^	(caret)	for a centered label
\	(backslash)	for a repeating label (use the slash on the left side of the keyboard not the right.)

Be aware that if you do not include a label-prefix character, 1-2-3 will automatically left-align your label unless it begins with any one of the following characters:

0 1 2 3 4 5 6 7 8 9 + – . (@ # $

If your label begins with one of these characters, and you forget the label-prefix, 1-2-3 will misinterpret your label and assume that you are entering a number or a mathematical formula.

To avoid this confusion, be sure to precede all labels that start with any of the number or punctuation symbols shown above with a label-prefix character. If your label begins with a letter you do not need to type a label prefix; 1-2-3 assigns it automatically. You will know that you are correctly

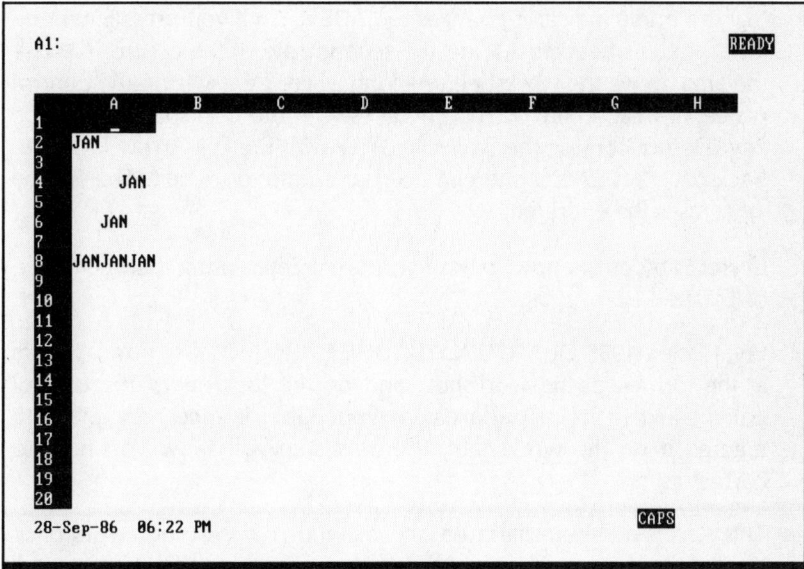

Figure 7.2: *Examples of Labels in Four Positions*

entering a label because the mode indicator will change from **READY** to **LABEL.**

How to Enter Labels on the Worksheet

To construct a quarterly budget

When you need to type the label-prefix characters (except for the apostrophe), use the Shift key. Use the Caps Lock key to enter the rest of the labels in capitals.

1. The pointer should be in cell A1. Press the CapsLock key when you want capitals. As you type the following label, use the numbers at the top of your keyboard. Type:

   '1986 QUARTERLY BUDGET PROJECTION

   Do not press Enter yet. Notice that you needed a single-apostrophe label prefix. This is because the label starts with a number. Notice also that the mode indicator changes to **LABEL**. Until you press Enter, the label remains beneath **A1**: on the second row of the control panel—the area above the worksheet. As long as your entry is on the control panel, you can easily correct mistakes with the Backspace or Escape key. (Do not confuse the Backspace key with the Left-Arrow key.) The Backspace key erases one character at a time to the left. The Escape key erases the entire entry.

2. Correct any errors now, before you press Enter, using the Backspace or Escape key.

3. Press Enter. **1986 QUARTERLY BUDGET PROJECTION** now appears at the top left of the worksheet and on the top row of the control panel, next to its cell address. If your label is incorrect and you entered it on the worksheet, the next step will show you how to correct it.

4. This step is added to illustrate one method of correcting errors once they are entered on the worksheet. You move the pointer to the cell containing the error, retype the entry on the control panel, and press Enter. Move the pointer to A1, if it is not already there. Type:

   '1987 QUARTERLY BUDGET PROJECTION

   Press Enter. The revision is entered on the worksheet. The label will span beyond cell A1 unless the cells to the right of it are already filled. Should this be the case, the label would be cut off.

5. Using the Down- and Right-Arrow keys, move the pointer to cell B3. The cell address on the control panel reflects the move.

6. Type:

   "QTR1

   Notice that you used double quotes to align the label on the right. Do not press Enter.

7. Correct errors while the entry is on the control panel. Do not press Enter.

8. Instead of pressing Enter, there is a more efficient method of entering: pressing the Right-Arrow key. In one step, instead of two, the label is entered on the worksheet and the pointer moves to the next cell.

9. Proceed to enter the next labels in cells C3, D3, E3, and F3 in the same way that you entered "QTR1. Be sure to look for mistakes on

the control panel before you press the Right-Arrow key. Remember to use the Shift key to type the quotation mark (") before each label. Type:

- **"QTR2** and press the Right-Arrow key
- **"QTR3** and press the Right-Arrow key
- **"QTR4** and press the Right-Arrow key
- **"TOTAL** and press the Enter key

10. Move the pointer to B4.
11. Type:

    *

    Be sure you use the correct slash key. The backslash is the label prefix for repeating a label within a cell.
12. Press the Right-Arrow key.
13. Repeat steps 11 and 12 for cells C4, D4, E4, and F4 until you have a row of asterisks beneath all the labels.
14. Move the pointer to A5.
15. Press the CapsLock key. The **CAPS** message disappears from the bottom of the screen. Type and check for errors:

    Sales

    Since the label starts with a letter and you want it aligned on the left, it is not necessary to use a label prefix.
16. Press the Down-Arrow key.
17. In A6, type and check for errors:

    Cst/Gds
18. Press the Down-Arrow key.
19. Enter the following labels in the same way. Check for errors as you type each label on the control panel. Use the CapsLock key to switch between capitals and lowercase labels.

    - in cell A7—**GROSS MARGIN**

      Press the Down-Arrow key. (This label extends past the column; you will correct this later.)

- in cell A8—**Expenses:**
  Press the Down-Arrow key.
- in cell A9—**Overhead**
  Press the Down-Arrow key.
- in cell A10—**Salaries**
  Press the Down-Arrow key.
- in cell A11—**Marketing**
  Press the Down-Arrow key.
- in cell A12—**Lgl Fees**
  Press the Down-Arrow key.
- in cell A13—**TTL EXPENSES**
  Press the Down-Arrow key. (This label also extends past the column. You will correct this too, later.)
- in cell A14—**PROFIT**
  Press the Down-Arrow key.

When you've completed these steps, the worksheet will look like the one in Figure 7.3.

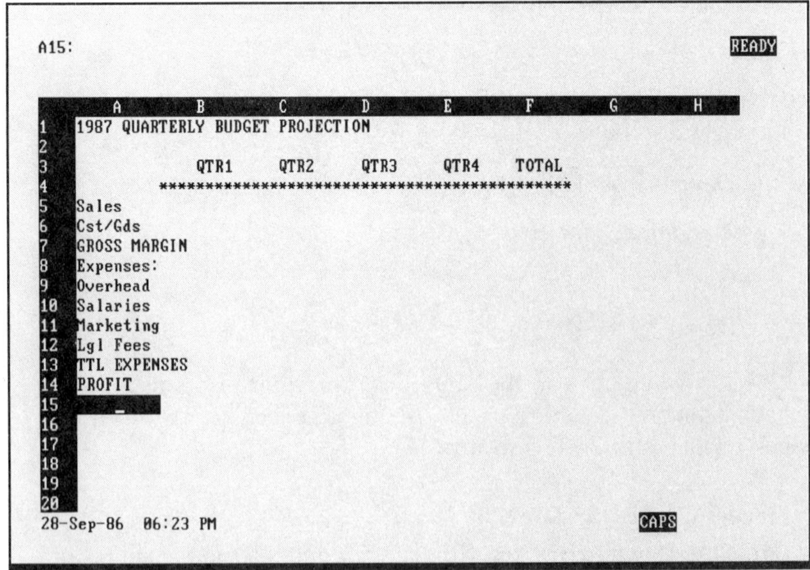

Figure 7.3: *Labeled Worksheet*

Now go back and correct any errors by typing and entering the corrections over the errors. If you entered some labels into the wrong cells altogether, leave them for the time being. You will learn how to erase them later.

8
Help! What Do I Do Next?

FEATURING:

the F1 (Help) function key to display Help screens

1-2-3 has a lifeguard built in to the program to save you from drowning in confusion. In case you don't know or can't remember how to proceed, there are more than 200 "pages" or Help screens instantly available.

A common problem at this stage is forgetting which label-prefix character to use. Suppose, for example, that you are confident about your new computer skills and you want to experiment by labeling your own worksheet beneath the first one on the screen. Perhaps you want a monthly rather than a quarterly projection, or perhaps you prefer to break down your overhead expenses into such categories as space and equipment rental. And you want the new labels to be centered or aligned on the right, instead of the standard left-aligned format. You decide to start by typing a label in column A.

Suddenly, you can't remember which label prefix to use. Although you could look it up in the previous section of this book, there's a more efficient way: referring to the Help screens in 1-2-3.

Any time you are in the midst of a problem, you can leave what you are doing on the screen, press the F1 (Help) function key on the left side of your keyboard, read the relevant Help screen, and return to your work, ready to proceed with the answer to your question.

To explore the Help screens, use the arrow, Backspace, Enter, Escape, and F1 keys, (shown in Figure 8.1), most of which you are already familiar with.

How to get Help using the Help screens

1. Press the F1 function key, and read the screen. Do not type the letter F and the number 1; there is a single key marked F1. Don't worry if you don't understand everything on the screen. Notice that the exact information you need is to the right of the word **Label** in the middle of the Help screen. The mode indicator in the top right corner now says **HELP**. Any time you have a question as to how to proceed, 1-2-3 can instantly provide a Help screen that applies to the task at hand.
2. To explore the Help screens further, use the Down-Arrow key and move the pointer to the phrase **Help Index**.
3. Press Enter, and read the screen.
4. Move the pointer to the phrase or topic that applies to what you need, in this case, **Cell Formats – Number Vs. Label**, since you want to know how to enter labels.
5. Press Enter, and read the screen.
6. For more specific information, move the pointer to **Label Formats**.
7. Press Enter, and read the screen.
8. Press Backspace to review the previous Help screen. If you wanted, you could continue to read other Help screens and 1-2-3 would

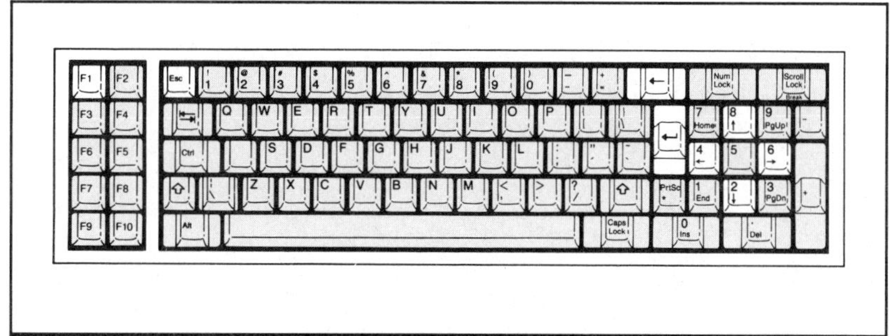

Figure 8.1: *The Arrow, Backspace, Enter, Escape, and F1 Keys*

remember up to 15, each of which you could review again by pressing Backspace.

9. After you finish reading, press F1 again to return to the first screen that you viewed.
10. Go to the Help Index and select the screen **Using the Help Facility.** Review the use of the Help screen.
11. To return to your work exactly where you left off, press the Escape key.

9
Correcting Mistakes

FEATURING:

the F2 (Edit) function key

In 1-2-3, there are often several ways to do one thing, such as correcting a mistake. Until now, you could correct an error by using the Backspace or Escape key before entering on the worksheet or by overwriting an entry already on the worksheet. However, by using the Edit function key, F2, you can correct a single error more easily.

For example, if you type **BUDET** on the control panel, instead of **BUDGET**, you would have to erase the **T** and **E** and type in **GET** before you entered it on the worksheet. Or, if it were already on the worksheet, you would have to type the entire word over and reenter it. Instead, using the **EDIT** mode, you simply insert the **G** where it belongs.

The F2 key enables you to make corrections any time you notice a mistake. If the error has not been entered on the worksheet, you can press F2 and correct it while it is still on the control panel. Once the entry is on the worksheet, you simply move the pointer to the cell that needs correcting, press F2, and the entry is "pulled up" to the control panel for editing. In effect, all errors, whether they are on the control panel or are entered on the worksheet, are corrected on the control panel.

At this stage, forgetting to enter a label prefix and making an incorrect entry are the most common errors. The following instructions show you how to correct these problems, using the **EDIT** mode to enter and delete characters.

How to Correct Errors with the F2 Function Key

1. To practice on a new screen, tap the PgDn key on the right side of the keyboard. This will bring up rows 21 through 40 where you can enter mistakes in order to learn how to correct them.

If you forget to enter a label-prefix character

2. Press the CapsLock key. **CAPS** is displayed. In the cell where the pointer currently resides, A35, type:

   1987 BUDGET

   Do not type a label-prefix character. Notice that the mode indicator changes to **VALUE**, not **LABEL**.

3. Press Enter. 1-2-3 beeps, your entry remains on the control panel, and the **EDIT** mode is automatically invoked because, although it doesn't recognize all errors, 1-2-3 knows when you forget to enter a label prefix if the label begins with any one of the following characters and contains letters.

   0 1 2 3 4 5 6 7 8 9 + . (@ # $

   An entry beginning with one of these characters is normally interpreted as a number or a mathematical formula. This is called a *value*. However, because there are letters in the entry, 1-2-3 recognizes the error and knows that you intended to enter a label.

4. When you are in the **EDIT** mode, the pointer-movement keys respond differently. The Right- and Left-Arrow keys now move a small *cursor* along the second line of the control panel. Move the cursor to the **1** in **1987 BUDGET**, and type a single apostrophe.

5. Press the Down-Arrow key. **1987 BUDGET** is entered as a label and aligned on the left, and you are in the **READY** mode.

If you enter a word or number incorrectly on the worksheet

6. In cell A36, rather than typing **RENTAL COSTS**, type the following incorrect entry:

   TENTA COSTD

7. Press Enter. **TENTA COSTD** appears on the worksheet.
8. Press F2. **'TENTA COSTD** is pulled up to the second line of the control panel. 1-2-3 automatically adds the label prefix.
9. Move the cursor to the first letter: **T**.
10. Press the Del(ete) key located below the arrow keys on the right side of the keyboard. The first letter **T** is deleted.
11. Type:

    R

    The **R** is inserted before the **ENTA** which shifts to the right.
12. Move the cursor to the space between **A** and **C**.
13. Type:

    L

    The **L** is inserted before the blank space.
14. Press the End key on the right side of the keyboard. In the **EDIT** mode, it moves the cursor to the space after the last character. (Pressing the Home key moves the cursor to the first character in the line.)
15. Press Backspace to delete the previous character.
16. After the **T** on **COST**, type:

    S

17. Press Enter. The corrected entry, **RENTAL COSTS**, appears on the worksheet. Having pressed Enter, you are back in **READY** mode.

10 Entering Numbers on the Worksheet

Now that the worksheet is labeled, you are ready to begin entering numbers. By the time you finish, your worksheet should contain the numbers in Figure 10.1, all of which represent dollar figures.

How to Enter Numbers

If you make mistakes as you type, use either the Backspace or Delete keys to correct the error while it is still on the control panel, or press F2 and edit the error.

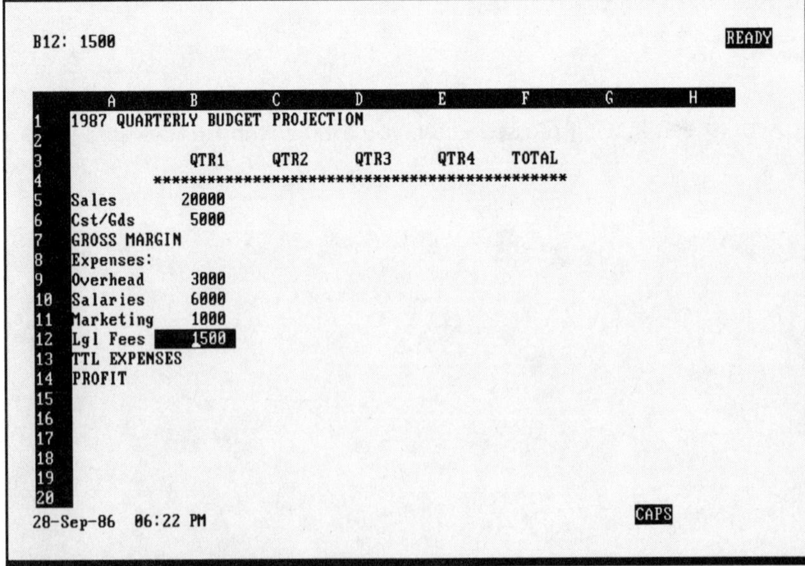

Figure 10.1: *Worksheet with Numbers*

1. Return to cell A1. A quick way is to use the Home key.
2. Move the pointer to B5. Without adding a comma, type:

   20000

   VALUE appears as the right-hand mode indicator.
3. Press the Down-Arrow key. **20000** appears on the worksheet.
4. Without adding a comma, in B6, type:

   5000
5. Press the Down-Arrow key. **5000** appears on the worksheet.
6. Move the pointer to B9, leaving B7 and B8 empty.
7. In the same way that you entered **20000** and **5000**, enter the following numbers:
   - in B9: **3000** (Press the Down-Arrow key.)
   - in B10: **6000** (Press the Down-Arrow key.)
   - in B11: **1000** (Press the Down-Arrow key.)
   - in B12: **1500** (Press the Down-Arrow key.)

   Never place a label prefix before a number that is to be calculated.

11

Entering Formulas and Functions and Playing "What if"

FEATURING:

formulas and the @SUM Function

If you only used 1-2-3 to store information, it wouldn't be much more than a very expensive ledger pad. However, with *formulas,* some as simple as the ones you learned in Algebra 1, you can begin to calculate, analyze, compare, and project.

Placed in individual cells, formulas tell 1-2-3 to perform calculations that can vary in complexity. A formula may be simple, such as one that adds numbers, or it may be complex, such as one that calculates your monthly mortgage payments.

Take a look at the worksheet you've built so far. When you look down through the rows, you will notice three empty cells that are crucial to this particular budget. They raise several questions: What is the profit on sales after the cost of goods is subtracted? What are the total expenses? What is the overall profit? Some simple formulas, entered in those cells, will provide the answers for you. Later, you can play "what if" by changing the numbers on the worksheet, and 1-2-3 will automatically adjust its findings to reflect your changes.

When you enter a formula, 1-2-3 interprets it as a *value,* which includes both formulas and numbers. A value is one of two kinds of entries possible on the worksheet; the other kind is a label, which you are already familiar with.

If you aren't careful, however, 1-2-3 will misinterpret your formula as a label. Since you can use a number's cell address, such as D9, in a formula, rather than the number itself, formulas often begin with letters. This leads 1-2-3 to assume your formula—D9+D10—is a label. The result is that 1-2-3 simply enters the formula on the worksheet; it doesn't store the formula as a direction to perform a calculation.

To avoid this, you need to precede the formula with a specific *operator.* An operator is a symbol representing a mathematical operation, such as a subtraction or division sign. Normally, you will precede your formula with a plus sign, as in +D9+D10. This way, you don't have to pay attention to whether or not your formula begins with a letter or a number.

There are other operators in addition to the ones already mentioned. The following are some of the most common.

^	Exponentiation
+,−	Positive, Negative
*,/	Multiplication, Division
+,−	Addition, Subtraction
<,>	Less than, Greater than (referred to as logical operators)

Most of these operators are probably familiar to you. However, some vary slightly from their counterparts in algebra books. For example, rather than use a traditional division sign, 1-2-3 uses the slash (/). Actually, this is quite logical. Since the fraction one-half means one divided by two, writing the operation like the fraction, 1/2, makes sense.

The operators are listed in order of precedence, that is, in the order in which 1-2-3 calculates them in a formula. 1-2-3 doesn't always calculate a formula from left to right. Instead, it follows the normal algebraic order of operations. Thus, for example, it calculates multiplication and division before it calculates addition and subtraction. This can seem confusing until you learn how to enter a formula correctly.

To illustrate the problem, let's assume that you want to project sales profits over the next two years. Being conservative, you project it at the current rate of sales. Using the worksheet you've built so far, you would apply the formula: Sales−Cst/Gds*2 years, or +20000−5000*2, or for the sake of efficiency, +B5−B6*2, where the cell addresses are used to represent the numbers on the worksheet. Calculated by hand, the answer is 30,000 since you know to subtract before you multiply. Calculated by 1-2-3, the answer is 10,000 since 1-2-3 multiplies before it subtracts. Obviously, there's a problem.

The solution is a simple one. If you place parentheses around whatever you want 1-2-3 to calculate first, it will do so. Thus, when it calculates (B5 – B6)*2, it will provide the correct answer: 30,000. (The left parenthesis functions the same way as a plus sign here so the initial plus sign is not needed.)

Something else to consider when entering a formula is the length of the formula. Sometimes a formula can get cumbersome. For example, if you want to calculate overall profits, you would add your expenses and subtract them from the sales profit. One way of writing this formula would be:

Sales – Cst/Gds – (Overhead + Salaries + Marketing + Lgl Fees)

or

+B5 – B6 – (B9 + B10 + B11 + B12)

Although this formula is quite long, a large spreadsheet might well have many more profit and expense entries. To avoid lengthy, time-consuming formulas, *functions* are used to represent part or all of a formula. For example, the previous formula can be written as +B5 – B6 – @SUM(B9..B12), using the *sum* function. Now the formula reads: the sales income minus the cost of the goods minus the sum of the expenses. The sum function tells 1-2-3 to add all the figures between and including two cells. In addition to the sum function, there are more than 50 other functions, some of which do special tasks, such as rounding off numbers. For a list of all the functions used by 1-2-3, see the appendix in your Lotus 1-2-3 manual.

To enter a function, always precede it by @, identify it by name, and enclose the cells included in the formula in parentheses. Whenever a formula starts with a function, you do not need to use a plus sign; the @ symbol serves the same purpose. Neither formulas nor functions can contain any blank spaces. There are two plus keys and two minus keys on the keyboard. You may use any of them in building formulas.

How to Enter Formulas and Functions

To calculate GROSS MARGIN using the formula: +B5 – B6

1. Move the pointer to B7, to the right of **GROSS MARGIN**.

2. Type:

   +B5 − B6

   Notice that the mode indicator changes to **VALUE**. It does not matter whether you use capital or lowercase letters when building formulas.

3. Press Enter. As in Figure 11.1, **15000** appears on the screen. Although the formula does not appear on the screen, 1-2-3 remembers it, and any time you change either of the two cell entries, 1-2-3 will recalculate **GROSS MARGIN**. (The **GIN** in **GROSS MARGIN** disappeared; you will correct this later.)

To calculate TOTAL EXPENSES using the function: @SUM(B9. .B12)

(Refer to the discussion of *functions* at the beginning of this chapter.)

4. Move the pointer to B13.

5. So far, you have been entering formulas by typing. You will now use the second method of entering a formula, *pointing*. Pointing offers a more visual method of identifying cells to include in the formula. First, type:

   @SUM(

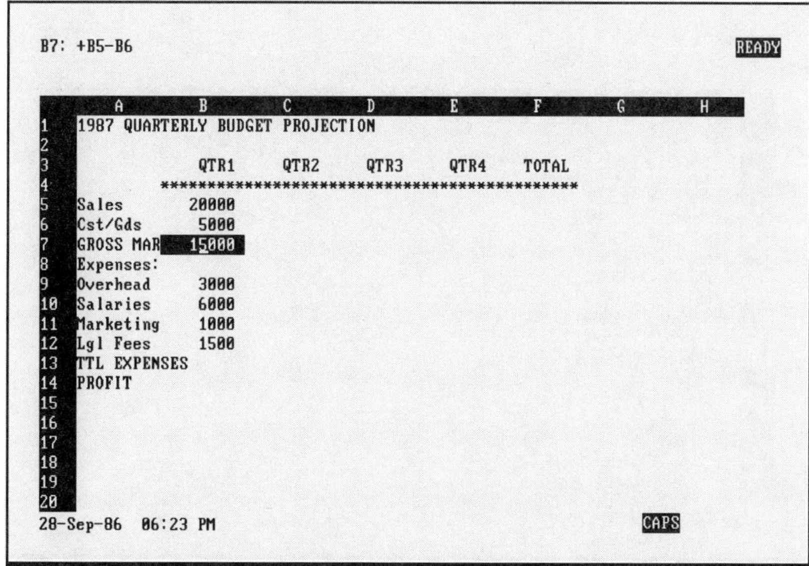

Figure 11.1: *Gross Margin Formula*

6. Now, point to B9 by moving the pointer to its cell using the Up-Arrow key.
7. Type a period to *anchor* B9 as the first cell in the formula. Two periods and another B9 appear on the screen. Typing a period prevents the first cell address on the control panel from changing when you move the pointer.
8. Point to B12 by moving the pointer to its cell. The four cells are highlighted. Notice that the second B9 is replaced by B12.
9. Type a right parenthesis to close the formula. **@SUM(B9..B12)** is displayed.
10. Press the Down-Arrow key. As in Figure 11.2, **11500** appears on the screen. Any time you change one of the cell entries, 1-2-3 will recalculate this figure. (The **SES** is erased from **TTL EXPENSES**. This too will be corrected later.)

To calculate PROFIT using the formula: +B7−B13

11. Be sure the pointer is in B14.
12. Type only a plus sign. Remember: you can use either of the plus keys and either of the minus keys when building formulas.

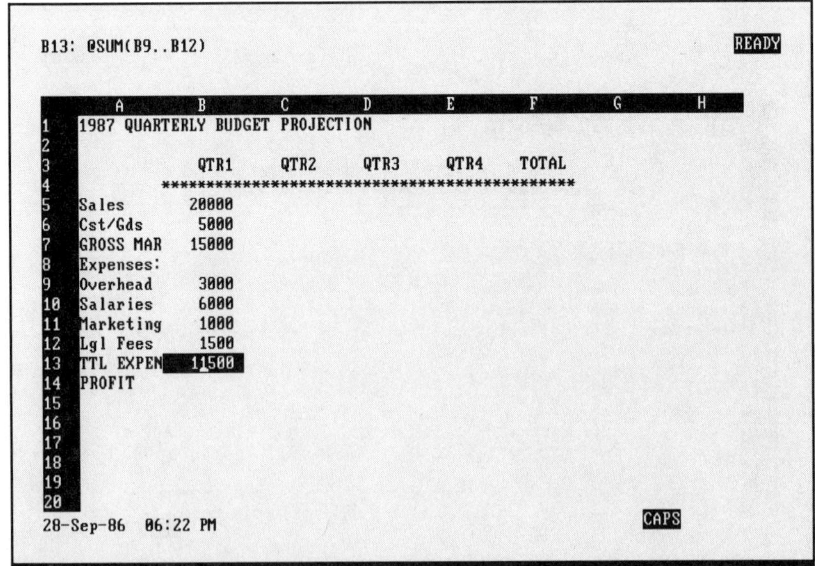

Figure 11.2: *Total Expenses Formula*

13. Point to B7 by moving the pointer to its cell.
14. Type a minus sign. The pointer will return to the original cell B14.
15. Point to B13 by moving the pointer to its cell.
16. Press Enter. **3500** is displayed on the screen. Since the formula for profit includes all of the cell entries, a change in any one will be reflected in the profit.

To play "What if"

17. Move the pointer to B5.
18. Type:

    30000

19. Press Enter. Notice that the totals for **GROSS MARGIN** and **PROFIT** are automatically recalculated to reflect the change.
20. In B5, type:

    20000

21. Press Enter. **20000** returns to the screen, and the totals are recalculated again. See Figure 11.3.

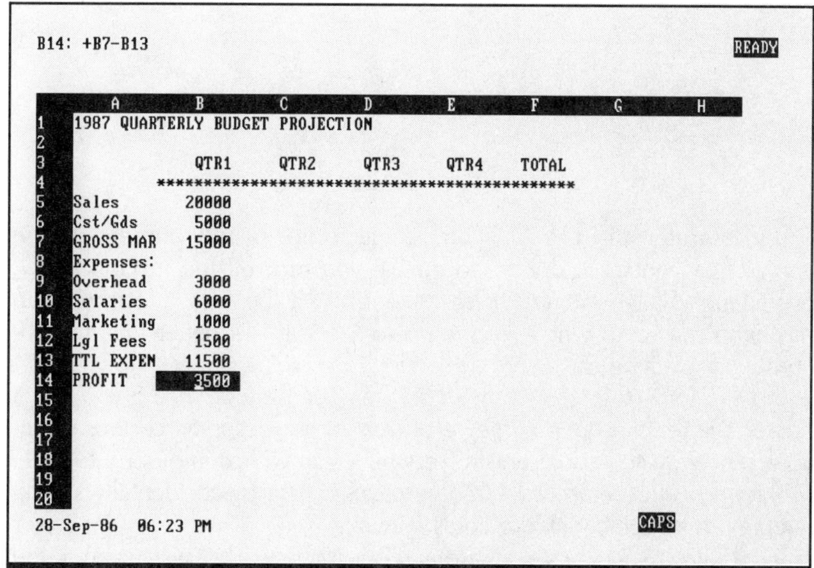

Figure 11.3: *Profit Formula*

12

Saving a File and Quitting 1-2-3: How to Stop Without Losing Everything You've Done

FEATURING:

the Slash (/) and Break keys and the File Save and Quit commands

You've gotten this far, and you decide to go to bed. Or you decide you've had enough and want to quit. If you turn off the machine now, everything you've entered up to this point will be erased. Rather than having to start over when you return to 1-2-3, it is a better idea to save your work on a disk.

You'll just skip this step for now? You may be disappointed if you do. A power failure, a sudden surge of power, or an observer curious about your power switch could erase everything you've accomplished to date. (Ironically, we just erased the last ten pages of text by accidentally knocking the power cable with the Lotus manual.)

To be safe, periodic "saves" are a good practice. That way, even if you accidentally turn off the machine as you reach for another cup of coffee or lean to pick up the phone, you will have the last version of your work stored on a disk. Storing is also a good idea if you want to file away one worksheet for later reference while you build another.

To store your work, you use a series of *commands.* Commands help you do a variety of operations that are indispensable in the creation of a spreadsheet, such as storing, printing, and retrieving the worksheet, displaying it as a graph, transferring information from one worksheet to another, and erasing data.

Commands are divided into categories by function and are assigned a corresponding name. There are ten major command categories, all of which you will have used by the time you finish this book. The commands needed to print worksheets are called **Print** commands. Commands that affect the entire appearance of the worksheet, such as the one that changes a column width, are called **Worksheet** commands; those that affect only part of the worksheet are called **Range** commands. There is a **Copy** command to copy one part of the worksheet to another part, and a **Move** command to move data within the worksheet. The commands that relate to creating a data base are called **Data** commands, and those that have to do with creating a graph are called **Graph** commands. The **System** command (new to Version 2.0) allows you to exit 1-2-3 temporarily without losing your work, so that you can run other programs or use DOS commands such as FORMAT, COPY, RENAME, and ERASE. The **Quit** command ends the worksheet session, erasing the worksheet in the process. To store a worksheet, you use **File** commands; more specifically, you use the **File Save** command. This is easy to remember if you think of saving as storing your work away in a filing cabinet. The major command catégories are listed in the *command menu,* shown in Figure 12.1.

To access commands, you press the slash (/) key. But be prepared! Pressing the slash key in 1-2-3 is like travelling down the tunnel to Wonderland with Alice. Suddenly, a vast hierarchy of commands is available to you.

How to Move Through the Command Menu

1. Press the slash (/) key. Be sure you press the right (/) slash, not the left (\). The command menu appears on the two lines of the control panel, listing the nine major categories of commands. The mode indicator changes to **MENU**.

2. Before proceeding to save your work, familiarize yourself with operating the command menu. Using the Right- and Left-Arrow keys,

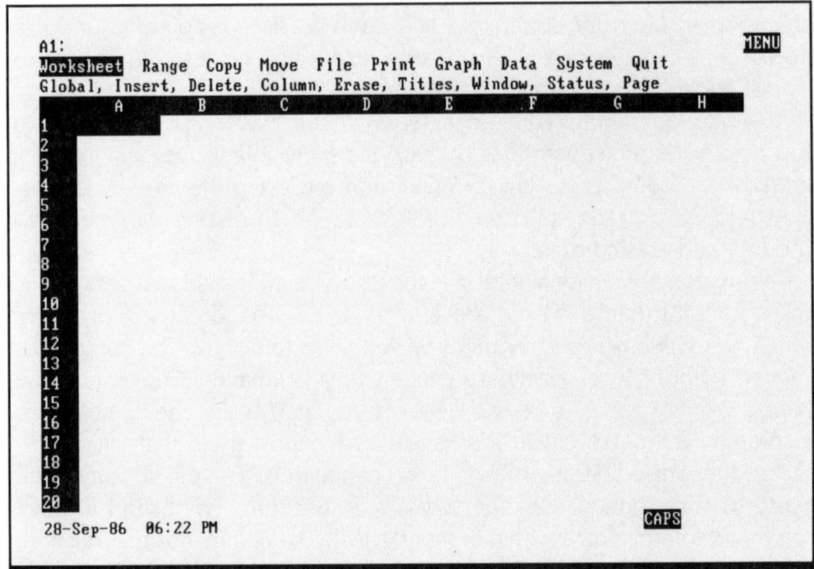

Figure 12.1: *The Command Menu*

which now move from command to command, move among the different command options. Notice that the second line on the control panel offers new options and/or explanations for each command.

3. Move the pointer to **File**. Read the second line on the control panel.
4. Press Enter. The options that were below **File** are now on the top line of the control panel. Each time you choose a command, there are additional explanations or commands on the second line that relate to the highlighted option above. These layers of commands, or submenus, form a tree structure. Choosing one opens up a number of branches; choosing again opens up more branches.
5. Press Escape. You return to the previous command menu. Enter and Escape allow you to move in and out of the command menu, one level at a time.
6. Press Enter again.
7. To exit instantly, rather than one level at a time, hold down the Control key above the left Shift key and tap the Break key in the top right corner. (*Break* may be written on the front side of the Scroll Lock key.) Do this now.

How to Save Your Work

8. If you have a hard-disk drive, read only the next paragraph about the **System** command, and proceed to step 9. If you have a floppy-disk drive, place a formatted disk in drive B and proceed to step 9. If you do not have a formatted disk, do the following:

   To format a disk without exiting 1-2-3, Version 2.0 now has the new **System** command. To format a disk now, press **/**, move to **System** and press Enter. The **A>** is displayed. Place your DOS disk in drive A. Type **FORMAT B:** and press Enter. When prompted, place a blank disk in drive B and press Enter again. When formatting is complete, type **N** and press Enter. Type **Exit** at the **A>** prompt and your worksheet will be displayed. Replace the DOS disk in Drive A with the 1-2-3 System disk, and leave the newly formatted disk in drive B. If you have only one floppy-disk drive, you will need to swap the System disk with the blank disk when prompted.

9. Press the slash (**/**) key again.

10. Move the pointer to **File**.

11. Press Enter. The **File** command menu, shown in Figure 12.2, appears on the screen. You use these commands to **Retrieve** a file that you **Save** on a disk, to **Combine** part or all of a saved worksheet with the worksheet on the screen, to **Xtract** part of your worksheet to a new file on the disk, to **Erase** a file, to display the names of the files that you've saved (**List**), to incorporate text or numbers from another software program into the worksheet (**Import**), and to save or retrieve from a disk and/or subdirectory (if you have a hard-disk system) other than the one you are currently using (**Directory**).

12. Move the pointer to **Save**.

13. Press Enter. The prompt **Enter save file name:** appears on the screen.

14. Choose a name for your worksheet. Be sure to choose a relevant title, such as 87BUDGET, so that when you read through the file names in the directory at a later date, you'll know what you filed under each name. It doesn't matter if you give the file a nickname, a date, a name, or a number, as long as it makes sense to you. But note the following rules:

    - 1-2-3 only will remember the first eight characters that you type.
    - You can use only letters of the alphabet, numbers, and the underline key.
    - You cannot use punctuation or blank spaces.

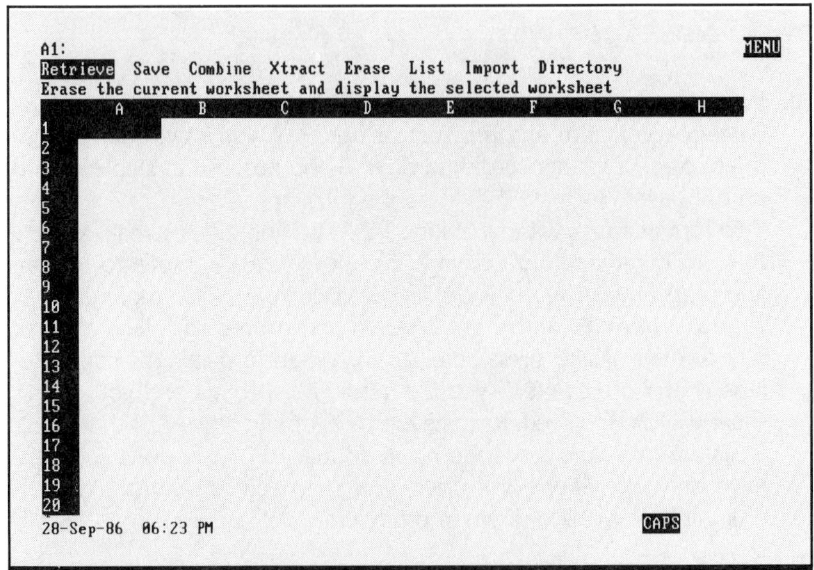

Figure 12.2: *File Command Menu*

15. If you have a floppy-disk system, type:

    B:87BUDGET

    If you have a hard-disk system, type:

    C:\123\87BUDGET

    If you named your subdirectory with a name other than 123 use that name instead.

16. Press Enter. When the mode indicator says **READY**, the worksheet or file is saved. The next time you save the same file, 1-2-3 will automatically enter the name of the file to save, and then the prompt **Cancel Replace** will appear. This gives you the opportunity to cancel the command. Instead of **Cancel**, you would select **Replace**, press Enter, and 1-2-3 would save the file. From now on, it is a good idea to save your work after each step in this book unless otherwise instructed. This will prevent you from having to retype more than a few steps if you accidentally erase the screen. If you want to stop working, now is the best time to do so—after you have saved your work.

Changing the default directory

17. Complete the following steps to eliminate having to type B: or C:\123\ every time you want to save a file. You must change 1-2-3's

default setting, the setting that came with the program, so that 1-2-3 knows to save to and retrieve from the correct drive. This needs to be done only once.

a. Press the slash (**/**) key.

b. Since the pointer is on **Worksheet**, press Enter.

c. Since the pointer is on **Global**, press Enter. 1-2-3 displays a menu including all the items that have settings that affect the entire worksheet. These are explained in detail for both floppy- and hard-disk users in Section 30, "Checking and Changing 1-2-3 Default Settings."

d. Move the pointer to **Default**.

e. Press Enter.

f. Move the pointer to **Directory**.

g. Press Enter.

h. For floppy-disk systems, type:

B:\

For hard-disk systems, type:

C:\123

i. Press Enter.

j. Move the pointer to **Update**.

k. Press Enter. This changes the 1-2-3 program.

l. Move the pointer to **Quit**.

m. Press Enter. The mode indicator changes to **READY**.

Saving a Worksheet under a Different Name—a Quick and Painless Way to Back Up Your Work

18. When you save a worksheet again, 1-2-3 suggests the drive, directory, and file name that it was originally saved under. To save a worksheet under a different name, just type in a new name.

    Use **/File Save** to display the current file name. Type in a new name: **BUDGET2**. Notice that **87BUDGET** was overwritten by the new name. Press Enter to save the worksheet.

19. To save a worksheet in a different area of your hard disk or on a different floppy drive, go through the following steps.

    Use **/File Save** to display the current file name, now **BUDGET2**. Press Escape once to display all worksheet files on the current drive in the current directory.

    If you have a floppy-disk computer, you will see:

    B:*.wk?

    If you have a hard-disk computer and the default directory is named 123, you will see:

    C:\123*.wk?

    A list of worksheet files is displayed. The ***.wk?** lists both 1-2-3 version 2.0 worksheet files (with **.wk1** extensions) and 1-2-3 version 1A files (with **.wks** extensions).

    Note: Once you have retrieved a version 1A worksheet, it may only be saved as a version 2.0 worksheet, with an extension of .wk1.

20. Press Escape again to display *all* files on the disk, not just worksheet files. You will see: B:\ or C:\123\

21. Press Escape one more time to clear the drive and directory. The following is displayed.

    Enter save file name:

22. Now type in the new destination.

    For a floppy-disk system, place another "backup" diskette in drive A. (Temporarily take out the System disk—it is only necessary when starting 1-2-3 or when using the Help screens.) Then type (after **Enter save file name:**) **A:\BUDGET2** and press Enter. This will create a backup copy on the other diskette. Now reinsert the System disk in drive A. If you do not have a backup disk at this time, skip this step. Press Escape to return to the Ready mode.

    For a hard-disk system, you can save the worksheet on a floppy as in the prior step for floppy-disk systems, or you can save it in a different directory on the same disk. At **Enter save file name:**, type **C:BUDGET2**. This saves the worksheet in the main, or *root,* directory.

23. Now save the worksheet once more under its original name and in the default directory. Using **/File Save**, save it as **B:\87BUDGET** for floppy-disk systems or **C:\123\87BUDGET** for hard-disk systems.

24. You will need to **Replace** the first version of the worksheet with the new one.

Quitting the Worksheet

25. To leave the worksheet use the **Quit** command. Press slash (**/**).
26. Move to **Quit**.
27. Press Enter. The Access menu is displayed. You can turn off your computer, exit to DOS in order to run another program, return to 1-2-3, or use any of the utility programs available from the Access menu.

13 Retrieving Work that You've Saved

FEATURING:

the File Retrieve command

You stored your worksheet, turned off your computer, went out for a luncheon appointment, and returned to your desk, ready to review your work. Another file command, **File Retrieve**, quickly returns your worksheet to the screen.

How to Retrieve a File

1. Bring up the blank worksheet on the screen. If you turned off the computer in the last section, you must turn it on again, then enter the date and time, if necessary. In the Lotus Access menu, press Enter to bring up the 1-2-3 worksheet. For further instructions, see Section 5, "Bringing Up the Worksheet on Your Screen."
2. Press the slash (**/**) key.
3. Move the pointer to **File**.
4. Press Enter.

5. Since the pointer is already on **Retrieve**, press Enter. If you have a floppy-disk system, the following is displayed unless you are using another directory or drive:

   Name of file to retrieve: B:*.WK?

   If you have a hard-disk system, the following is displayed unless you are using a different directory or drive:

   Name of file to retrieve: C:\123*.WK?

   Beneath the prompt will be a list of any worksheet files that were saved previously. To see additional files, use the Right-Arrow or Left-Arrow key to scroll through the list to the right or left.

6. When you find **87BUDGET**, press the Enter key to retrieve it. (Instead of *pointing* to a file name you can just type in the name.)

If, at a later date, you are viewing one worksheet and want to retrieve another worksheet that you've saved, remember to *save the worksheet you are viewing before you attempt to retrieve a file. If you don't, the current worksheet will be erased.* For instructions on how to save a file, refer to the previous section.

14 Changing a Column Width and Hiding and Displaying Columns

FEATURING:

the Worksheet Column and Worksheet Hide and Display commands

You have a problem. When you entered numbers in column B, some of the labels in column A were cut off. In order to read the complete labels, you have to widen the column. Since changing a column affects the appearance of the entire worksheet by shifting all of the columns to the right, you use a **Worksheet** command, rather than a **Range** command that is reserved for changes affecting only part of the worksheet.

How to Change a Column Width

1. Move the pointer to any cell in the column that you want to widen. In this case, move it to **A5**.
2. Press the slash (**/**)key.

3. Since the pointer is already on **Worksheet**, press Enter. The **Worksheet** command menu, shown in Figure 14.1, appears on the screen. You use these commands to check **Status** and change **Global** settings—such as column-width—that affect the appearance of the entire worksheet, to **Insert** and **Delete** columns and rows, to change the width or hide or display a column (**Column Set-Width, Column Hide, Column Display**), to **Erase** the entire worksheet, to split the screen into two screens or **Windows**, and to ensure that your labels don't scroll off the screen when you move the pointer (**Titles**). In 1-2-3 version 2.0 you can now use the **Worksheet Page** command to set a *page break* anywhere in your worksheet.

4. Move the pointer to **Column**.

5. Press Enter.

6. The following menu is displayed:

   Set-Width Reset-Width Hide Display

   Since the pointer is on **Set-Width**, press Enter. The prompt **Enter column width (1..240): 9** appears. Nine is the preset, or *default*, width of a column.

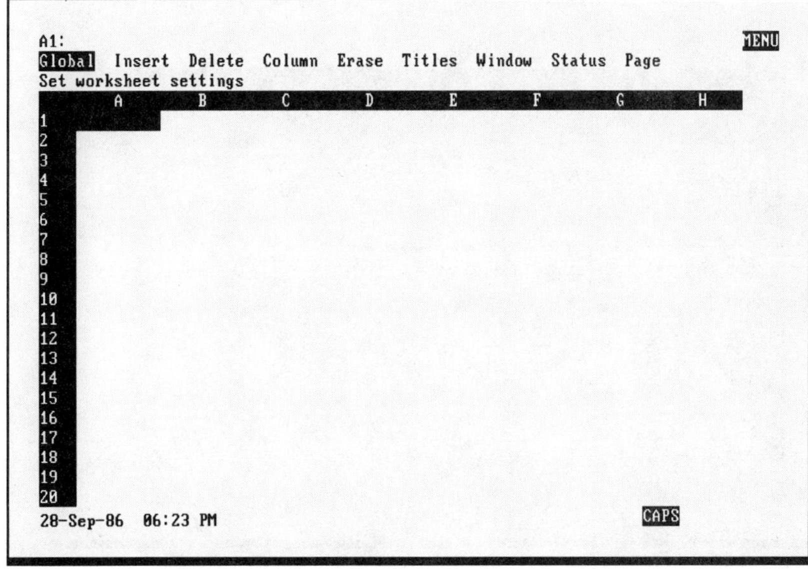

Figure 14.1: *Worksheet Command Menu*

7. Using the Right-Arrow key, widen column A to 13. The labels that were cut off in column A reappear. If you didn't need to see the display first, you could also type 13.

8. Press Enter. The worksheet now matches the one in Figure 14.2. Notice that **[W13]** is displayed above the worksheet in the Control Panel. This shows that column A has been set with Worksheet Column for a width of 13. At this point, if you wanted to change the column back to its original width, called the **global default** setting—*global* because it affects the entire worksheet, *default* because it is the original setting that comes with the 1-2-3 program—you would select **Reset**, instead of **Set** after doing **/Worksheet Column** again. After pressing Enter, 1-2-3 would automatically return the column back to its original setting.

How to Hide and Display a Column

With the new version of 1-2-3, you can now hide one or more columns so they are not displayed on the screen or included when the worksheet is printed. This can keep sensitive data secure while the data is used to build and calculate worksheets that will be distributed to others.

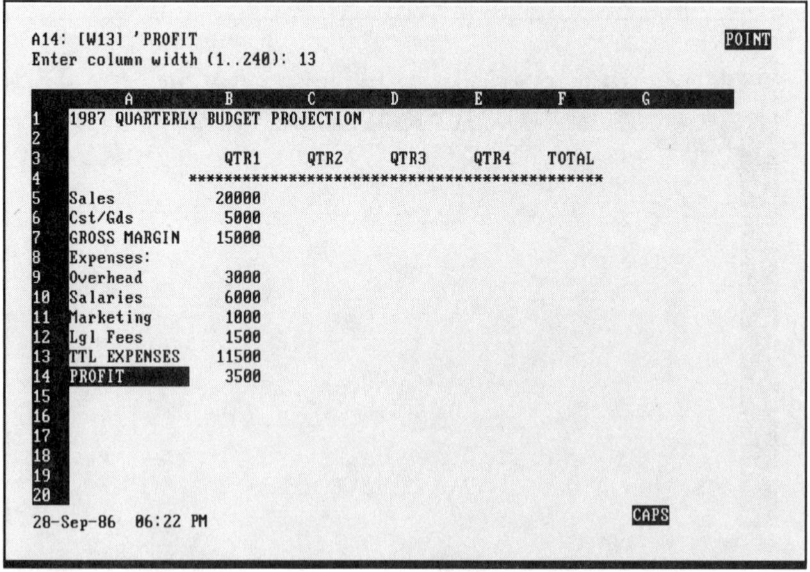

Figure 14.2: *Widening the Column*

9. Use **Worksheet Column** again to hide a column. Press **/**.
10. Press Enter at **Worksheet**.
11. Move the pointer to **Column** and press Enter again.
12. Move the pointer to **Hide** and press Enter.
13. The screen displays: **Enter current column: A5**. Press Enter. Column A will disappear.
14. To redisplay the column, use **/Worksheet Column Display**. Column B will be prompted. Move to column A and press Enter. Column A is displayed again.

15

Copying Data from One Area of the Worksheet to Another

FEATURING:

the Copy command

Often while building a worksheet, you run into the problem of having to retype formulas and/or data that you have already entered on another part of the same worksheet. The **Copy** command eliminates tedious retyping by copying information for you. It enables you to copy a single cell or a group of cells across the worksheet or down through a column.

Let's assume, for the sake of illustration, that the company for which you are building the 1987 Budget Projection is extremely consistent; in fact, it is so consistent that you expect the income and expenses to stay the same for the remaining three quarters. To save yourself time, you would copy all the figures across the worksheet, from **QTR1** into the remaining three columns or quarters.

As soon as you finish entering the figures for all four quarters, though, other questions will come to mind. What are the total sales for the year? What are the total salary costs? The total marketing costs? Column F is the place to answer these questions. After entering a formula in F5, and copying the formula down through the column, you will have the annual totals for every item in column A.

How to Copy Data from One Part of the Worksheet to Another

Hint: If you lose your way in the following steps remember that the Escape key takes you out of any menu. Also, you can always start over by retrieving the file 87BUDGET if you need to.

If you want to copy a single cell across to several cells

1. Move the pointer to the cell you want to copy; in this case, it is B5.
2. Press the slash (**/**) key.
3. Move the pointer to **Copy**.
4. Press Enter. The prompt **Enter range to copy FROM: B5. .B5** appears on the screen, and the mode indicator changes to **POINT** indicating that you will point to or type the *range*. A range is either a single cell or a group of cells arranged in a rectangular block, such as part of a column or row, or a combination of both. Since the pointer was already on B5 when you pressed the slash (**/**) key, 1-2-3 assumes that it is the only cell you are copying. There are no others between B5 and B5.
5. Since you are copying B5, press Enter. The prompt **Enter range to copy TO: B5** appears. 1-2-3 assumes you are copying to the same cell until it is told otherwise.
6. Move the pointer to C5.
7. Type a period to **anchor** the cell. Two periods appear.
8. Move the pointer to E5. All the cells into which you are copying are highlighted. **C5. .E5** is also displayed on the control panel.
9. Press Enter. The number 20000 is copied to cells C5, D5, and E5, as shown in Figure 15.1, and the pointer returns to the original cell.

If you want to copy more than one cell across the worksheet

Now copy the rest of the numbers in column B to columns C, D, and E all at once.

10. Move the pointer to B6, **5000**.
11. Press the slash (**/**) key.

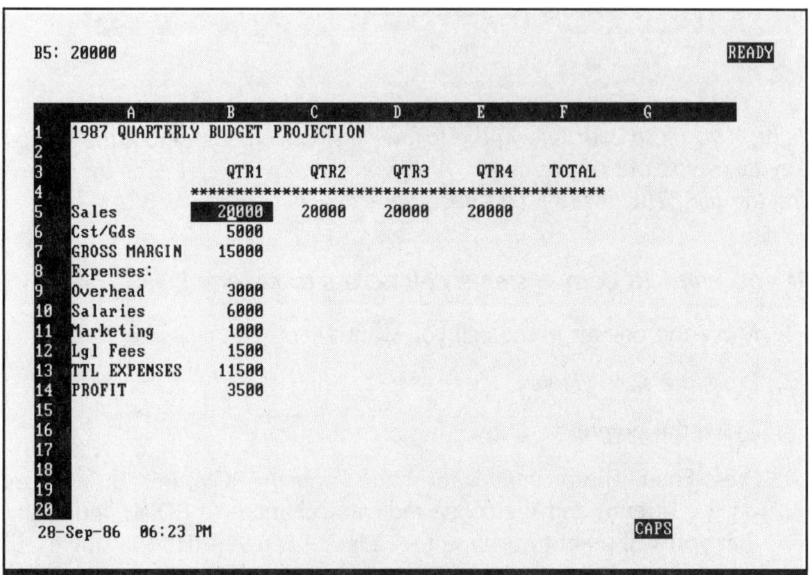

```
B5: 20000                                                          READY

     A              B         C         D         E         F         G
1   1987 QUARTERLY BUDGET PROJECTION
2
3                   QTR1      QTR2      QTR3      QTR4      TOTAL
4                ********************************************
5   Sales           20000     20000     20000     20000
6   Cst/Gds          5000
7   GROSS MARGIN    15000
8   Expenses:
9   Overhead         3000
10  Salaries         6000
11  Marketing        1000
12  Lgl Fees         1500
13  TTL EXPENSES    11500
14  PROFIT           3500
15
16
17
18
19
20
20-Sep-86  06:23 PM                                          CAPS
```

Figure 15.1: *Worksheet with Copied Numbers*

12. Move the pointer to **Copy**.
13. Press Enter. 1-2-3 displays **Enter range to copy FROM: B6..B6**
14. Since you are copying more than one cell, move the pointer to B14 before pressing Enter. Cells B6 through B14 are highlighted.
15. Press Enter. The **copy-TO** prompt appears. Notice that this prompt does not display the cell addresses separated by periods. You must decide at this point whether you want to move the pointer first, *before* anchoring it to a particular cell.
16. Move the pointer to C6.
17. Type a period to anchor it.
18. Move the pointer to E6. When you copy a column, you only need to specify the top of the range you are copying to. When you copy a row down, you only need to specify the left side of the range you are copying to.
19. Press Enter. The numbers and formulas are copied across the worksheet, as in Figure 15.2, and the pointer returns to the original cell. Now save the budget in case you make mistakes in the following steps. If this happens, you can then abandon the later version and retrieve what you have done so far.

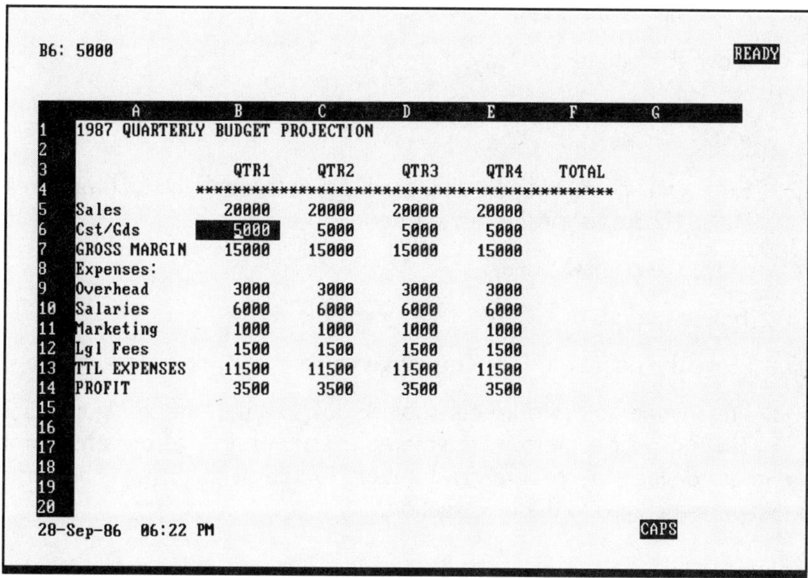
B6: 5000 READY

	A	B	C	D	E	F	G
1	1987 QUARTERLY BUDGET PROJECTION						
2							
3		QTR1	QTR2	QTR3	QTR4	TOTAL	
4		************	************	************	************	********	
5	Sales	20000	20000	20000	20000		
6	Cst/Gds	5000	5000	5000	5000		
7	GROSS MARGIN	15000	15000	15000	15000		
8	Expenses:						
9	Overhead	3000	3000	3000	3000		
10	Salaries	6000	6000	6000	6000		
11	Marketing	1000	1000	1000	1000		
12	Lgl Fees	1500	1500	1500	1500		
13	TTL EXPENSES	11500	11500	11500	11500		
14	PROFIT	3500	3500	3500	3500		
15							
16							
17							
18							
19							
20							

28-Sep-86 06:22 PM CAPS

Figure 15.2: *Second Worksheet with Copied Numbers*

20. Use **/File Save.**
    Press slash (**/**).
21. Move to **File** and press Enter.
22. Move to **Save** and press Enter.
23. Press Enter to accept the same name. Since you have already saved the budget once, you must **Replace** it with the new version. Move to **Replace** and press **Enter.**

If you want to copy down through a column

There are two ways to create formulas in column F that will total the quarterly amounts into yearly amounts. One way is to type in one formula for each row of numbers; the other is to type in one formula and copy it into the other rows. The second way is more efficient.

24. Cell F5 is empty. Before you copy it, you need to enter a formula. Since you want to total each row, type the @SUM function in F5:

    @SUM(B5. .E5)

25. Press Enter. **80000** appears in F5.

26. Press the slash (**/**) key.
27. Move the pointer to **Copy**.
28. Press Enter. 1-2-3 asks you to identify the range you are copying from. It suggests **F5. .F5**.
29. Since you are copying the single cell down through the column, press Enter. 1-2-3 asks for the range to copy to.
30. Move the pointer to F6.
31. Type a period.
32. Move the pointer to F14. The range you are copying to is highlighted.
33. Press Enter. Your worksheet should look like the one in Figure 15.3. The totals for each row are entered in column F. A zero is entered in row 8 since there were no numbers to add in this row. Proceed to erase the zero in the next section.

```
F5: @SUM(B5..E5)                                                    READY

         A            B         C         D         E         F         G
1   1987 QUARTERLY BUDGET PROJECTION
2
3                   QTR1      QTR2      QTR3      QTR4     TOTAL
4              *********************************************
5   Sales          20000     20000     20000     20000     80000
6   Cst/Gds         5000      5000      5000      5000     20000
7   GROSS MARGIN   15000     15000     15000     15000     60000
8   Expenses:                                                  0
9   Overhead        3000      3000      3000      3000     12000
10  Salaries        6000      6000      6000      6000     24000
11  Marketing       1000      1000      1000      1000      4000
12  Lgl Fees        1500      1500      1500      1500      6000
13  TTL EXPENSES   11500     11500     11500     11500     46000
14  PROFIT          3500      3500      3500      3500     14000
15
16
17
18
19
20
28-Sep-86  06:22 PM                                            CAPS
```

Figure 15.3: *Worksheet with the Total-Column Numbers*

16 Erasing Part of the Worksheet

FEATURING:

the Range Erase command

A few seconds ago, a colleague walked into your office with revised figures. It turns out that you've been making predictions with outdated information. With **Range Erase**, you can quickly erase all the old figures before you enter the new data.

Depending on your needs, you can erase one or many cells with **Range Erase**. You may have noticed that you can't completely erase a cell with the F2 Edit key; you can only change the entry. You must use **Range Erase** if you want to leave one or several cells completely blank.

How to Erase Part of the Worksheet

If you want to erase a single cell

1. Move the pointer to F8.
2. Press the slash (**/**) key.

3. Move the pointer to **Range**. The **Range** command menu, shown in Figure 16.1, appears on the screen. You use these commands to change the **Format** of some of the numbers (by adding dollar signs for example), to move labels within their columns (**Label**), to **Erase** part of the worksheet, to assign a **Name** to a group of cells, to perform some rudimentary text editing to labels (**Justify**), to set a cell so you can't enter anything in it (**Protect**)—unless you change the setting (**Unprotect**)—and to enter data only in the unprotected cells (**Input**). Version 2.0 has added two additional Range commands. The **Value** command converts formulas into their values. It is similar to the Copy command. However, when you use the Value command to copy a formula only the actual number displayed on the screen, the value of the formula, is copied. The formula itself is left behind. The **Transpose** command exchanges columns and rows on a worksheet. In this budget, we could transpose the four quarters to the left side of the worksheet in column A and the budget categories to the top in row 3. The numbers would be switched accordingly to match the new headings.
4. Press Enter.
5. Move the pointer to **Erase**.
6. Press Enter. The prompt **Enter range to erase:F8. .F8** appears. 1-2-3 always suggests the single cell where the pointer currently resides.

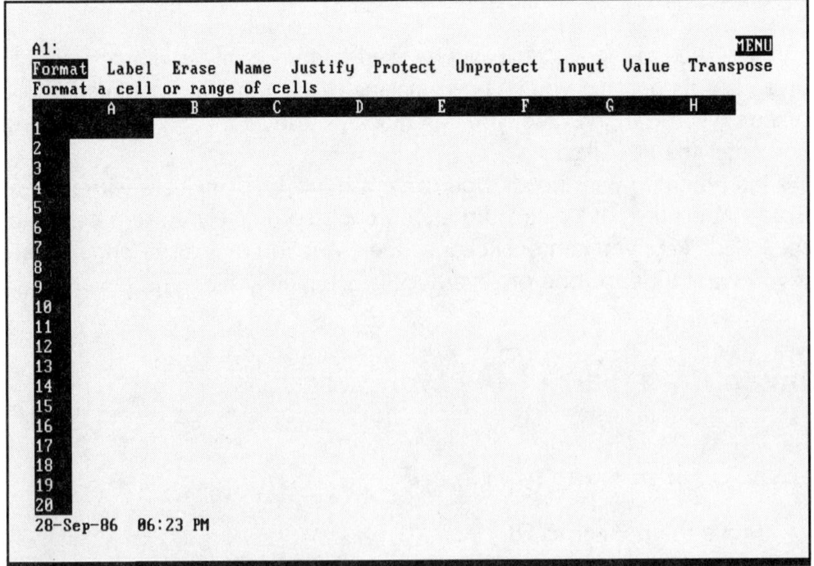

Figure 16.1: ***Range*** *Command Menu*

7. Press Enter to erase **F8**.

If you want to erase a range of cells

8. Press the slash (**/**) key.
9. Move the pointer to **Range**.
10. Press Enter.
11. Move the pointer to **Erase**.
12. Press Enter. The range-to-erase prompt appears again.
13. Press Escape. The second half of the range is erased from the prompt. You have just *unanchored* the range.
14. Move the pointer to the cell where you practiced making corrections earlier, A35.
15. Type a period to anchor A35.
16. Use the Down-Arrow key to include A36. The cells are highlighted, and the control panel reflects the range.
17. Press Enter. The range is erased.
18. Press the Home key.
19. Be sure to save your worksheet now. You will be erasing the entire worksheet in the next section. Saving it will enable you to return to the worksheet as it appears at this time. 1-2-3 will ask you if you want to **Cancel** or **Replace** the worksheet that was already saved on the disk. **Replace** it with your new version of the worksheet.
20. Now erase some numbers in your budget. Move to B5.
21. Press **/**, move to **Range**, and press Enter.
22. Move to **Erase** and press Enter. 1-2-3 displays **Enter Range to erase: B5..B5**.
23. Move the pointer to E6. The Sales and Cst/Gds numbers are highlighted.
24. Press Enter to erase the range.
25. Do the same with Expenses. Do not erase the formulas, however.
26. Proceed to the next section. Do not save the worksheet since you saved a completed version of your budget in step 19.

17

Erasing the Entire Worksheet

the Worksheet Erase command

When you've finished with a worksheet, and saved it, you can erase it by using the Worksheet Erase command.

How to Erase the Entire Worksheet

1. Press the slash (**/**) key.
2. Since the pointer is already on **Worksheet**, press Enter.
3. Move the pointer to **Erase**, press Enter. There is no range to specify. Instead, the prompt **No Yes Do not erase the entire worksheet; return to READY mode** appears as a safeguard to prevent you from erasing the worksheet in case you forgot to save it first.
4. Move the pointer to **Yes**.
5. Press Enter. The entire worksheet is erased—not only the entries, but also the column-width setting that you changed.

Do not save your worksheet now. Whenever you save, the previously saved file is overwritten with the new save. This means that you would be saving the blank worksheet. Since you want to retrieve the worksheet that you saved earlier, not a blank worksheet, don't save it now.

18

Formatting the Entire Worksheet: Changing the Way Numbers Are Represented on the Entire Worksheet

FEATURING:

the Worksheet Global Format command

At some point, you may want to share a worksheet with your co-workers. Before you do, though, you will want it to be as clear and straightforward as possible. A few changes will enhance its appearance.

Whenever you change the appearance of the cell entries, you are *formatting* the worksheet. There are a variety of ways to format the worksheet. You can change the appearance of all the cells with **Worksheet Global Format** commands, or you can change only part of the worksheet using **Range Format** commands.

An important point to remember about formatting is that **Range** commands take precedence over **Worksheet** commands. Once you alter part of the worksheet with a **Range** command, it will not be affected by **Worksheet** commands. In other words, you can't display some of the numbers on the worksheet as currency and then expect to display all of the numbers, including the currency, as percentages. Therefore, although you can change your mind and the worksheet several times, it is easier if you plan your changes so that you use **Worksheet Global Format** commands before you use **Range Format** commands.

Returning to your worksheet, you will first want to change the way your figures are represented on the entire worksheet. You can choose any of the following nine formats:

Fixed displays numbers with a specified number of decimal places (e.g., 2.0).

Scientific displays all numbers in exponential form with a specified number of decimal places (e.g., 2.00E+01).

Currency displays all numbers with a **$**, commas, and a specified number of decimal places (e.g., $2,000.00).

, displays all numbers with commas and a specified number of decimal places (e.g., 2,000.00).

General displays numbers in the most abbreviated way possible (e.g., 2000). This is the standard format, also known as the default format.

+/− displays numbers as a pictograph; that is, positive numbers are represented by plus signs (5= + + + + +) and negative numbers are represented by minus signs (−3= − − −). Zeros are displayed as periods. As always, numbers that are too large for the column are not displayed; instead, asterisks fill the column.

Percent displays numbers as multiples of 100 with a percent sign, and with a specified number of decimal places (e.g., 2=200.0%).

Date takes special numbers and converts them into one of five date formats or one of four time formats. The special numbers for the date format range from 1 (which represents January 1, 1900) to 73049 (which represents December 31, 2099). The numbers represent the days from January 1, 1900, counted sequentially. For times the numbers are fractions of a day. For example, noon is represented by 12/24 or 0.5. To generate the number that represents a particular date, use the **@DATE** or the **@NOW** functions. To generate a number that represents a particular time, use **@TIME** or **@NOW**. (Refer to Section 57, on "Applying Commonly-Used Functions," for further explanation.)

Text displays formulas as they were entered on the screen and displays numbers in **General** format.

Hide allows you to hide the contents of one or more cells from the screen or from print.

Before you can format the worksheet, you need to retrieve the completed budget. To bring it back on the screen, see Section 13, "Retrieving Work that You've Saved."

How to Format the Entire Worksheet

To add commas and decimal places to the numbers

1. Retrieve the worksheet first using **File Retrieve**. Then press the slash (**/**) key.
2. Use **Worksheet**, **Global**, and **Format**, remembering to press Enter.
3. Now move the pointer to the comma. Press Enter. The prompt **Enter number of decimal places (0. .15):2** appears.
4. Since the numbers represent dollar figures, leave the **2** on the control panel. Press Enter. Your worksheet will match the one in Figure 18.1. The comma format adds four characters to each number. Those numbers that are now too large are replaced by asterisks. To correct this, you use the **Worksheet Global Column-Width** command, introduced in the next section.

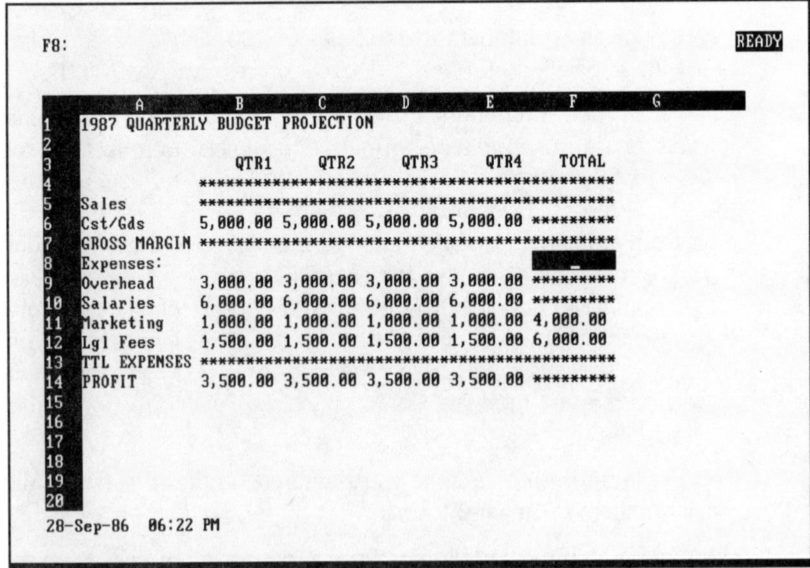

F8: READY

	A	B	C	D	E	F	G
1	1987 QUARTERLY BUDGET PROJECTION						
2							
3		QTR1	QTR2	QTR3	QTR4	TOTAL	
4		*********	*********	*********	*********	*********	
5	Sales	*********	*********	*********	*********	*********	
6	Cst/Gds	5,000.00	5,000.00	5,000.00	5,000.00	*********	
7	GROSS MARGIN	*********	*********	*********	*********	*********	
8	Expenses:						
9	Overhead	3,000.00	3,000.00	3,000.00	3,000.00	*********	
10	Salaries	6,000.00	6,000.00	6,000.00	6,000.00	*********	
11	Marketing	1,000.00	1,000.00	1,000.00	1,000.00	4,000.00	
12	Lgl Fees	1,500.00	1,500.00	1,500.00	1,500.00	6,000.00	
13	TTL EXPENSES	*********	*********	*********	*********	*********	
14	PROFIT	3,500.00	3,500.00	3,500.00	3,500.00	*********	
15							
16							
17							
18							
19							
20							

28-Sep-86 06:22 PM

Figure 18.1: *Formatted Worksheet*

19 Widening All the Columns on the Worksheet

FEATURING:

the Worksheet Global Column-Width command

Since many display formats add several characters to each number—commas, decimal points and places, and dollar signs—numbers often become too large for their column. Thus, it is necessary to widen all the columns. But wait a minute! You already learned how to adjust a column width in an earlier section. Why do you need to learn how to do it again?

The reason is because when you widened column A to fit all of the labels, the rest of the worksheet only shifted to the right; the other columns didn't get any wider. Now, you will widen all the columns.

How to Widen all the Columns

1. Press the slash (/) key.
2. Since the pointer is on **Worksheet**, press Enter.

3. Since the pointer is on **Global**, press Enter.
4. Move the pointer to **Column-Width**.
5. Press Enter. The prompt **Enter column width (1. .72): 9** appears. As explained earlier, nine is always the number of characters in a 1-2-3 column unless you specify otherwise; it is the default setting.
6. Use the Right-Arrow key to expand the columns to 11. You could also type the desired width.
7. Press Enter. Your worksheet will now match the one in Figure 19.1. Notice that column A didn't widen. This is because you widened it earlier with the **Worksheet Column-Width** command, which takes precedence over the **Worksheet Global Column-Width** command. To adjust column A, you need to use **Worksheet Column Reset**.

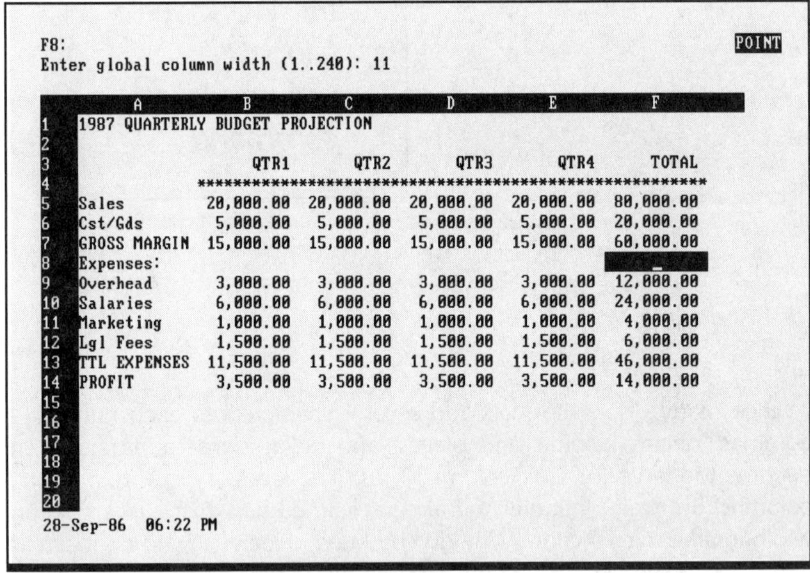

F8: POINT
Enter global column width (1..240): 11

	A	B	C	D	E	F
1	1987 QUARTERLY BUDGET PROJECTION					
2						
3		QTR1	QTR2	QTR3	QTR4	TOTAL
4		**********	**********	**********	**********	**********
5	Sales	20,000.00	20,000.00	20,000.00	20,000.00	80,000.00
6	Cst/Gds	5,000.00	5,000.00	5,000.00	5,000.00	20,000.00
7	GROSS MARGIN	15,000.00	15,000.00	15,000.00	15,000.00	60,000.00
8	Expenses:					
9	Overhead	3,000.00	3,000.00	3,000.00	3,000.00	12,000.00
10	Salaries	6,000.00	6,000.00	6,000.00	6,000.00	24,000.00
11	Marketing	1,000.00	1,000.00	1,000.00	1,000.00	4,000.00
12	Lgl Fees	1,500.00	1,500.00	1,500.00	1,500.00	6,000.00
13	TTL EXPENSES	11,500.00	11,500.00	11,500.00	11,500.00	46,000.00
14	PROFIT	3,500.00	3,500.00	3,500.00	3,500.00	14,000.00
15						
16						
17						
18						
19						
20						

20-Sep-86 06:22 PM

Figure 19.1: *Worksheet with Widened Columns*

20

Formatting Part of the Worksheet: Changing the Way Numbers are Represented on Part of the Worksheet

FEATURING:

the Range Format command

Perhaps, for more impact, you want to emphasize particular areas of the worksheet. Using **Range Format** you have the same options that you had in **Worksheet Global Format**, but you can use them to change the way a single cell or range of cells is displayed. For example, you can play up the most relevant details on the worksheet by adding dollar signs to the gross margin, total expenses, and profit figures.

How to Format Part of the Worksheet

To change the GROSS MARGIN, TTL EXPENSES, and PROFIT rows to currency

1. Press the slash (/) key.
2. Move the pointer to **Range**.

3. Press Enter.
4. Since the pointer is on **Format**, press Enter. The **Range Format** menu, shown in Figure 20.1, appears on the screen. Notice that there is one command in **Range Format** that is not in **Worksheet Global Format: Reset.** It is used to return the range setting that you specify back to the global format—in this case, the comma format.
5. Move the pointer to **Currency.**
6. Press Enter. The prompt **Enter number of decimal places (0. .15): 2** appears.
7. Since you still want two decimal places, press Enter. A prompt asking you to enter the range to format appears.
8. Press Escape. The range is unanchored.
9. Move the pointer to the first cell in the range; in this case, it is B7.
10. Type a period to anchor the cell again.
11. Move the pointer to F7.
12. Press Enter. Dollar signs are added to the figures in row 7. **(C2)** appears on the control panel above the worksheet. It tells you that

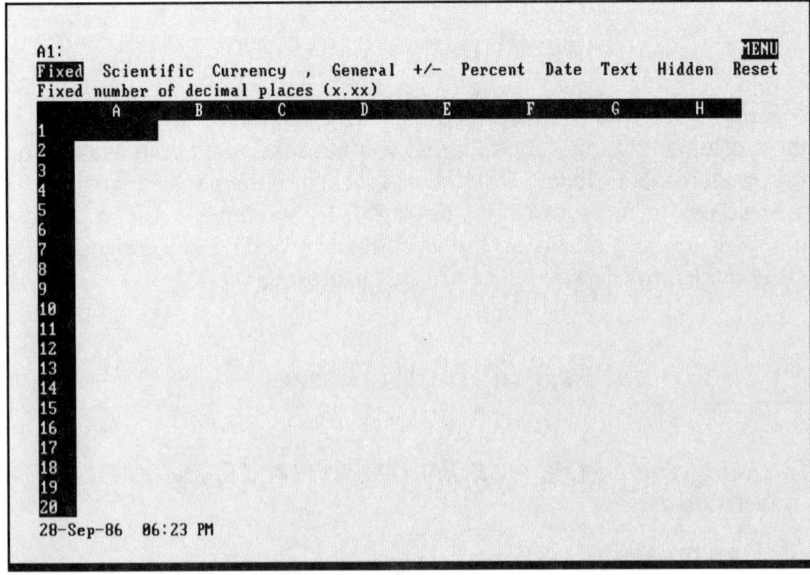

Figure 20.1: *The Range Format Menu*

the cell is range-formatted with currency and two decimal places. This only appears in front of cells that are range-formatted. (To see this, you must move the pointer to a cell in row 7 if it is not already on one.)

13. To add dollar signs to the **TTL EXPENSES** and **PROFIT** rows, repeat the process beginning with step 1 and type in or point to the appropriate cell ranges. When you are done, the worksheet will look like the one in Figure 20.2.

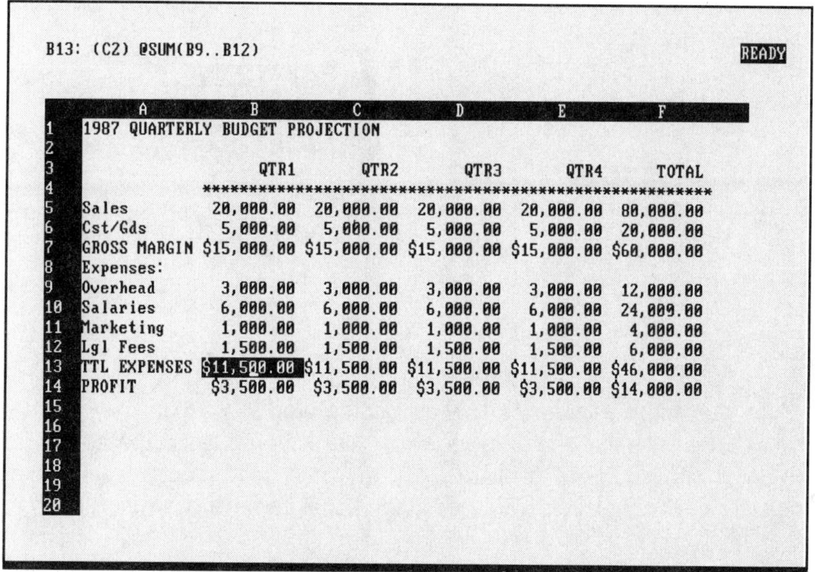

B13: (C2) @SUM(B9..B12)   READY

	A	B	C	D	E	F
1	1987 QUARTERLY BUDGET PROJECTION					
2						
3		QTR1	QTR2	QTR3	QTR4	TOTAL
4		************	************	************	************	************
5	Sales	20,000.00	20,000.00	20,000.00	20,000.00	80,000.00
6	Cst/Gds	5,000.00	5,000.00	5,000.00	5,000.00	20,000.00
7	GROSS MARGIN	$15,000.00	$15,000.00	$15,000.00	$15,000.00	$60,000.00
8	Expenses:					
9	Overhead	3,000.00	3,000.00	3,000.00	3,000.00	12,000.00
10	Salaries	6,000.00	6,000.00	6,000.00	6,000.00	24,009.00
11	Marketing	1,000.00	1,000.00	1,000.00	1,000.00	4,000.00
12	Lgl Fees	1,500.00	1,500.00	1,500.00	1,500.00	6,000.00
13	TTL EXPENSES	$11,500.00	$11,500.00	$11,500.00	$11,500.00	$46,000.00
14	PROFIT	$3,500.00	$3,500.00	$3,500.00	$3,500.00	$14,000.00
15						
16						
17						
18						
19						
20						

Figure 20.2: *Partially Reformatted Worksheet*

21 Shifting Labels Within Their Columns

the Range Label command

After you have entered your labels on the worksheet, you may decide that you want to shift them, especially if you have widened the columns. Although you could go back to individual cells and reenter each label to center it, shifting labels with the **Range Label** command is much faster.

How to Shift Labels Within their Columns

1. Press the slash (**/**) key.
2. Move the pointer to **Range**.
3. Press Enter.
4. Move the pointer to **Label**.
5. Press Enter. You now have a choice of making all the labels centered or aligned on the left or the right.
6. Move the pointer to **Center**.
7. Press Enter. A prompt asks you to enter the range.
8. Press Escape to unanchor the range on the control panel.

9. Move the pointer to B3.
10. Type a period to anchor the cell.
11. Move the pointer to F3.
12. Press Enter. The labels are centered. At a later date, if you decide you want all of your labels automatically aligned on the right or centered, use the **Worksheet Global Label-Prefix** command to change the default setting so that 1-2-3 doesn't automatically align them on the left. You must use this command before you enter any labels because it will not realign labels already on the worksheet.

Preformated for label alignment:
Left, Center, Right
use Worksheet, Global, Label Prefix Command

To Align existing labels,
use Range Label Command
(Range label takes President)

22 Inserting Columns and Rows

FEATURING:

the Worksheet Insert command

After you finish building the worksheet, or while you are still in the midst of building it, you may want to insert columns or rows. Perhaps you need to add figures you neglected to include, or you might want to move a column or row that you've already entered, or set apart a column or row by surrounding it with blank space. You don't simply want to add to the right or bottom of the worksheet; you want to insert columns and rows between columns and rows that already contain information.

For example, looking at the budget, you realize you haven't answered an important question: What percent of the total expenses does each item represent? And you still don't like the appearance of the worksheet; the numbers are too crowded. What can you do? You need to add another column of figures and insert some blank rows so there is more space between the rows of numbers.

Where should you put the new column? One option is to add the figures between the fourth quarter and total columns. But first, you have to insert a blank column between the two columns. To do so, you use the **Worksheet Insert** command. The same command enables you to add blank rows above and below **GROSS MARGIN** and **TTL EXPENSES.**

How to Insert Columns and Rows

1. Move the pointer to F3.
2. Press the slash (**/**) key.
3. Since the pointer is on **Worksheet**, press Enter.
4. Move the pointer to **Insert**.
5. Press Enter. The prompt **Column Row Insert one or more blank columns to the left of the cell pointer** appears.
6. Since you want to insert a column to the left of the **TOTAL** column, to the left of column F, you press Enter. The prompt **Enter column insert range:F3. .F3** appears. You need only specify one cell in the column. 1-2-3 always inserts an entire column. You expand the range to the right only if you want to insert more than one column.
7. Since you only want to insert one column, press Enter.
8. Move the pointer to the right to see that everything from column F shifts to the right to make room for the blank column. (Had there been more columns with entries, they too would have shifted to the right.) All the formulas are adjusted to reflect the change. The worksheet now looks like the one in Figure 22.1.

To insert a blank row

9. Press the slash (**/**) key.
10. Since the pointer is on **Worksheet**, press Enter.
11. Move the pointer to **Insert**.
12. Press Enter. 1-2-3 offers you the option of inserting a column or a row.

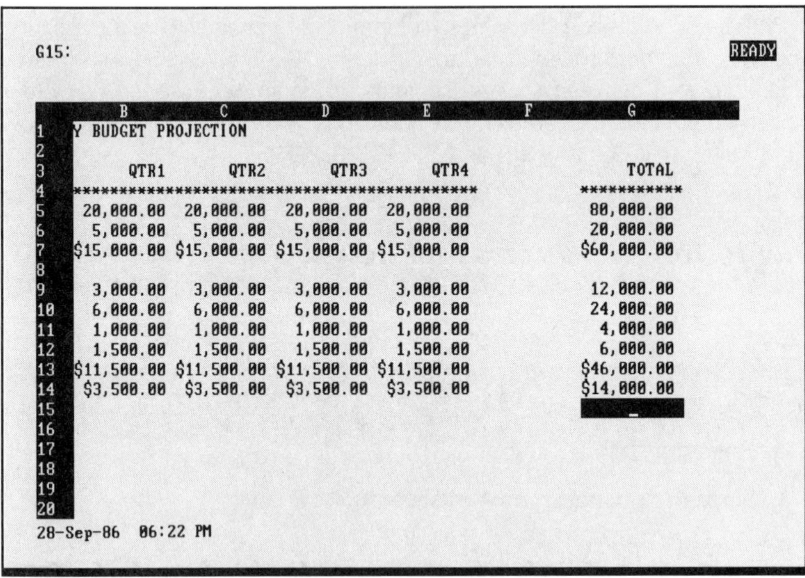

Figure 22.1: *Worksheet with a Blank Column*

13. Move the pointer to **Row**.
14. Press Enter. 1-2-3 asks you to identify the range of the row and suggests the cell where the pointer currently resides.
15. Press Escape to unanchor the range.
16. Move the pointer to a cell in the row where you want to insert a row. Move it to A7. It's not necessary to specify any more than one cell in the row. 1-2-3 automatically inserts an entire row. You expand the range only when you want to insert more than one row.
17. Press Enter. A blank row appears between **Cst/Gds** and **GROSS MARGIN**, and the worksheet shifts down. Formulas adjust automatically to reflect the change.
18. Repeating steps 9 through 17, insert blank rows between **Expenses** and **GROSS MARGIN**, between **TTL EXPENSES** and **Lgl Fees**, and **PROFIT** and **TTL EXPENSES**. Remember as you enter each row, that 1-2-3 adds a blank row *above* the row that you specify.
19. Press the Home key. The budget should now look like the one in Figure 22.2.

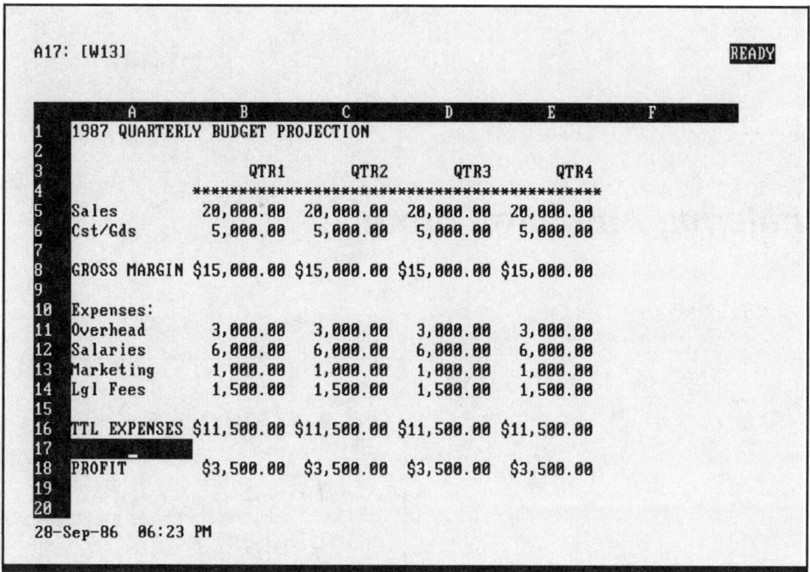

Figure 22.2: *Worksheet with Blank Rows*

23 Entering Absolute Formulas

FEATURING:

the F4 (Absolute) function key

Column F is empty. You still need to calculate each expense item as a percentage of the total expenses. To arrive at the percentages, you need to enter a formula and copy it down through the expenses, similar to the way you entered and copied formulas across the worksheet. However, there is one major difference that has to do with the cell addresses being *relative* or *absolute.*

When you first entered formulas, you typed or pointed to the different cell addresses to create the gross margin, total expenses, and profit formulas. You then copied them, along with the rest of the figures, across the worksheet.

When you copied, 1-2-3 automatically adjusted, or made relative, the cell addresses in the formula. More specifically, 1-2-3 adjusted the total expenses formula in column B—@SUM(B9..B12)—to @SUM(C9. .C12) for column C, @SUM(D9. .D12) for column D, and @SUM(E9. .E12) for column E. 1-2-3 does this automatically to all formulas whether it's copying across the worksheet or down through columns.

Because of this, a problem arises when you build the formula to calculate the percent of total expenses. In the formula, Expense Item/Total Expenses, the cell address for total expenses must remain constant, while the expense items change. Therefore, you need to instruct 1-2-3 not to automatically adjust the total expenses figure when it copies the formula. To do this, you precede both parts of the cell address with a dollar sign and the formula is written: +G11/$G$16. This makes the cell address of the total expenses absolute, rather than relative.

Not only is it possible to make a cell address absolute, but it is also possible to make part of it absolute. Since a cell address consists of two parts, a column letter and a row number, you can make either component absolute. This is called a *mixed cell address.*

Why would you want to do this? Suppose you want to know how much of the sales for each quarter is spent on marketing. After you find what percentage of the total expenses is represented by marketing, you would multiply sales by the percentage figure—+B5*G11.

If you want the percentage for the sales figures for every quarter, though, you need to enter a formula in which the columns change, but the rows do not so that you can copy the formula across the worksheet. In this case, you designate the row number as absolute with the column letter remaining relative. Thus, when you enter the formula +B$5*$G$11, the formulas are copied across as +C5*G11,+D5*G11, and +E5*G11. Only the column changes because the first cell address in the original formula is a mixed cell address.

Mixed cell addresses are considered to be a more advanced use of 1-2-3. In this section, you will be using only absolute cell addresses. However, as you become more skilled, understanding mixed cell addresses will help you put them into practice.

How to Enter Absolute Cell Addresses

1. First, enter the following labels:

   in F3 **% of TOTAL**

   in F4 *

2. In F11, type a plus sign to begin the formula.
3. Move the pointer to the right, to the first expense total in G11.
4. Press the slash (**/**) key. The right slash key, not the left. This time, it acts as a division sign because you are building formulas and you are in the **VALUE** mode. Also, the pointer returns to the original cell.

5. Move the pointer to the entire year's total expenses, G16. Notice that you are pointing to cells, not typing in their cell addresses. *The Absolute function key [F4] only works when pointing in order to build formulas.* If you type in a formula and press the F4 (Absolute) function key, 1-2-3 beeps. When you type in formulas, instead of pointing, and are in the **EDIT** or **VALUE** mode, you must type the dollar signs to designate a cell address as absolute.

6. Press the F4 function key on the left side of the keyboard. The following appears on the control panel:

   +G11/$G$16

   G16 is now absolute. The F4 function key can also be used to enter a mixed or relative cell address. Pressing it once, as you did, makes both the column and row absolute. Pressing it once or twice more makes the cell address mixed, and pressing it a fourth time returns the cell to its original relative setting.

Press once	Absolute	**$G$16**
Press twice	Mixed:Relative column, absolute row	**G$16**
Press three times	Mixed:Absolute column, relative row	**$G16**
Press four times	Relative	**G16**

   Return to absolute by pressing F4 once more.

7. Press Enter. **0.26** appears in F11, and you return to the **READY** mode.

8. To copy the formula for the other three expenses, press the slash (**/**) key, move the pointer to **Copy**, and press Enter. Do not change the range to copy from.

9. Press Enter to enter the range to copy to.

10. Designate **F12..F16**.

11. Press Enter. The percentages appear, and the worksheet now matches the one in Figure 23.1. Use **/Range Format** to display the four numbers in **Percent** format with two decimals. Highlight all four numbers. Use **/Range Erase** to erase the zero in row 15.

12. Move the pointer up and down through the four cells. Notice, on the control panel, that the first cell address changes but the second does not. It remains absolute.

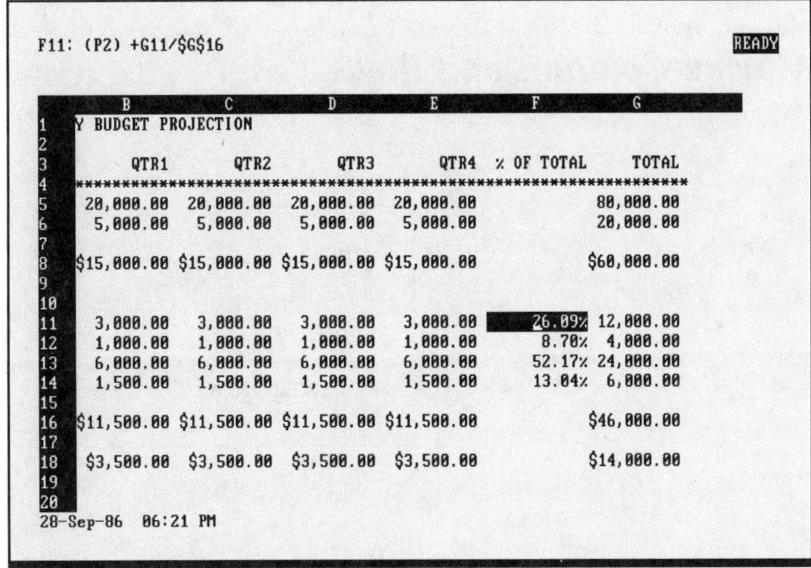

F11: (P2) +G11/$G$16 READY

	B	C	D	E	F	G
1	Y BUDGET PROJECTION					
2						
3	QTR1	QTR2	QTR3	QTR4	% OF TOTAL	TOTAL
4	************	************	************	************	************	************
5	20,000.00	20,000.00	20,000.00	20,000.00		80,000.00
6	5,000.00	5,000.00	5,000.00	5,000.00		20,000.00
7						
8	$15,000.00	$15,000.00	$15,000.00	$15,000.00		$60,000.00
9						
10						
11	3,000.00	3,000.00	3,000.00	3,000.00	26.09%	12,000.00
12	1,000.00	1,000.00	1,000.00	1,000.00	8.70%	4,000.00
13	6,000.00	6,000.00	6,000.00	6,000.00	52.17%	24,000.00
14	1,500.00	1,500.00	1,500.00	1,500.00	13.04%	6,000.00
15						
16	$11,500.00	$11,500.00	$11,500.00	$11,500.00		$46,000.00
17						
18	$3,500.00	$3,500.00	$3,500.00	$3,500.00		$14,000.00
19						
20						

28-Sep-86 06:21 PM

Figure 23.1: *Worksheet with Percentages*

24
Moving Columns and Rows

FEATURING:

the Move command

Note: Save your worksheet again before you begin this section and after you finish each of the following sections. A small error in these sections can delete valuable information.

You inserted the **% of TOTAL** column between the **QTR4** and **TOTAL** columns, and now you don't like how it looks. It would make more sense, you think, to put it after the **TOTAL** column. You also want to move **Marketing** above **Salaries**, since both marketing and overhead expenses have risen dramatically this year while salaries and legal fees haven't changed. With the **Move** command that transfers a range of cells to any position on the worksheet, you can do both.

How to Move Columns and Rows

To move a column

Since you are moving the **% of TOTAL** column to the right end of the worksheet, there is space. You do not have to insert a blank column first.

1. Press the slash (/) key.
2. Move the pointer to **Move**.
3. Press Enter. 1-2-3 asks you where you want to move from.
4. Press Escape. The range is now unanchored.
5. Move the pointer to F3.
6. Type a period. The cell is now anchored again.
7. Move the pointer down to row F14. The range of cells to move is highlighted.
8. Press Enter. 1-2-3 asks you where you want to move to.
9. Move the pointer to H3. You do not have to specify more than the first cell in the column you are moving to.
10. Press Enter. The column moves to the right of the **TOTAL** column, and a blank column is left in its place. The worksheet now looks like the one in Figure 24.1.

To move a row

11. Since you are moving the row up, above **Salaries**, you first need to insert a blank row. Using the **Worksheet Insert** command, do so now in cell A12. If you've forgotten how, see Section 22, "Inserting Columns and Rows."
12. Press the slash (/) key.
13. Move the pointer to **Move**.
14. Press Enter. 1-2-3 asks you where you want to move from and displays a range.
15. Press Escape.
16. Move the pointer to A14. The range is unanchored and shows a single **Marketing** cell

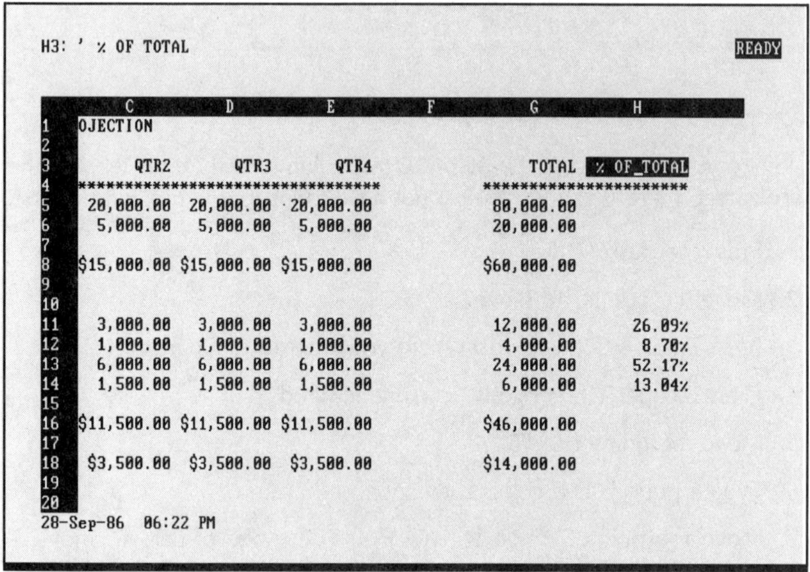
H3: ' % OF TOTAL READY

	C	D	E	F	G	H
1	OJECTION					
2						
3	QTR2	QTR3	QTR4		TOTAL	% OF_TOTAL
4	**********	**********	**********		**********	**********
5	20,000.00	20,000.00	20,000.00		80,000.00	
6	5,000.00	5,000.00	5,000.00		20,000.00	
7						
8	$15,000.00	$15,000.00	$15,000.00		$60,000.00	
9						
10						
11	3,000.00	3,000.00	3,000.00		12,000.00	26.09%
12	1,000.00	1,000.00	1,000.00		4,000.00	8.70%
13	6,000.00	6,000.00	6,000.00		24,000.00	52.17%
14	1,500.00	1,500.00	1,500.00		6,000.00	13.04%
15						
16	$11,500.00	$11,500.00	$11,500.00		$46,000.00	
17						
18	$3,500.00	$3,500.00	$3,500.00		$14,000.00	
19						
20						

28-Sep-86 06:22 PM

Figure 24.1: *The Worksheet after Moving a Column*

17. Type a period. The cell is anchored.
18. Move the pointer to H14. The range of numbers to move is highlighted.
19. Press Enter. 1-2-3 asks you where you are moving to.
20. Move the pointer to A12, the blank cell. You do not have to specify more than the first cell in the range.
21. Press Enter. The row moves up, and row 14 is left blank. The worksheet now appears like the one in Figure 24.2.
22. Save your worksheet. *Note:* In this case, no formulas are disrupted. However, if you moved a row containing a cell that had been entered as the first or last cell in a formula, you would disrupt the formula and produce inaccurate results or get an error message. For example, the Legal Fee amounts in row 14 could not have been moved without causing an **ERR** message in the Total Expenses and Profit formulas. The same is true with the row of Overhead figures. This is because the Total Expense formulas refer directly to rows 11 and 14 which are the Overhead and Legal Fee rows. Thus, if you were to move either of them you would get one of these formulas: **@SUM(ERR..B14)**, **@SUM(B11..ERR)**, or **@SUM(ERR..ERR)**. In the future, if you move

cells that contain formulas, be aware that you might have to correct the formulas to reflect the moves.

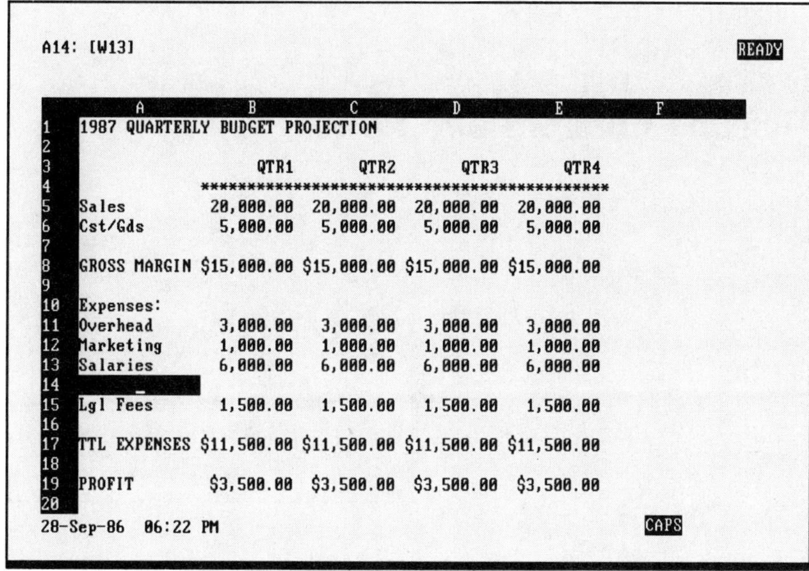

A14: [W13]　　READY

	A	B	C	D	E	F
1	1987 QUARTERLY BUDGET PROJECTION					
2						
3		QTR1	QTR2	QTR3	QTR4	
4		************	************	************	************	
5	Sales	20,000.00	20,000.00	20,000.00	20,000.00	
6	Cst/Gds	5,000.00	5,000.00	5,000.00	5,000.00	
7						
8	GROSS MARGIN	$15,000.00	$15,000.00	$15,000.00	$15,000.00	
9						
10	Expenses:					
11	Overhead	3,000.00	3,000.00	3,000.00	3,000.00	
12	Marketing	1,000.00	1,000.00	1,000.00	1,000.00	
13	Salaries	6,000.00	6,000.00	6,000.00	6,000.00	
14						
15	Lgl Fees	1,500.00	1,500.00	1,500.00	1,500.00	
16						
17	TTL EXPENSES	$11,500.00	$11,500.00	$11,500.00	$11,500.00	
18						
19	PROFIT	$3,500.00	$3,500.00	$3,500.00	$3,500.00	
20						

28-Sep-86 06:22 PM　　CAPS

Figure 24.2: *The Worksheet after Moving a Row*

25 Deleting Columns and Rows

FEATURING:

the Worksheet Delete command

Having moved a column and a row, you are left with a blank column and row on the budget. Obviously, they both need to be deleted. The **Worksheet Delete** command handles this task.

Deleting part of the worksheet is not the same as erasing it. Erasing entries simply leaves the cells blank. Deleting does more. It erases the entries in a column or row *and* deletes the space occupied by the column or row.

How to Delete Columns and Rows

Note: In case of an accidental deletion, retrieve the worksheet that you saved in the last section.

To delete a column

1. Press the slash (**/**) key.
2. Since the pointer is on **Worksheet**, press Enter.
3. Move the pointer to **Delete**.

4. Press Enter. You have the choice of deleting columns or rows.
5. Since the pointer is on **Column**, press Enter. 1-2-3 asks you the range of columns to delete.
6. Press Escape.
7. Move the pointer to a cell in column F. You only need to specify one cell in the column.
8. Press Enter. The blank column disappears from the screen, and the columns on the right shift to the left.

To delete a row

9. To delete row 14, repeat the steps above, but select **Row** instead of **Column**, and designate a cell in row 14. When you've finished, the worksheet will look like the one in Figure 25.1.

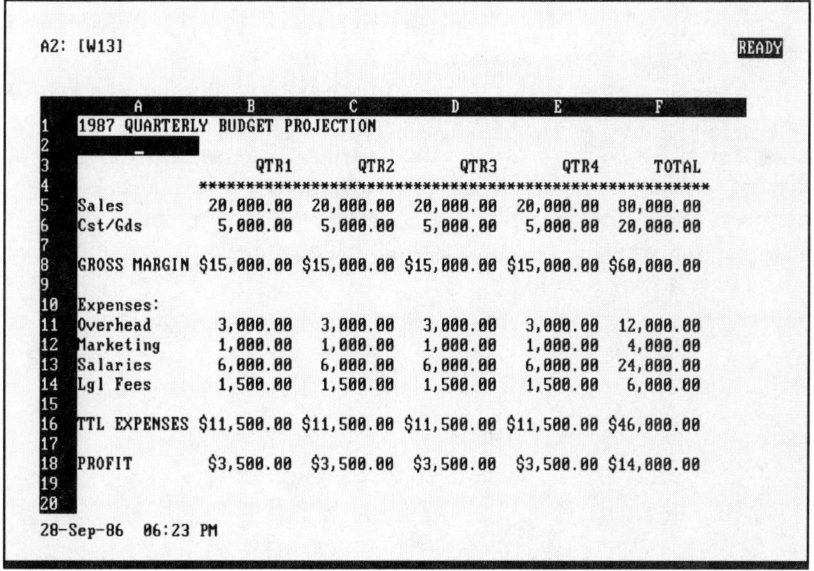

A2: [W13] READY

	A	B	C	D	E	F
1	1987 QUARTERLY BUDGET PROJECTION					
2						
3		QTR1	QTR2	QTR3	QTR4	TOTAL
4		************	************	************	************	************
5	Sales	20,000.00	20,000.00	20,000.00	20,000.00	80,000.00
6	Cst/Gds	5,000.00	5,000.00	5,000.00	5,000.00	20,000.00
7						
8	GROSS MARGIN	$15,000.00	$15,000.00	$15,000.00	$15,000.00	$60,000.00
9						
10	Expenses:					
11	Overhead	3,000.00	3,000.00	3,000.00	3,000.00	12,000.00
12	Marketing	1,000.00	1,000.00	1,000.00	1,000.00	4,000.00
13	Salaries	6,000.00	6,000.00	6,000.00	6,000.00	24,000.00
14	Lgl Fees	1,500.00	1,500.00	1,500.00	1,500.00	6,000.00
15						
16	TTL EXPENSES	$11,500.00	$11,500.00	$11,500.00	$11,500.00	$46,000.00
17						
18	PROFIT	$3,500.00	$3,500.00	$3,500.00	$3,500.00	$14,000.00
19						
20						

20-Sep-86 06:23 PM

Figure 25.1: *The Worksheet Without the Blank Column and Row*

26

Keyboard Shortcuts: A Faster Way to Enter Commands

Now that you're experienced, it's time to start saving time. Just as you can type in or point to a cell to enter its address on the control panel, you can type in or point to a command. Typing, however, saves keystrokes and time.

How do you type in a command? Simply type the first letter of the command. This selects the command and enters it automatically. For example, if you want to save a file, you only need to press the slash (**/**) key and type **FS**, for **File Save**, before you enter the file name.

Throughout the remaining sections of the book, you will be asked to *select* commands, rather than move the pointer to the command and press Enter. Whenever you see the instruction to select, you have a choice: you can move the pointer to the command name and press Enter, or you can save time by typing the first letter of each command.

Be careful, though! It's much easier to enter a wrong command by typing than it is by pointing.

27

Splitting the Screen: Viewing Two Parts of the Worksheet Simultaneously

FEATURING:

the Worksheet Window command and the F6 (Window) function key

A worksheet can get very large, with most of its columns not visible on the screen. This can be inconvenient, especially if you want to compare figures in a visible area to figures that are not on the screen. Scrolling through the worksheet isn't the solution since you have to scroll back and forth every time you want to look at a number off the screen.

Instead, you can divide the screen in two—horizontally (as shown in Figure 27.1) or vertically—with the **Worksheet Window** command. This way you can scroll through two areas of the worksheet and analyze distant figures side by side. To move the pointer back and forth between the two screens or windows, you press the F6 (Window) function key on the left side of the keyboard.

How to View Two Areas of the Worksheet Simultaneously

To split the screen horizontally

1. Press Home to display the beginning of the worksheet if it is not already on your screen.
2. Move the pointer to a cell in the row where you want to split the screen; in this case, move it to A5.
3. Press the slash (/) key.
4. Select **Worksheet Window**. Remember: You can move the pointer to the command and press Enter or type the first letter of the command. The **Window** menu, shown in Figure 27.2, appears on the screen.
5. Select **Horizontal**. The screen is divided into two windows. Notice that the column letters are inserted across the middle of the screen.
6. Move the pointer down. Now the pointer moves only in the top window.
7. Press the F6 function key. Notice that the pointer switches windows.

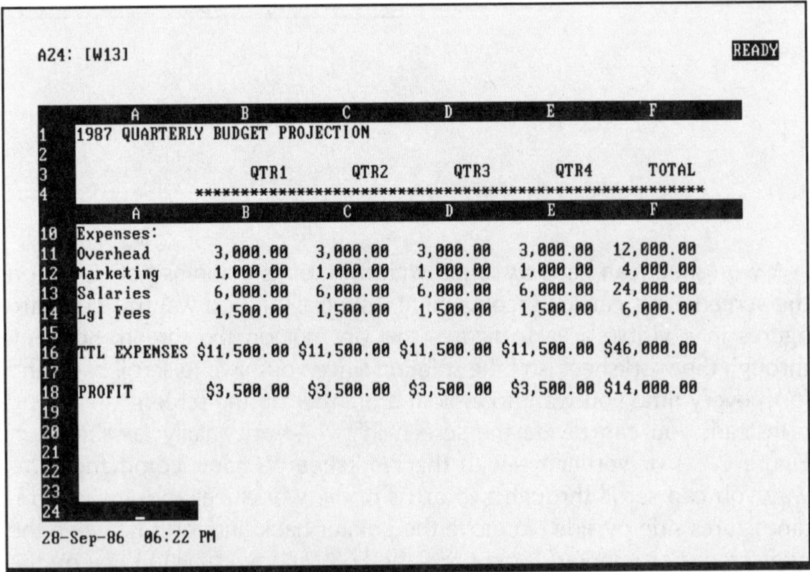

Figure 27.1: *Horizontally Split Screen*

8. Move the pointer down again.
9. Press F6. The pointer switches back to the top window.

To return to one window

10. Press the slash (**/**) key again.
11. Select **Worksheet Window Clear**. The single window returns to the screen.

To split the screen vertically

12. Press Home.
13. Move the pointer to a cell in the column where you want to split the screen; in this case, move it to column B.
14. Press the slash (**/**) key.
15. Select **Worksheet Window Vertical**. The screen splits vertically.
16. Move the pointer to the right. Only the left window scrolls. Press the Home key.

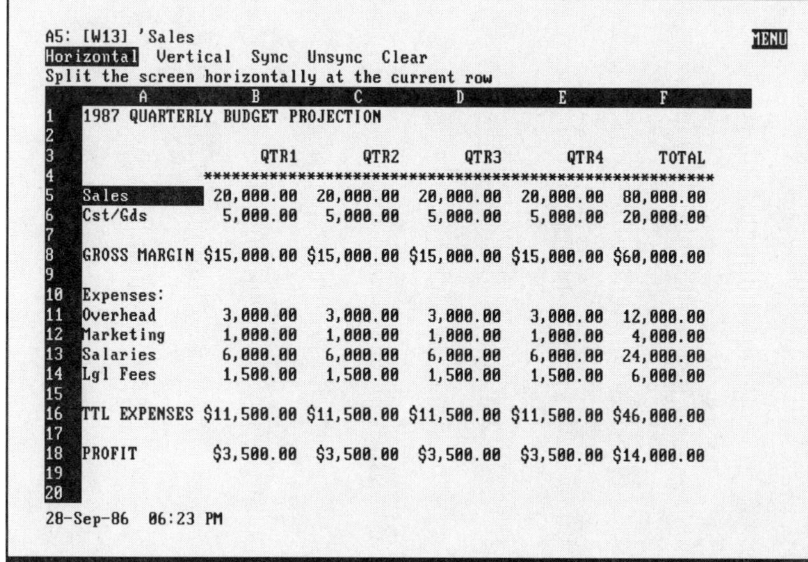

A5: [W13] 'Sales MENU
Horizontal Vertical Sync Unsync Clear
Split the screen horizontally at the current row

	A	B	C	D	E	F
1	1987 QUARTERLY BUDGET PROJECTION					
2						
3		QTR1	QTR2	QTR3	QTR4	TOTAL
4		**********	**********	**********	**********	**********
5	Sales	20,000.00	20,000.00	20,000.00	20,000.00	80,000.00
6	Cst/Gds	5,000.00	5,000.00	5,000.00	5,000.00	20,000.00
7						
8	GROSS MARGIN	$15,000.00	$15,000.00	$15,000.00	$15,000.00	$60,000.00
9						
10	Expenses:					
11	Overhead	3,000.00	3,000.00	3,000.00	3,000.00	12,000.00
12	Marketing	1,000.00	1,000.00	1,000.00	1,000.00	4,000.00
13	Salaries	6,000.00	6,000.00	6,000.00	6,000.00	24,000.00
14	Lgl Fees	1,500.00	1,500.00	1,500.00	1,500.00	6,000.00
15						
16	TTL EXPENSES	$11,500.00	$11,500.00	$11,500.00	$11,500.00	$46,000.00
17						
18	PROFIT	$3,500.00	$3,500.00	$3,500.00	$3,500.00	$14,000.00
19						
20						

28-Sep-86 06:23 PM

Figure 27.2: *The Window Menu*

17. Press the F6 key to move the pointer into the right window.
18. Move the pointer to the right. Only the right window scrolls.

To scroll through both windows at the same time

19. Press the slash (**/**) key.
20. Select **Worksheet Window Sync.**
21. Move the pointer down to row 40. Notice that both windows scroll together and the labels scroll off the top of the worksheet. (When the screen is split horizontally, you can scroll both windows to the left and right.)

To release the synchronized scrolling

22. Press the slash (**/**) key.
23. Select **Worksheet Window Unsync.**
24. Move the pointer up or down. Notice that you are scrolling through only one window.
25. Press the slash (**/**) key, and select **Worksheet Window Clear** to return to one window.

28

Fixing Titles So They Don't Scroll Off the Worksheet

FEATURING:

the Worksheet Titles command

When you view column G, the labels in column A scroll off the screen. Unless you have the labels for each column and row memorized, this can be disconcerting. It becomes difficult, if not impossible, to interpret or alter unidentified figures.

The **Worksheet Titles** command remedies this before or after you split the screen by ensuring that designated columns and/or rows—called *titles*—remain on the screen or are *fixed;* hence, the term *fixing titles.* A worksheet with fixed titles is shown in Figure 28.1. Normally, you would fix labels or headings; however, you can designate more than one column or row as long as it borders the top or left edges of the worksheet.

How to Fix Titles

To fix rows across the top (horizontal titles)

1. Press Home. Move the pointer to a cell in the row *below* the titles you want to remain fixed. To fix all the labels on the top of the worksheet, move the pointer to row 5.
2. Press the slash (**/**) key.
3. Select **Worksheet Titles Horizontal.**
4. Move the pointer to row 35. Notice that rows 1 through 4 do not scroll off the top of the screen.

To release fixed rows and/or columns

5. Press the slash (**/**) key.
6. While you are still in row 35, select **Worksheet Titles Clear.** Notice that the titles have disappeared off the top of the screen. Press Home.

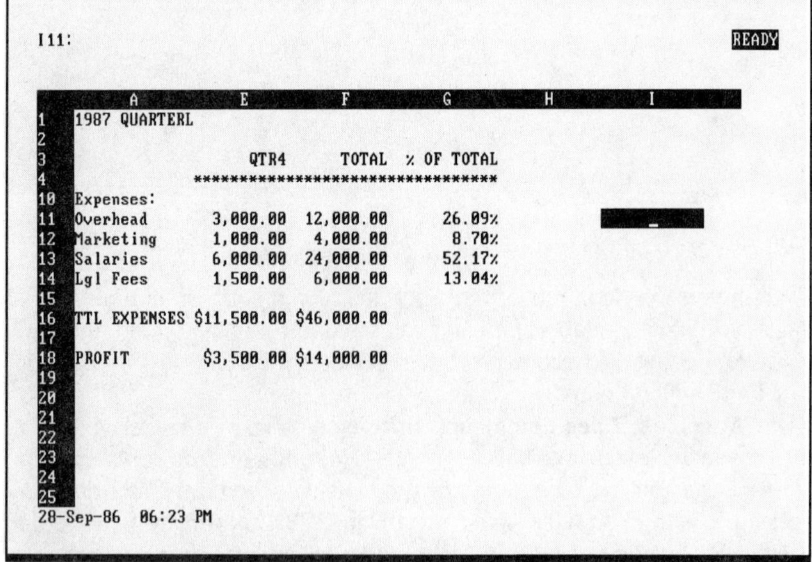

I11: READY

	A	E	F	G	H	I
1	1987 QUARTERL					
2						
3		QTR4	TOTAL	% OF TOTAL		
4		**********	**********	**********		
10	Expenses:					
11	Overhead	3,000.00	12,000.00	26.09%		
12	Marketing	1,000.00	4,000.00	8.70%		
13	Salaries	6,000.00	24,000.00	52.17%		
14	Lgl Fees	1,500.00	6,000.00	13.04%		
15						
16	TTL EXPENSES	$11,500.00	$46,000.00			
17						
18	PROFIT	$3,500.00	$14,000.00			
19						
20						
21						
22						
23						
24						
25						

28-Sep-86 06:23 PM

Figure 28.1: *Worksheet with Fixed Titles*

To fix a column on the left (vertical titles)

7. Move the pointer to a cell in the column to the right of what you want to remain fixed. To fix the left column, move the pointer to column B.
8. Press the slash (**/**) key.
9. Select **Worksheet Titles Vertical**.
10. Move the pointer to column L. Notice that column A remains on the screen.
11. Release the left column using **Worksheet Titles Clear** again. Press Home.

To fix both rows and columns simultaneously

12. Move the pointer below and to the right of everything that you want to remain fixed. To fix all of the labels on the budget, move the pointer to B5.
13. Press the slash (**/**) key.
14. Select **Worksheet Titles Both**.
15. Move the pointer to column L. Notice that everything in column A remains.
16. Press Home. The pointer returns to B5.
17. Move the pointer down to row 35. Now everything in the top four rows remains fixed.
18. Press Home. Notice that the pointer does not return Home, to A1. It is in B5 again. This is because pointer-movement keys will not move the pointer into fixed titles. Other than clearing titles, the only way to move into a title, to edit for example, is to use the F5 (GoTo) function key.
19. Press the F5 function key. 1-2-3 asks you to enter the cell address of the cell you want to go to.
20. Press the Left-Arrow key once. Notice that a copy of the fixed titles is brought out for editing. Press Enter to complete the process.
21. Move the pointer down to **Cst/Gds**. Change the title to **Cost/Goods**, using the F2 (Edit) function key. When you finish, press Enter.
22. Move down to **Lgl Fees**. Again using the Edit function key, change this to read **Legal Fees**. When you finish, press Enter.

23. To eliminate duplicate titles, move to column E.

To release fixed columns and rows

24. Use **/Worksheet Titles Clear.**

29

Protecting the Worksheet: Making Some Entries Permanent

FEATURING:

the Worksheet Global Protection, the Range Unprotect, and the Range Input commands

If you plan to update only some of the cells on the worksheet, while others, particularly formulas, remain unchanged, it is a good idea to *protect* those cells which will remain constant. By protecting them, you cannot change or erase cell entries, accidentally or otherwise, without first *unprotecting* the cells.

Protecting is a safety measure to ensure that you, or other people who have access to your files, don't alter certain entries. For example, you may want to be sure that if your co-workers enter new sales figures on the worksheet, they won't accidentally erase the formulas.

Protecting cells is a two-step process: First, you protect the entire worksheet with the **Worksheet Global Protection** command. Then, you unprotect the cells where you will continue to work with the **Range Unprotect** command. You can also do the reverse: unprotect the cells you want to work in and then protect the rest of the worksheet; the result will be the same.

How to Protect the Worksheet

1. Press the slash (**/**) key.
2. Select **Worksheet Global Protection**. The menu in Figure 29.1 is displayed on the screen. Until you change it, **Worksheet Global Protection** is disabled, that is, not in effect.
3. Select **Enable**. The entire worksheet is now protected; you cannot make any changes. Later, if you wanted to turn off the protection, you would select **Disable**.
4. Move the pointer to B5, and type your first name.
5. Press Enter. 1-2-3 beeps and **ERROR** and **Protected cell** appear on the screen. 1-2-3 is reminding you that you cannot enter anything in that cell.

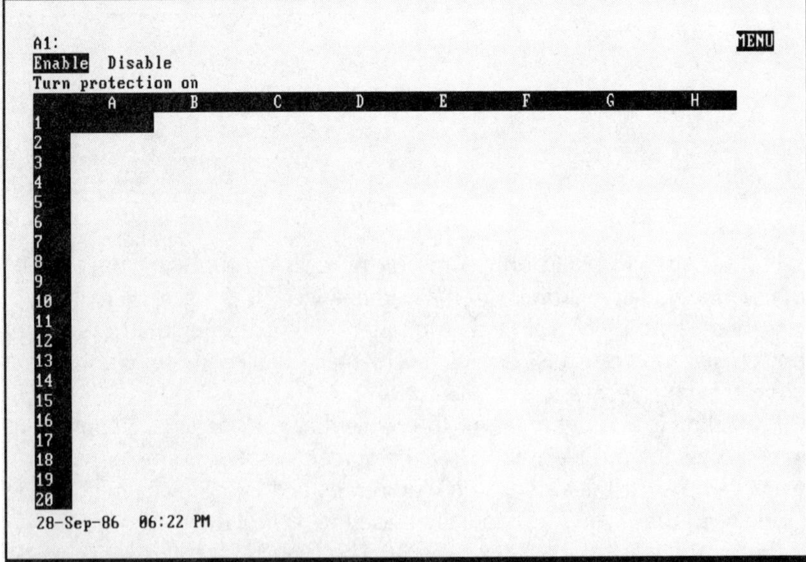

Figure 29.1: *Global Protection Menu*

6. Press Escape to clear the control panel. When you get an error message, pressing Escape returns you to the **READY** mode.

To unprotect individual cells

7. Press the slash (**/**) key.
8. Select **Range Unprotect**. 1-2-3 asks you to identify the range that you want to unprotect.
9. Press Escape to unanchor the range.
10. Move the pointer to B5, if it's not already there.
11. Type a period.
12. Move the pointer to include rows 5 and 6 from column B through column E.
13. Press Enter. Notice that the unprotected cells are highlighted after you press Enter.
14. Repeat steps 7 through 13 to specify a second range. Include rows 11 through 14 from column B across to column E.
15. Press Enter. The cells in these two ranges do not have labels or formulas.

To disable global protection

16. Use **/Worksheet Global Protection** to **Disable** protection. The unprotected ranges will remain highlighted. **/Range Protect** would change this, though it is not necessary.

30
Checking and Changing 1-2-3 Default Settings

FEATURING:

the Worksheet Status command and the Worksheet Global Default command

The budget you have built is not so large that you have to worry about running out of memory (RAM) inside the computer. However, long before you fill all of 1-2-3's 8,192 columns and 256 rows, you'll confront a **Memory full** message. How can you find out, before you run out, how much memory is available? And, if you don't remember, how can you find out whether the global column-width is set at 9 or 11? And what about the global format? Is it set at a comma with two decimal places or is it set at **Currency?**

The **Worksheet Status** command displays the answers to all of these questions on the screen. In addition to indicating available memory, it displays global settings—that is, the settings for the features that affect the entire worksheet, such as recalculation, format, label-prefix, column-width, and protection.

The **Worksheet Global Default Status** command displays the startup—or default—settings whenever you begin working with 1-2-3. It comes in handy when you want to know how 1-2-3 is set up for printing, saving and retrieving files, and for displaying formats for dates, times, and numbers. The **Worksheet Global Default** commands enable you to change these settings.

How to Check Worksheet Status

1. Press the slash (**/**) key.
2. Select **Worksheet Status**. 1-2-3 displays the menu in Figure 30.1. Since you have already changed several settings, such as **Global Column Width** and **Global Protection**, these settings are not necessarily the default settings—or the settings that originally came with the Lotus program. Descriptions of the various settings follow.

    Available Memory: Conventional is the amount of memory (RAM), up to 640kb, that is available in your computer after the disk operating system (DOS), 1-2-3 itself, and the current worksheet have been loaded.

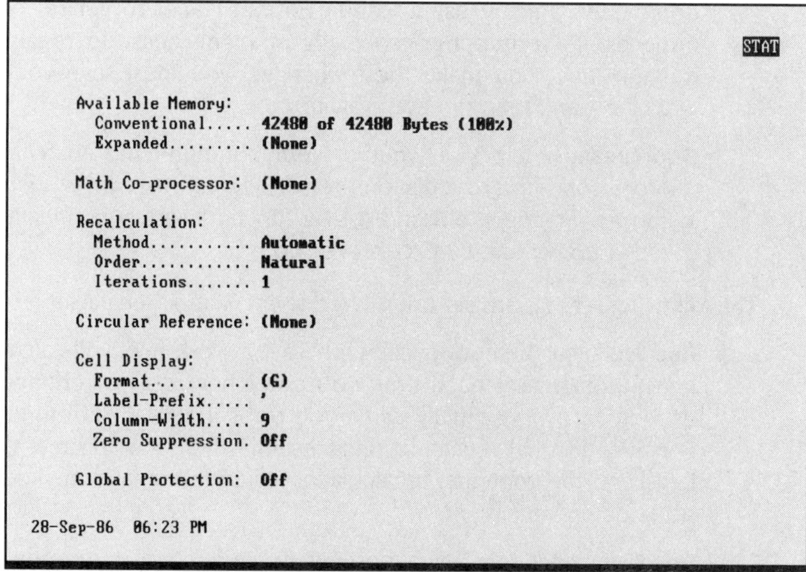

Figure 30.1: *Worksheet Status Settings*

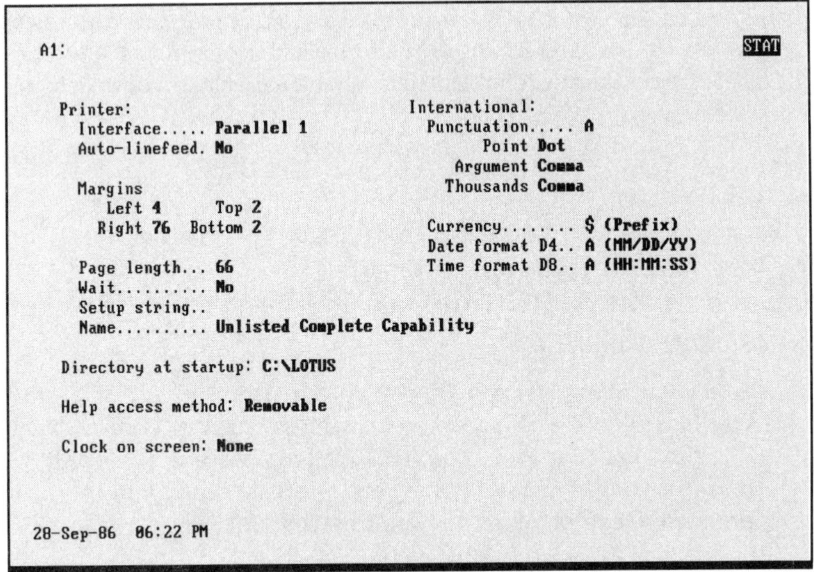

Figure 30.2: */Worksheet Global Default Status Screen*

Available Memory: Expanded is the amount of memory above 640kb and up to 4 megabytes that is available. (*Note:* You can increase the amount of memory available by erasing data you don't need and by using **Range Format Reset** to get rid of unnecessary formatting, especially of blank cells. To regain memory after you make these changes, you must save your worksheet and then retrieve it again.)

Coprocessor: Tells you whether your computer has an 8087 coprocessor. Some calculations, especially complex ones such as those using the **@IRR** and **@NPV** functions, are substantially speeded up with an 8087 coprocessor.

The following settings are set using **/Worksheet Global Recalculation**.

Recalculation: Method specifies whether a worksheet will calculate **Automatically** each time you enter new data or change existing data, or **Manually** when you press the F9 (CALC) function key. Manual recalculation is useful when a worksheet is large and the continual recalculation of the automatic method slows down your work.

Recalculation: Order will almost always be left to **Natural** order. When calculating a formula that depends on the results of another formula, this setting makes 1-2-3 wait until the results of the first formula have been calculated. Exceptions may occur when you have translated a worksheet from another software program that depends on **Column** or **Row** order, or if a 1-2-3 worksheet has been set specifically to calculate in one of these alternative orders.

Recalculation: Iterations is useful when a worksheet needs to be calculated a number of times in order to derive correct results. For example, this is useful if you use formulas that calculate internal rates of return. You can set up the number of times you want a worksheet to be calculated.

Circular Reference displays any cell address where a formula refers to itself. For example, a formula in cell B4 that reads +B2+B3+B4 is a circular reference. In many cases circular references will produce inaccurate results. **CALC** will display on the screen whenever there is one or more circular references. If there are multiple circular references, correcting the one that is displayed in the Status menu will display any others.

Cell Display: Format refers to the **/Worksheet Global Format** setting for all numbers and formulas. **Label Prefix** refers to the **/Worksheet Global Label Prefix** setting that determines if labels are centered, right-aligned, or left-aligned when first entered into the worksheet. **Column-Width** displays the Worksheet Global Column Width setting, and **Zero Suppression** refers to whether formulas will display a 0 or be displayed (and printed) as blank, when the value of the formula is 0. This is set using Worksheet Global Zero.

Global Protection displays whether Worksheet Global Protection has been enabled or disabled. Refer to Section 29, "Protecting You Worksheet."

3. To return to the worksheet, press any key.

How to Check and Change Lotus 1-2-3 Global Default Settings

4. Select **/Worksheet Global Default Status**. 1-2-3 displays the screen in Figure 30.2.

Printer: Settings displays the printer interface (serial or parallel), the default margins, page length, any setup codes, and the name of the printer driver, if other than 1-2-3. These default settings will be used for all worksheets unless they are changed here or changed individually in a worksheet using the **/Print Options** command.

Directory at startup displays the drive and subdirectory used for retrieving and storing files.

Help access method reflects whether 1-2-3 has been set up to allow removal of the System disk from Drive A, while still allowing use of the Help screens.

Clock on Screen reflects the type of time format displayed on-screen. This clock can be turned off.

International reflects the types of formatting for numbers, currency, dates, and times.

(Note: These settings can be changed using the other Worksheet Global Default commands: **Printer, Directory, Other.***)*

5. Press any key when you finish with this screen. The worksheet is displayed.
6. Experiment with changing some of the Global Default settings using the **Printer, Directory,** or **Other** selections.
7. If you want to change any settings permanently, save the changes with the **Update** command in **/Worksheet Global Default**. If you are using a floppy System disk, you must remove the write-protect tab first.

31

Handling Large Worksheets by Turning Off Automatic Recalculation

FEATURING:

the Worksheet Global Recalculation command and the F9 (Calculate) function key

As worksheets expand, 1-2-3's ability to calculate slows down. Usually this happens when a worksheet is many times the size of the one you have built.

Large worksheets force 1-2-3 to do more work. Each time you enter a piece of information—whether it's a label, number, or formula—1-2-3 automatically recalculates the entire worksheet. Although the only changes you see are the new entries and calculations, every formula has been recalculated. As a result, very large worksheets may take as much as a minute or more to recalculate after every entry.

To save time, you can turn off the automatic recalculation setting. When you do this, 1-2-3 does not recalculate until you press the F9 (Calc—for calculate) function key. So that you don't forget to calculate, before printing or saving for example, 1-2-3 reminds you by displaying **CALC** at the bottom of the worksheet.

How to Turn Off the Automatic Recalculation Setting

1. Press the slash (/) key.
2. Select **Worksheet Global Recalculation**. 1-2-3 offers these setting options: **Automatic**, **Manual**, **Natural**, **Columnwise**, **Rowwise**, and **Iteration**. These options were explained in the last section.
3. Select **Manual**.
4. Move the pointer to B5.
5. Type:

   30000

6. Press Enter. Notice that 1-2-3 did not recalculate any formulas and **CALC** appears at the bottom of the screen.
7. Press the F9 function key. All the formulas are recalculated, and **CALC** disappears.

To turn off manual recalculation

8. Press the slash (/) key.
9. Select **Worksheet Global Recalculation.**
10. Now select **Automatic.**
11. In B5, type:

    20000

12. Press Enter. 1-2-3 automatically recalculates.

32 Printing the Worksheet

FEATURING:

the Print command

Note: Even if you don't have a printer, follow the instructions in this section. The information will be useful when you do have access to a printer.

The **Print** command enables you to print all or part of the worksheet. In addition, 1-2-3 offers a variety of formatting options that transform the worksheet into a fancy report.

With printing options, you can add a *header* and/or *footer* to the worksheet page. Either one might include the report's title, author, date, and page number. You can also *fix* columns and rows at the top and left of each page of the report, just as you fixed titles on the screen, in case the worksheet is so large that parts of it are printed on separate pages. You can adjust the print-out to fit different paper sizes, making the report pages longer or shorter, wider or narrower. You can also vary the size of the characters, their type style, and the printing shade from light to dark, depending on your printer.

1-2-3 prints each page with margins on four sides and fits as many columns as it can within the standard or default left and right margins. Columns that don't fit are printed on a new page.

In this section, you will experiment with three types of print-outs. You will first print the worksheet simply, without any additions to the page. Then, you will print it using a variety of format options that change the appearance of the report. After that, you will print the formulas in the worksheet.

In the steps that remain, you will use the **Worksheet Global** command to change the printer default settings. Since many 1-2-3 users will consistently use certain print options, it makes sense to save time by making them permanent. For example, if the majority of your work consists of large budget projections, you will probably want to print as much as you can on wide paper, with a wide printer, and with small type. By changing the default settings to suit your needs, you don't have to set these options each time you want to print a worksheet.

How to print the Worksheet

To Print a simple report

1. Prepare your printer. Make sure that the top of the first page is lined up with the print head. Turn on your printer.
2. Save your worksheet. This is always a good idea before you print.
3. Press the slash (**/**) key.
4. Select **Print Printer**. (Selecting **Print File** saves the worksheet exactly as it appears on the screen, that is, without formulas. **Print File** enables you to include the worksheet in a document created by a word-processing program to create a report.) The **Print** menu, shown in Figure 32.1, appears. **Range** specifies the cells that you want to print. **Line** advances the printer a single line. **Page** advances the paper to the top of the next sheet. **Options** offers a menu of printing options, such as headers and footers. **Align** tells the printer where the top of the page is, once you've aligned the perforated area with the head. **Go** tells the printer to print, and **Quit** exits the **Print** menu. (In all menus except the main command menu, **Quit** takes you out of the menu currently on the control panel. On the main command menu, it ends the worksheet session and erases the screen.)
5. Select **Range**. 1-2-3 asks you to enter the print range and displays the cell where the pointer resides.
6. Press the Home key to move the pointer to the top left corner.

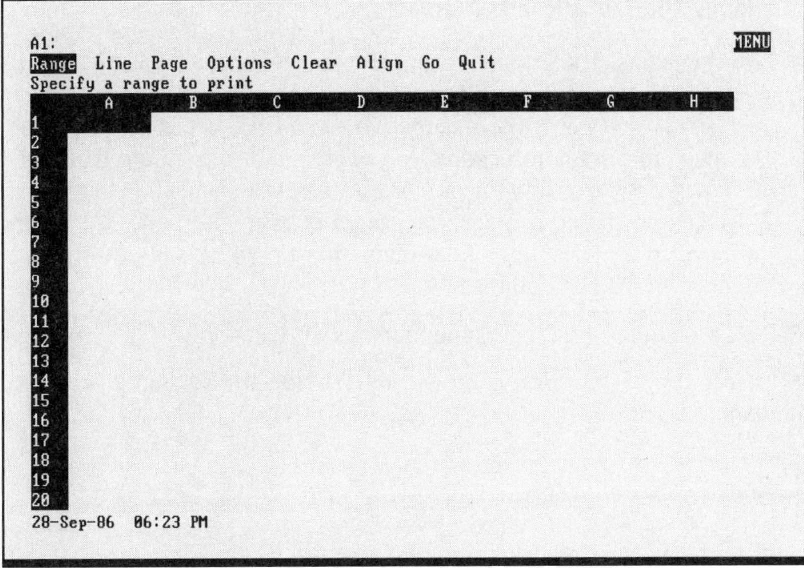

Figure 32.1: *Print Menu*

7. Type a period.
8. Move the pointer down to row 20 and across to column G.
9. Press Enter. The **Print** menu returns to the control panel.

To start and stop printing

10. Select **Align** to tell 1-2-3 that the top of the paper is aligned correctly in the printer. Then select **Go**. If you have a printer, the worksheet begins to print. If you don't, 1-2-3 will beep and **ERROR** will flash on the screen. If this happens, press Escape to return to the worksheet.
11. Hold down the Control key, and tap the Break key on the right side of the keyboard. The printer stops. The **Print** menu is erased. Bring it back up on the screen by pressing the slash (**/**) key and selecting **Print Printer** again.
12. Select **Page.** If you have a printer, the paper advances to the top; otherwise, nothing happens.
13. Select **Go** again. If you have a printer, the worksheet is printed.

To change the left and top margins

14. Select **Options**. The **Options** menu, shown in Figure 32.2, is displayed. Some of the options have been explained already. **Borders** adds a border to each page. For example, if the worksheet is so large that you need to print it in sections, you might want to print the labels on each page. **Setup** tells your printer the size, style, and shade of print. **Page-Length** is used to adjust the printer in case your paper is shorter or longer than 11 inches. **Other** offers more options, such as printing formulas instead of numbers.
15. Select **Margins**. 1-2-3 offers the four margin locations.
16. Select **Top**. 1-2-3 displays the standard or default setting: **2**, for two lines.
17. Type:

    10

18. Press Enter.
19. Select **Margins** again.
20. Then Select **Right**. 1-2-3 displays the right default setting: **75**, for 75 characters.

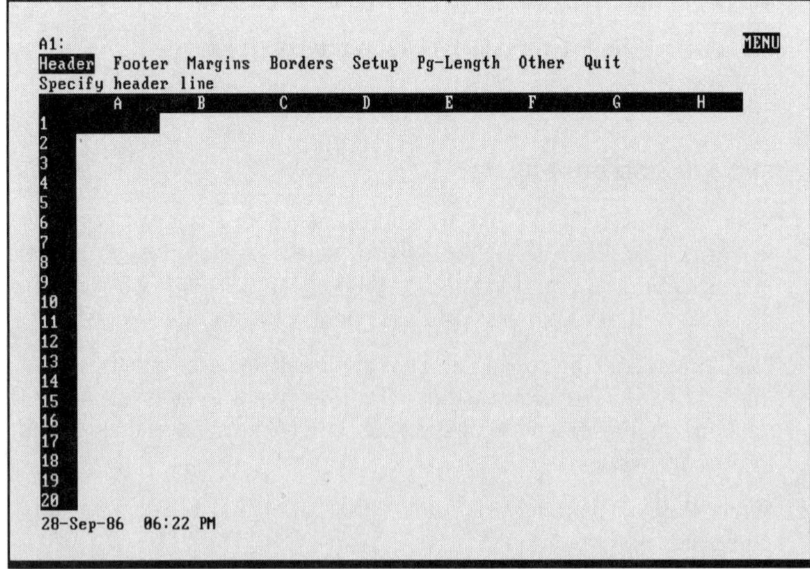

Figure 32.2: *Options Menu*

21. Type:

    136

    This expands the margins to include more characters.

22. Press Enter. The **Options** menu returns to the screen.

To add a header

23. Select **Header.** 1-2-3 asks you to enter the header.

24. Type:

    Widgets Division Budget &v &v @

    The vertical lines are added to tell 1-2-3 how to distribute the header across the page. They are created with the Shift and \ keys. The header is divided into three parts: the left third, the center third, and the right third. Anything that is typed before the first vertical line is printed on the left corner of the page. Whatever is entered between the vertical lines is centered, and what comes after is printed in the right corner. The @ symbol will print today's date, which is the date you entered at the beginning of this session. The two vertical lines tell 1-2-3 to place Widgets Division Budget in the left third and the date in the right third. (One vertical line centers the header; no vertical line aligns it on the left.)

25. Press Enter. The **Options** menu returns to the screen.

To add a footer

26. Select **Footer.** 1-2-3 asks for the footer.

27. Type:

    ¦#

    This tells 1-2-3 to print page numbers in the center of the bottom of each page.

28. Press Enter. The **Options** menu returns to the screen.

To change the size of the print

29. Select **Setup.** 1-2-3 asks you to enter the **Setup String.** The **Setup String** tells 1-2-3 how to print your worksheet characters (e.g., bold or italic).

30. To compress the print to roughly half the size, type:

    \015

    This is the setup code for compressed print for IBM and Epson dot-matrix printers. Printers differ as to how they interpret setup codes. Consult your printer manual for the correct setup codes, referred to as *printer control characters.* Then, translate the printer's control characters into 1-2-3's setup codes, following the "Printer Control Codes" in the appendix of the Lotus manual. You will probably want to know which characters will direct your printer to print compressed print, emphasized or bold print, and italicised print.

31. Press Enter.

32. To return to the main **Print** menu, select **Quit**.

33. Select **Go**. If you have a printer, 1-2-3 prints the new version of the report. Select **Page** to advance the page.

To print the formulas of a worksheet

34. Select **Options Other**. 1-2-3 displays four options:

    As-Displayed Cell-Formulas Formatted Unformatted

    As-Displayed prints the worksheet as it is displayed on the screen. **Cell-Formulas** prints what is displayed on the control panel for each cell. **Formatted** tells 1-2-3 to print the worksheet with the standard and/or selected options, such as headers, footers, and margins; **Unformatted** tells 1-2-3 to print it without any options, including the standard margins and page length, in case, for example, you want to print the worksheet in a report.

35. Select **Cell-Formulas**. This can be helpful if you need to trouble-shoot or to set up another worksheet and you want to know what formulas you used previously. The **Options** menu returns.

36. Press Escape to return to the **Print** menu.

37. Select **Go**. If you have a printer, 1-2-3 prints the worksheet. When it's finished, select **Options Other** to return the setting to **As-Displayed** for normal printing later on. The **Options** menu returns to the screen.

38. Press Escape to return to the **Print** menu. Select **Page**.

To clear the print options

39. To return the worksheet to its default print settings to print other worksheets, you can clear the print options. Select **Clear**. 1-2-3 offers four choices:

    All Range Borders Format

    All cancels all options and the print range that you last used. **Range** cancels only the range. **Format** cancels the **Margins**, **Page-Length**, and **Setup** options. **Borders** cancels the column's and row's **Borders** option.

40. To clear **Options** but retain the **Print** range, select **Format**. The **Print** menu returns.

To make Options permanent by changing the print default settings

41. Press Escape twice to return to the main command menu.

42. Select **Worksheet Global Default**. 1-2-3 offers five choices:

    Printer Directory Status Update Other Quit

43. Select **Printer**. The **Default Printer** menu is displayed.

44. Select **Right**.

45. Type:

    136

    This widens the right margin.

46. Press Enter. The **Printer** menu returns.

47. Select **Quit** to return to the **Default** menu.

48. If you have a floppy-disk system, remove the write-protect tab from the 1-2-3 System disk. Place the System disk back in drive A.

49. Select **Update**. The new settings are permanently saved as part of the 1-2-3 program until you change them again.

50. Select **Quit**.

Note: If you are using a printer that can print only 80 columns, change the right margin setting back to the initial 75 setting. Use **Update** *to save the change.*

33 Naming Parts of the Worksheet

FEATURING:

the Range Name command and the F3 (Name) function key

It's possible, with the **Range Name** command, to use everyday English, rather than cell addresses, when you need to specify a range of cells.

Suppose, for example, you have a very large worksheet and you want to print only one section of it. Instead of having to remember the cell addresses of that one section, say C462. .P512, you can assign a name, say "Summary," to the entire range of cells. Later, when you want to print it, all you have to do is specify the name "Summary," not the range.

You can also use names in formulas. For example, if you hadn't already entered a **PROFIT** formula, you could assign a name to B8, the cell containing the **GROSS MARGIN** figure, and another name to B16, the cell containing the **TTL EXPENSES** figure. Then, instead of entering the **PROFIT** formula as +B16−B8, you could enter the formula in English: **+GROSS MARGIN−TTL EXPENSES.**

Once a range is named, you can also copy, move, or format the cells in the named range. Whenever 1-2-3 asks you to specify a range, you only need to enter its name.

What you name a range is entirely up to you. The only limitation is the number of characters: 15. Other than that, you can be as descriptive as you like.

How to Assign a Name to a Range

To print the Expenses summary

1. Press the slash (**/**) key.
2. Select **Range Name**. The following choices are displayed:

   Create Delete Labels Reset Table

   Create assigns a name to a range. **Delete** erases a range name. **Labels** allows you to use a label that already exists on the worksheet as a name for a range. **Reset** erases all the **Range Names** from the worksheet. **Table** creates a list of all the range names that you have created.
3. Select **Create**. 1-2-3 asks for the name of the range.
4. Type:

   EXPENSES
5. Press Enter. 1-2-3 asks for the range you want to name.
6. Press Escape to unexpand the range.
7. Move the pointer to the label, **Expenses:**, in cell A10.
8. Type a period.
9. Move the pointer to **TTL EXPENSES** in A16.
10. Move across to the **%of TOTAL** figures in column G, row 16.
11. Press Enter.

To print the named range

Even if you don't have a printer, complete the following steps.

12. Press the slash (**/**) key.
13. Select **Print Printer Range**. 1-2-3 asks for the range to be printed and displays the last range you printed. The entire worksheet is displayed.

14. Press the F3 (Name) function key. All the range names that have been created—in this case, one—are displayed.
15. Since the pointer is already on **Expenses:**, press Enter. You could also type the name on the control panel. The **Print** menu returns to the screen, and the new range is specified.
16. To check that the range is specified, press Enter again at the **Range** command. Although the name is not displayed, the range is. Notice that the Expense range you named is now highlighted as the Print range.
17. Press Enter to return to the **Print** menu.
18. To print the summary, select **Page** to advance the paper in the printer one sheet.
19. Select **Go**. If you have a printer, 1-2-3 prints the **Expenses** summary. Select **Page**.
20. To return to the **READY** mode, select **Quit**.

34 *Transferring Data from One Worksheet to Another*

FEATURING:

the File Combine command

It's often useful to transfer data from one worksheet file to another where the data will be combined with new information. For example, let's assume that you've created the budget projection for one of two stores and you would like to compare the two stores' profits in another worksheet file, one that summarizes the profit figures for all four quarters.

The **File Combine** command accomplishes this by transferring data from one worksheet into the worksheet on the screen without erasing it from the original worksheet.

First, you must name the range that you want to transfer before you can transfer it. Then, in order to compare profits for two stores, you will create a budget in a second file for the second store. Finally, you will create a third file into which you will transfer each store's profits using the **File Combine** command.

How to Transfer Data from One Worksheet to Another

To name the range

1. Press the slash (**/**) key.
2. Select **Range Name Create**. 1-2-3 displays the range that you've already named: **EXPENSES**.
3. Type:

   PROFIT
4. Press Enter. 1-2-3 asks you to specify the range you are naming.
5. Press Escape to unexpand the range.
6. Specify the **PROFIT** row or bottom-line figures (row 18), columns B through F. Do not include the label in Column A.
7. Press Enter.
8. Save the current worksheet. Use the **File Save** command, and save the worksheet under the name **STORE1** by typing in the name and pressing Enter.

To create the budget for the second store

9. Enter the following numbers in place of the current ones. (They will automatically be converted to the comma, decimal format.)

Sales	100000	110000	120000	130000
Cst/Gds	40000	45000	50000	55000
GROSS MARGIN				
Overhead	15000	15000	15000	15000
Marketing	10000	10000	10000	10000
Salaries	30000	30000	30000	30000
Lgl Fees	8000	8000	8000	8000
TTL EXPENSES				
PROFIT				

The gross margin, total expenses, and profits adjust automatically. Two numbers in column F are not displayed because they are too wide for the column; instead, asterisks are displayed.

10. Use **Worksheet Global Column-Width** to widen the columns to 12. Notice that column F shifts off the screen.
11. Using the **File Save** command again, save the current worksheet under the name **STORE2**. Notice that you did not have to define the Profit range again. You will use the one you defined earlier.
12. Use the **Worksheet Erase** command to erase the screen.
13. Enter the labels in Figure 34.1 on the new summary worksheet. Use **/Worksheet Global Label-Prefix Right** before typing in the labels. This will cause the QTR headings to be right-aligned properly above the numbers you will be using.
14. To prepare the worksheet before you transfer numbers, enter the following formulas in B8, to the right of **TOTAL**, and in F5, beneath **TOTAL**.

    In B8: **@SUM(B5. .B6)**

    In F5: **@SUM(B5. .E5)**

    After pressing Enter, a zero appears because no numbers have been entered in B5 or B6.

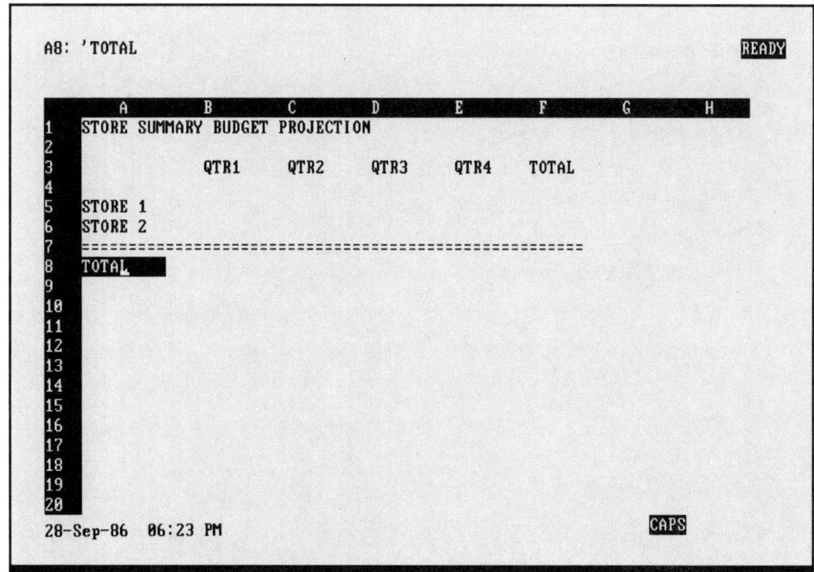

Figure 34.1: *Summary Worksheet Labels*

15. Use the **Copy** command to copy the formula in B8 across to the remaining columns, including the **TOTAL** column, and the formula in F5 down to F6. The worksheet now looks like the one in Figure 34.2. An alternative is to type in formulas manually beneath each quarter and the Total column. Use the two formulas in step 14 as models for the others, but change the cell addresses appropriately. Save the new worksheet as **SUMMARY**.

16. Move the pointer to the cell where **STORE1** and **QTR1** intersect: B5. This is the first cell of the range where you will use **File Combine** to copy in the profits.

17. Press the slash (**/**) key.

18. Select **File Combine**. 1-2-3 displays three choices: **Copy**, **Add**, and **Subtract**.

    Copy erases existing entries and replaces them with incoming data. **Add** adds incoming values to the existing values and produces totals. If the existing entries are labels, incoming values are discarded. **Subtract** is similar to **Add**, except that incoming values are subtracted from existing values. Use **Add** since **Copy** will incorrectly bring in the formulas from each store worksheet.

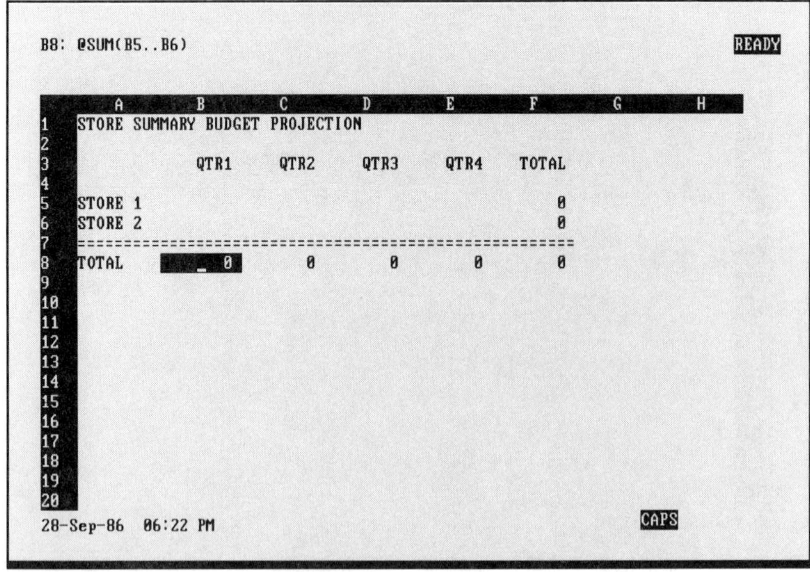

Figure 34.2: *Summary Worksheet with Formulas*

19. Select **Add.** 1-2-3 displays two more choices: **Entire-File** and **Named/Specified-Range.**
20. From **STORE1**, you will transfer the profit range that you named; therefore, select **Named/Specified-Range.**
21. Type:

    PROFIT

    After you press Enter, 1-2-3 asks you for the file name.
22. Select **STORE1**. After you press Enter, the worksheet will look like the one in Figure 34.3. If there were numbers already present in row 5, **File Combine Add** would add them to the numbers you are copying. In the future, be sure that you erase whatever is in the row you are copying to unless you want the figures added together.
23. Use **Worksheet Global Column-Width** to expand the columns to 12. After you finish, the worksheet will look like the one in Figure 34.4.
24. Move the cursor to the cell where **STORE2** and **QTR1** intersect: B6.
25. Press the slash (**/**) key. Select **File Combine Add Named/Specified-Range.**

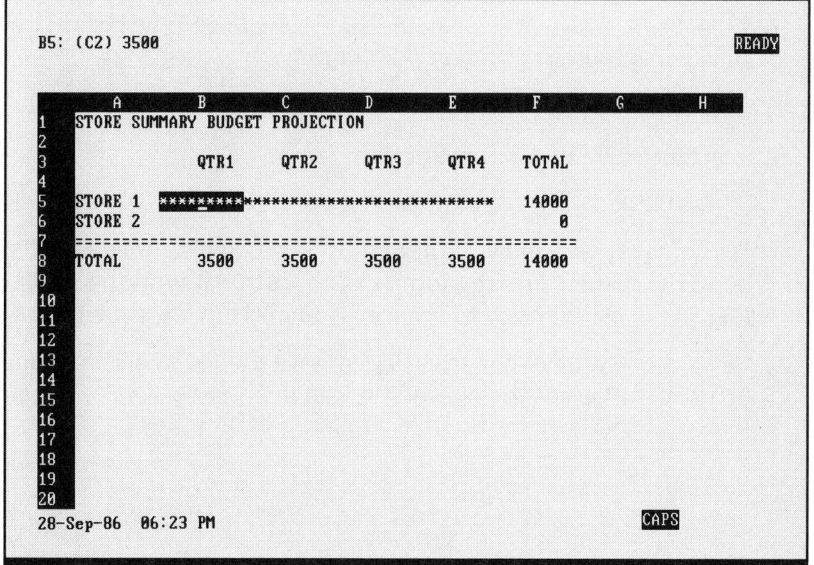

Figure 34.3: *Summary Worksheet with STORE1 Profit Figures*

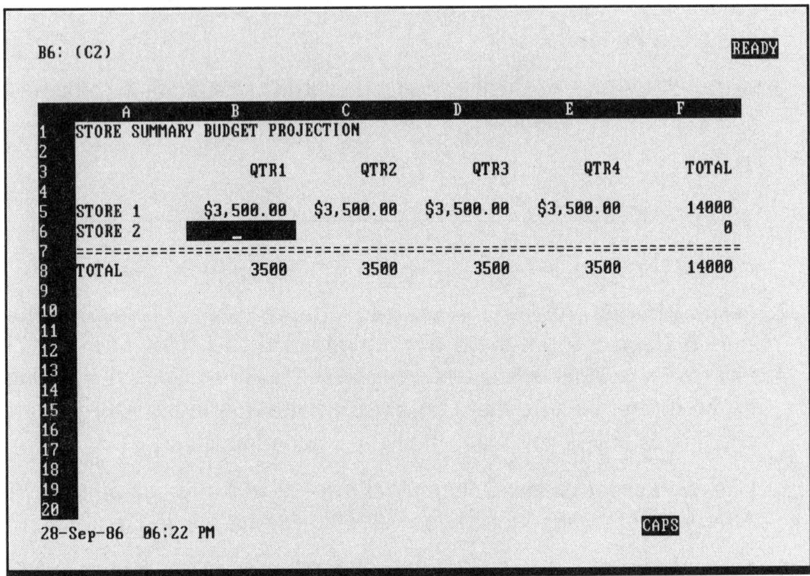

Figure 34.4: *Summary Worksheet with Expanded Columns*

26. Type the name of the second range:

    PROFIT

    Since the profit figures were in the same rows in each worksheet, the same name is used to transfer both ranges.

27. Press Enter.

28. Select the name of the second file:

    STORE2

    The summary file, shown in Figure 34.5, is complete. **File Combine** bring overs the **Currency** format of the **STORE** worksheets. Use **/Range Format Currency** to change all numbers to the same format.

29. Using the **File Save** command again, save the file under the name **SUMMARY. Replace** the old version with the new version.

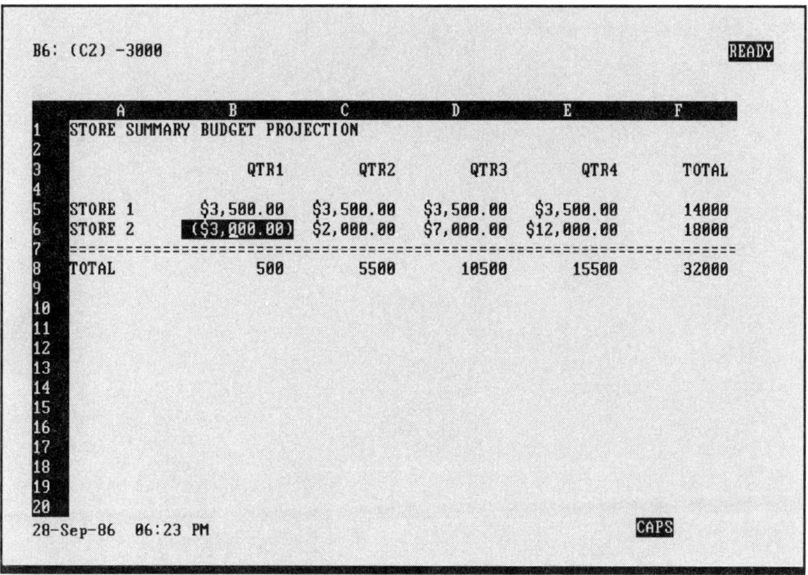

Figure 34.5: *Summary Worksheet*

123

Chapter Three

GRAPHING THE WORKSHEET

35 Converting the Worksheet to a Graph

FEATURING:

the Graph Type, Graph ABCDEF, and Graph View commands

A key feature of 1-2-3 is its ability to display worksheet data as a graph, both on the screen and in print. You can choose from a variety of graph types: line, bar, scatter, stacked bar, and pie chart. And, just as you added information to the worksheet to make it easier to interpret, you can enhance a graph's appearance by adding such things as titles, symbols, legends, and a horizontal or vertical background grid.

You can view a graph if you have a graphics "card" or a color/graphics "card" in your computer. You can view a graph and worksheet simultaneously if you have two monitors, and you can display a graph in color if you have a color monitor. You cannot view a graph with a monochrome card and monitor. You can print a graph regardless of what kind of monitor and card you have—even if you can't see it on screen, though the process will be tedious!

Converting the worksheet to a graph is simple, a matter of only a few steps. First, create the type of graph you want. Then, when you can see where labels need to be added, add the labels.

How to View the Graph

1. Use **File Retrieve** to retrieve **87BUDGET**.
2. Change the following cell entries on the worksheet

Change:	C5	to	**30000**
	D5	to	**40000**
	E5	to	**50000**
	C12	to	**7000**
	D12	to	**8000**
	E12	to	**9000**

You will need to widen column F. Use **Worksheet Column**.

3. Press the slash (**/**) key. Select **Graph**. The following menu appears on the control panel:

   Type X A B C D E F Reset View Save Options Name Quit

   In addition to choosing a **Type** of graph and **Viewing** the graph, you can add labels to the **X**-axis, graph up to six different ranges on the worksheet (**A-F**), **Reset** the ranges, save the graph for printing, **Save** the appearance of the graph with various symbols and labels, and **Name** the graph.

4. Select **Type**. 1-2-3 offers five graph types:

   Line Bar XY Stacked-Bar Pie

5. Select **Bar**. The Graph menu is displayed again.

6. Select **A**, and enter the first data range to be graphed, the **GROSS MARGIN** figures: B8. .E8.

7. Select **B**, and enter the second data range, the **TTL EXPENSES** figures: B16. .E16.

8. Select **C**, and enter the third data range, the **PROFIT** figures: B18. .E18.

9. Select **View**. The graph in Figure 35.1 is displayed. In order to view the graph, you must have a graphics card installed in your computer. If you don't, you can create and print the graph but you can't view it.

10. Press any key to return to the worksheet. The **Graph** menu remains on the screen above the worksheet until you press Escape or select **Quit**. This enables you to switch more rapidly between worksheet and graph, without having to press the slash (**/**) key first.

11. To view the same data displayed in a different type of graph, select **Type Stacked-bar** and select **View** again. The graph in Figure 35.2 is displayed. Notice that the scale has changed to include the three totals in one bar.

12. To return to the worksheet and graph commands, press any key.

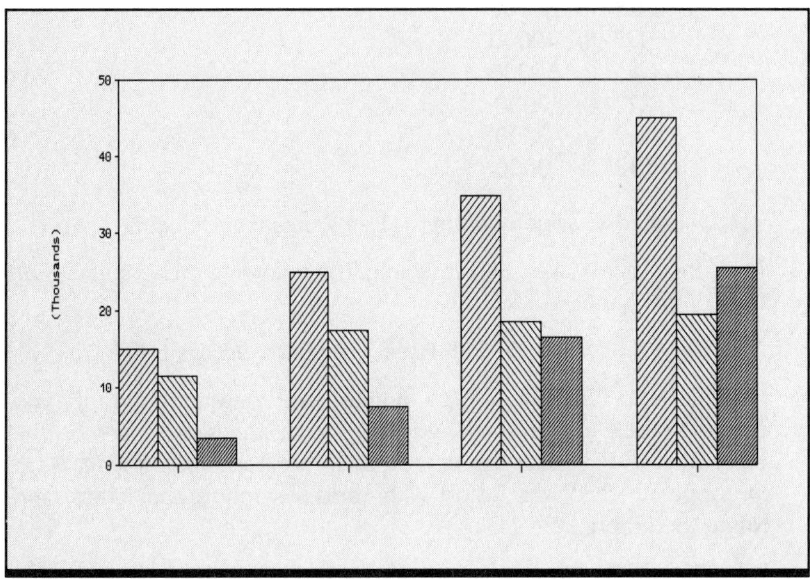

Figure 35.1: *Bar Graph*

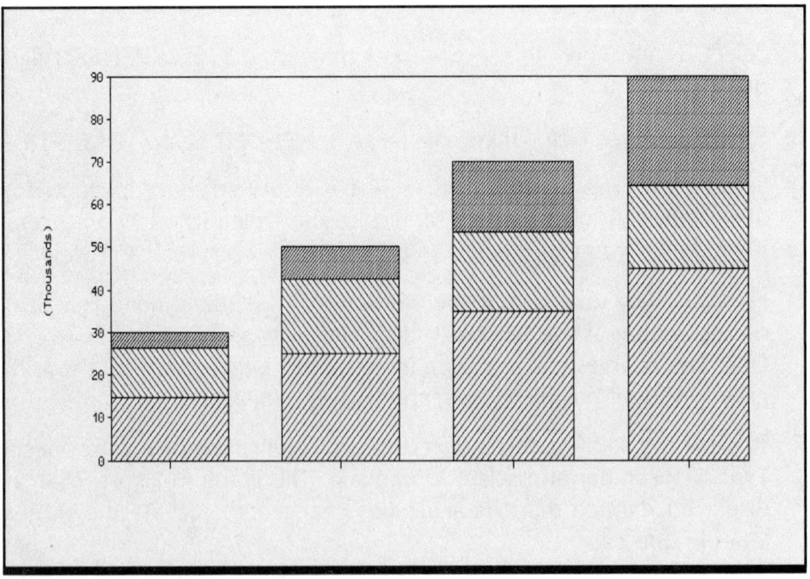

Figure 35.2: *Stacked-Bar Graph*

36 Labeling the Graph

FEATURING:

the Graph Options Legend, the Graph Options Titles, and the Graph X commands

Before you show the graph to anyone, especially if you plan to print it, it's a good idea to add labels. There are two types of labels: *titles* and *legends*. The graph is difficult to interpret without them.

Titles are added to put the entire graph into context. For example, on the graph you just viewed, you could add the title **Budget Projection** across the top. Along the bottom and left sides of the screen, not the graph, you could add titles such as **January-December** and **Dollars**, although these aren't really necessary to understand the graph.

Legends are added to explain what is inside the borders of the graph. With the stacked-bar graph, for example, you need to know which bar shadings refer to **MARGIN** and which refer to **TTL EXPENSES**.

With the **Graph X** command, you can add more specific titles along the X and Y axes. For example, you need to identify the four quarters in this graph. The **Graph X** command places these names directly beneath each data range.

How to Add Labels to the Graph

To add legends

The **Graph** menu should still be on your screen. If not, press the slash (**/**) key, and select **Graph**.

1. Select **Options**. The following menu appears:

   Legend Format Titles Grid Scale Color B&W Data-Labels Quit

   In addition to legends and titles, you can add a background grid, change the scale on the axes, display the graph in color or black and white, and add data-labels or labels within the graph.

2. Select **Legend**. A prompt asks you to set the legend for the first range, the A range. The only limitation is the number of characters: 19. However, because of space limitations, it's a good idea to use less than 19 characters. Legends appears at the bottom of the screen to show what is represented by the various bar shadings.

3. Select **A**.

4. Type the name of the A range:

   GROSS MARGIN

   You can also enter a legend by typing a backslash (\) followed by the cell address of a label that is on the worksheet. Thus, in the previous case, you would type: **\A8**. If you use the cell address and later change the label in the cell address, the legend on the graph will also change.

5. Press Enter. The pointer returns to **Legend**.

6. Select **Legend** again and repeat the process, typing the following names for the B and C ranges.

   TTL EXPENSES

   PROFIT

   When you finish, the pointer again returns to **Legend**.

To add titles

7. Select **Titles**. You have a choice of giving the graph a one- or two-line graph title. Again, the only limitation is the number of characters: 39 per line. As with legends, you can enter labels directly from the worksheet by typing a backslash (\) and the cell address.
8. Select **First**.
9. Type:

   BUDGET PROJECTION

10. After you press Enter, select **Titles** again.
11. Select **Second**.
12. Type:

    1987

13. Press Enter. At this point, it is also possible to title the X and Y axes; however, these titles are centered across the bottom and left side of the screen, not right next to the axes. To add labels close to the axes, you use the **Graph X** command.

To add titles along the axes

14. Select **Quit**. You need to leave the **Graph Options** menu and return to the **Graph** menu to add titles to the axes.
15. Select **X**.
16. Since you graphed the four quarters, you will now enter the titles you want on the X-axis. Specify the range for the **QTR** titles on the worksheet: **B3. .E3**.
17. Press Enter.
18. Select **View** to view the graph again, this time with labels. See Figure 36.1.
19. Press any key to return to the commands and the worksheet.
20. Select **Type Bar**.
21. Select **View** again. A Bar graph similar to Figure 36.1 is displayed.
22. Press any key.

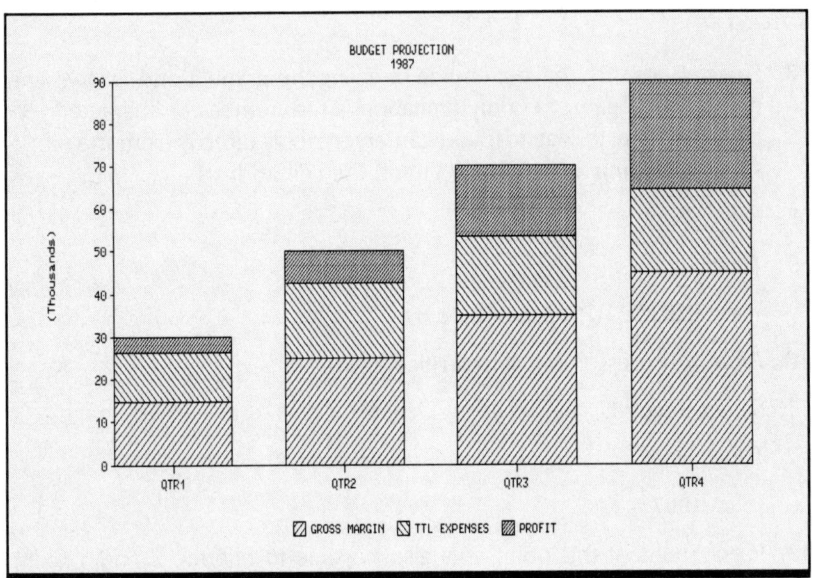

Figure 36.1: Graph with Labels

37 Changing the Scales on the Axes

FEATURING:

the Graph Options Scale command

Unless directed otherwise, 1-2-3 automatically scales the X- and Y-axes to accommodate the graphed range values. The high and low ends of each are based on the highest and lowest values in the data ranges that you entered from the worksheet. As with the other settings in 1-2-3, though, automatic scaling can be turned off. This enables you to set manually the scales on the axes.

When might you want to do this? Any time that you want two graphs to be scaled in the same way. For example, assume that you are preparing a report and you've included your 1987 Budget Projection graphs as a means of predicting trends in expenditures. To avoid any confusion in your readers, you adjusted the Y-axis manually so that all of the graphs are similar.

How to Change the Axes

1. Select **Options Scale** from the Graph menu. The menu enables you to set the scale of the numbers along the X or Y axes. You can also skip some of the X-axis labels. For example, you could display labels for QTR1 and QTR3 but leave QTR2 and QTR4 unlabelled.

2. Select **Y**. The following menu appears:

   Automatic Manual Lower Upper Format Indicator Quit

   Lotus "scales" the Y-axis **Automatically**. Selecting **Manual** allows you to set **Lower** and **Upper** scales. **Lower** refers to the number on the bottom of the scale. **Upper** refers to the number at the top of the scale. **Format** offers the same options available in the **Range Format** and **Worksheet Global Format** commands, such as **Currency** and **Percentages**. **Indicator** allows you to turn on and off the *ticks,* or indicator marks, along the X and Y axes.

3. Select **Manual**. The same menu returns, but 1-2-3's automatic scaling is not in effect so you must now set the upper and lower limits and the format for the numbers on the scale.

4. Select **Upper**.

5. Enter a number twice the highest **GROSS MARGIN** on your worksheet. Type:

   90000

6. Press Enter.

7. You will not change the lower scale. Select **Format**. The standard format menu appears.

8. Select **Currency**. This will display the numbers on the Y-axis with dollar signs and commas.

9. Type **0** decimals, press Enter.

10. Press the Escape key three times to return to the **Graph** menu—the menu that begins with the word **Type**.

11. To view the graph again, this time with the revised scale, select **View**. Notice in Figure 37.1 how the enlarged scale has changed the graph's appearance.

12. Press any key to return to the worksheet. The **Graph** menu remains on the control panel.

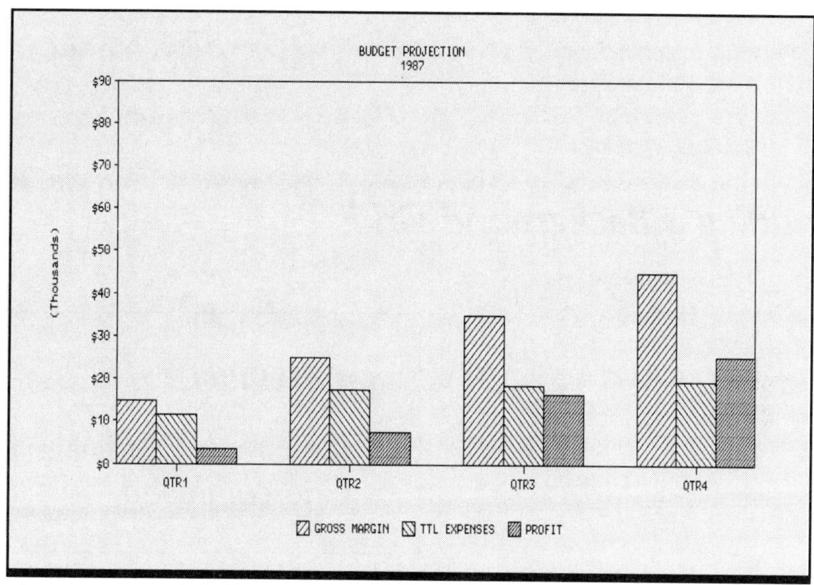

Figure 37.1: *Graph with Revised Scale*

38 Adding a Background Grid

FEATURING:

the Graph Options Grid command

In addition to changing the scale, you can add a background grid to your graph. You have the choice of adding either vertical or horizontal lines, or both. As you will see, the grid is another way of making interpretation easier. For example, with horizontal lines, it's much simpler to see which bar on a bar graph represents the largest figure—or the smallest.

How to Add a Background Grid

1. Select **Options Grid Both**. You will add both horizontal and vertical background lines to your graph.
2. Press Escape to return to the **Graph** menu.
3. Select **View**. The graph is now displayed with a background grid, as shown in Figure 38.1.
4. Press any key to return to the worksheet.

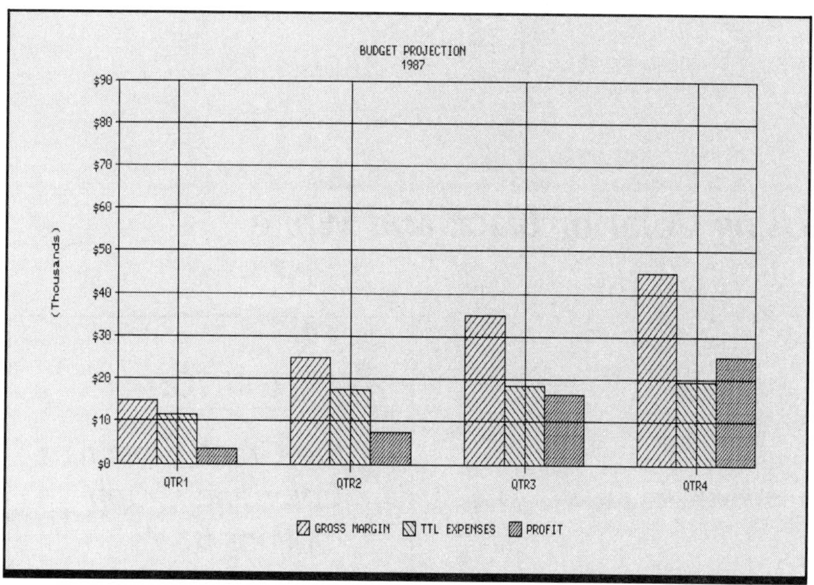

Figure 38.1: *Graph with Grid*

39 Using Color or Black and White

FEATURING:

the Graph Options Color and Graph Options B&W commands

If you are using a black-and-white (monochrome) monitor, use the **B&W** setting for viewing graphs in order to get the cross-hatching seen on the previous graphs. If you are using a color monitor, you can use either the **B&W** or the **Color** setting. Some monochrome monitors can use the **Color** setting and will display different shades instead of cross-hatching. In the exercise below, you will check to see if your monitor has this capability. So don't skip this section if you don't have a color monitor. You might be surprised to see what happens.

For printing, use the **B&W** setting unless you are using a color plotter or color printer. In that case use the **Color** setting.

How to Display in Color

1. Select **Options Color**.
2. **Quit** the Options menu.

3. Select **View**. Even if you have a monochrome monitor, the cross-hatching will be changed to solid bars for monochrome monitors, although the bars may not differ in shading for some. The graph will still print out in different colors, however, on a color plotter or color printer.
4. Return to the Graph menu.

To return to black and white

5. Select **Options B&W**.
6. **Quit** the **Options** menu.
7. View the original graph again. The cross-hatching has replaced the solid shades of green.
8. Return to the worksheet.

40 Naming, Saving, and Using Graphs

FEATURING:

the Graph Name and Graph Save commands

Saving graphs is one of the most misunderstood areas of 1-2-3 because the methods vary depending on what you want to do with your graph. You may want to view only one graph for a worksheet, view multiple graphs per worksheet, or save and print one or more graphs on a printer or plotter.

If you want to view a single graph, and not print it, you need only the **File Save** command to save it—the same command you use to save the worksheet itself. The graph settings are saved along with the worksheet, and you can view the graph when you retrieve the worksheet.

If you plan to save more than one graph per worksheet, you must use **Graph Name** to name them so that 1-2-3 will save the settings for each one.

If you want to print a graph, you must follow several steps: name the graph if you have more than one, save a *picture* of it with the **Graph Save** command, and save the settings with the **File Save** command.

How to Name, Save, and Use Graphs

To name the graph

1. The **Graph** menu should still be on your screen. Select **Name**, and press Enter. 1-2-3 displays a choice:

   Use Create Delete Reset

   Use is the command that calls up a particular graph you have already saved. You simply enter its name. You use **Create** to name the graph the first time you create it, and later on to rename the graph whenever you change settings—titles, legends, type. **Delete** and **Reset** delete either a single graph name or all graph names. Beware! Along with the name, all of the settings, including the graph, are also erased.

2. Select **Create**. 1-2-3 asks you to enter the name of the graph.
3. Type:

   BAR CHART

   When naming a graph, the only limitation is the number of characters: 14. Be sure, in the future, not to use a name that you have already used unless you want that graph replaced by the current graph.

4. Press Enter. The **Graph** menu returns to the screen.

To save the graph for printing

5. Select **Save**. 1-2-3 asks you to enter the name of the file.
6. Type:

   BARCHART

   Notice that there are no spaces in the **Graph Save** file name. Unlike the procedure for the **Graph Name**, the **Graph Save** file name is entered the same way as the other file names: eight characters that can be letters, numbers, or underlined, but no blank spaces and no punctuation. The graph file name is saved with a graph extension (.PIC), whereas a worksheet is saved with a .WK1 extension using **File Save**. You will not be able to retrieve and work with this graph file; it is a static picture created for the purpose of printing out the graph. If you change the graph at all on the screen, you must use **Graph Save** to save the graph again, with the same or a different name, in order to reflect the changes.

7. Press Enter.

To name and save additional graphs

8. To create another graph, such as a stacked-bar chart, you must change the type, name the graph with a new name so as not to overwrite the original bar chart settings, and then save the graph as a new graph file. First, select **Type.**
9. Select **Stacked-Bar. View** the Graph. Press any key to return.
10. Select **Name Create.**
11. Type in the following graph name:

    STACKED BAR CHART
12. Press Enter. The settings for this graph have now been assigned a name.
13. Select **Save.**
14. Type in the following graph file name:

    STACKBAR

    Again, no spaces are allowed in a file name.
15. Press Enter. The graph is saved to the disk.

Using named graphs

16. Now that you've named two graphs, it is easy to switch between the two for viewing. In the Graph menu select: **Name.**
17. Select **Use.** The two graph names are listed.
18. Move the pointer to **BAR CHART** and press Enter. The bar chart is displayed.
19. Press any key to return to the **Graph** menu.
20. Select **Name Use** again.
21. Point to **STACKED BAR CHART** and press Enter. The stacked bar chart is now displayed.

To save the graphs along with the worksheet

22. Select **Quit** to leave the Graph menu.
23. Use **File Save** to save the entire worksheet, including all the graph settings and names you have created.
24. Use the current file name, **87BUDGET**.
25. **Replace** the old version with the new one.

41 Playing "What if": Reflecting Worksheet Changes on the Graph

FEATURING:

the F10 (Graph) function key

Just as 1-2-3 automatically recalculates figures after new data is entered on the worksheet, it automatically updates graphs to reflect the new worksheet entries. Thus, "what if" scenarios on the worksheet can also be displayed graphically. To do so, you return to the worksheet, alter numbers, and press the F10 (Graph) function key that instantly displays the current graph. Pressing the F10 key saves you from having to enter the **Graph** command menu to view the graph.

How to Reflect Worksheet Changes on the Graph

1. Change the following cell entries on the worksheet.

Change:	B5	to	30000
	B6	to	7000
	B11	to	1300
	B12	to	3000
	C5	to	25000
	C6	to	6000

2. Press the F10 function key. The changes are reflected in the graph, as shown in Figure 41.1.

3. Press any key.

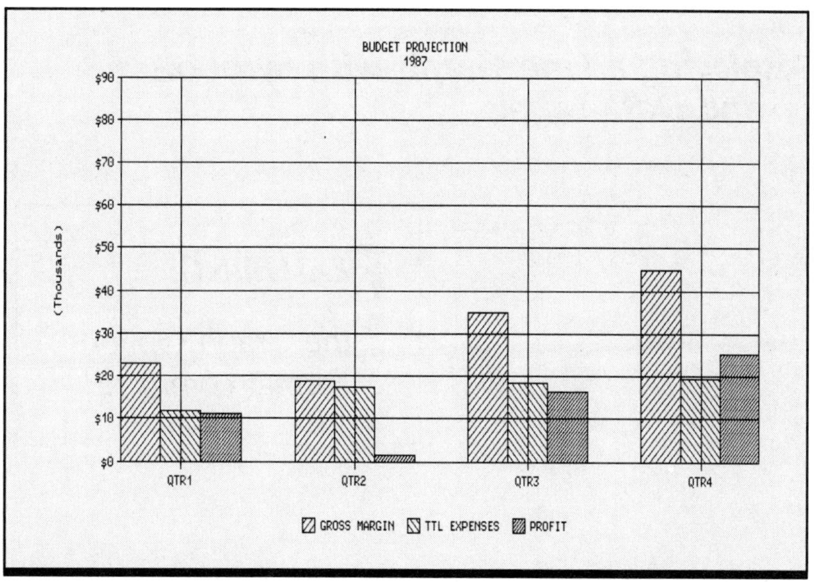

Figure 41.1: *Updated Graph*

42 Displaying a Line Graph with Symbols and Data-Labels

FEATURING:

the Graph Options Format command

To experiment further with graphs, you can create a line graph using several options. You can add a variety of symbols to represent each range, instead of bar shadings as you saw in your bar graphs. This is possible only with line and XY graphs. In addition, you can display all of the numbers that you graphed to make the graph more specific. You can do this with all graph types, except pie graphs.

How to Create a Line Graph with Symbols and Data-labels

To create a line graph

1. Press the slash (**/**) key.
2. Select **Graph Type Line**. Select **Options Grid Clear** to clear the grid. **Quit** the Options menu.

3. **View** the graph. See Figure 42.1. The lines are based on the previous graph, or the graph after you made the worksheet changes. Notice that each line or data range has a unique set of symbols placed at each quarter's data point. The bottom line, the profit line, intersects each quarter with diamonds. The total expenses line intersects with crosses. And the gross margin line intersects with squares.

4. Press any key to return to the Graph menu. Use **Options Scale Y-Axis Automatic** to reset the Y scale to automatic scaling. **Quit** the Scale Menu. **Quit** the Options menu. **View** the graph again.

To change the symbols inside the graph

5. Press any key to return to the Graph menu. Select **Options Format.** You have the choice of:

    Graph A B C D E F Quit

    Graph is used to set the format of the entire graph. Each letter is used to set the format for individual ranges.

6. Select **Graph.** You now have the following choice:

    Lines Symbols Both Neither

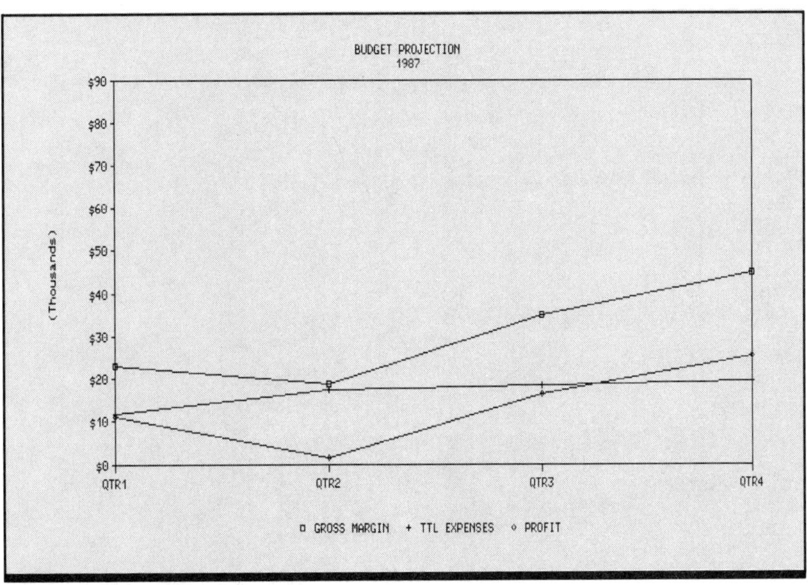

Figure 42.1: *Line Graph*

Graph Format does not have the same meaning as **Worksheet Global Format** or **Range Format**. Now **Format** refers only to lines and symbols. The graph is already displayed with both. You may choose one or the other; however, in this case, lines alone would make the graph impossible to interpret since only the symbols have legends.

7. Select **Symbols**.
8. **Quit** the **Format** and **Options** menus to return to the **Graph** menu.
9. View the graph. As shown in Figure 42.2, now only the symbols are displayed on the graph.
10. Press any key to return to the worksheet.

To add Data-Labels

11. Select **Options Data-Labels**. 1-2-3 displays the letters **A** through **F**. Each letter refers back to the data range you entered when you first created the bar graph.
12. Select **A**.
13. Specify the original A-range, the GROSS MARGIN figures: **B8..E8**. This will display the actual Gross Margin numbers right on the graph.

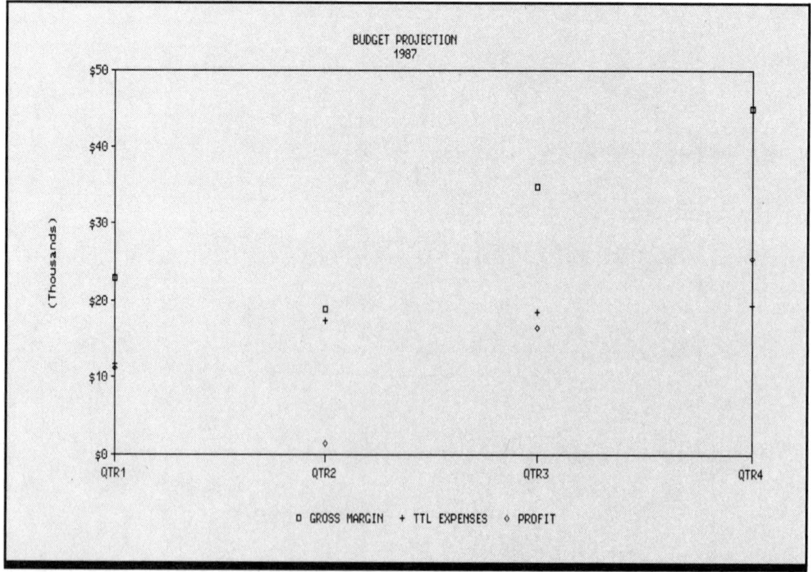

Figure 42.2: *Graph with Symbols*

14. Press Enter.
15. To specify the data labels, select **Right**.
16. Select **Quit**.
17. **Quit** again to the main **Graph** menu.
18. **View** the graph. The gross margin figures from the worksheet are now displayed on the graph directly to the right of the gross margin data points, as shown in Figure 42.3. (Some of the data-labels may run off the screen. They will be printed correctly, however.)
19. Return to the **Graph** menu.
20. Select **Options Data-Labels** to create labels for the B (Total Expenses) and C (Profit) ranges.
21. Select **B** to set the labels for the B-range.
22. Type in or point to **B16..E16**.
23. Press Enter.
24. Specify **Above** to display the labels above the data points.
25. Select **C** to set the labels for the C-range.

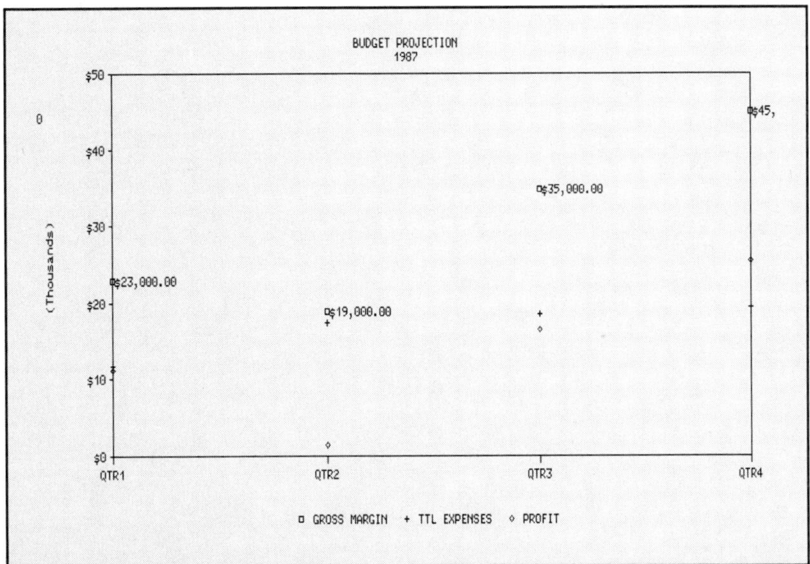

Figure 42.3: *Graph with Data-Labels*

26. Type in or point to **B18..E18**.
27. Press Enter.
28. Specify **Below**.
29. Select **Quit** twice until you return to the Graph menu.
30. **View** the graph.
31. Save the graph using **Save**. If you don't remember how, refer back to Section 40 for instructions. Save the graph under the name **DATALBLS**. (Remember that file names have a maximum of eight characters.)
32. Name the graph using **Name Create**. Again, refer back to Section 40 if necessary. Name the graph as **DATA LABELS**. (Remember that graph names can be up to 14 characters long, including spaces.)
33. Leave the Graph menu by using the Escape key or select **Quit**.

43 Printing the Graph

FEATURING:

the PrintGraph program disk to access Print commands

Printing a graph requires several more steps than simply viewing it. Whether you have a hard- or floppy-disk system, you must leave the worksheet and use a separate 1-2-3 program: PrintGraph. Floppy-disk users will be using a new program disk.

Before you can print a graph, you must save it with the **Graph Save** command, as you did in Section 40, "Saving the Graph." Complete this section even if you don't have a printer.

How to Print the Graph

1. Be sure that your printer is on and ready.
2. You have already saved the graph using the **Graph Save** command. Next, save the current worksheet using the **File Save** command. Save it as **87BUDGET**.

3. When you have saved the worksheet, press the slash (/) key.
4. Select **Quit**. 1-2-3 asks you if you are sure you want to quit the current worksheet session. This is because, in addition to quitting the worksheet session, you will erase whatever is currently on the screen.
5. Select **Yes**. The Lotus Access menu appears. See Section 3, "Installing 1-2-3," for further discussion about the Access System.
6. Select **PrintGraph**. If you have a floppy-disk system, 1-2-3 will ask you to insert the PrintGraph disk in drive A and press Enter. Do so now. The PrintGraph menu should appear:

   Image-Select Settings Go Align Page Exit

   You may get a message stating that the "printer driver" is incompatible with the PrintGraph program. If so, exit this menu and return to the Access menu. Use **Install** to specify a graphics printer. Refer to Section 3 on installing 1-2-3 on your computer.

   Image-Select allows you to select one or more of the graph files that you create and save in the 1-2-3 worksheet. **Settings** enables you to change the graph's size, color, rotation, and type fonts, and to identify the printer(s) in use and the directories in which the graph files are located. **Go** instructs printing to begin. **Align** synchronizes the PrintGraph program with your printer before printing. **Page** advances the paper in the printer. **Exit** takes you out of the PrintGraph program.

To set up the PrintGraph program for your computer and printer

The following steps (7–17) need to be done only if the PrintGraph program is not yet set up. If you are unsure, do these steps; otherwise, skip to step 18.

7. Before selecting graphs, use the **Settings** command to instruct 1-2-3 where to look for them. Select **Settings**. 1-2-3 displays:

   Image Hardware Action Save Reset Quit

8. Select **Hardware**. 1-2-3 displays:

   Graphs-Directory Fonts-Directory Interface Printer Size-Paper Quit

9. Select **Graphs-Directory**. 1-2-3 prompts you to type in the directory that contains the graphs. If you have a floppy-disk system, type:

   B:

   If you have a hard-disk system, you must specify the directory where the graph files have been saved. If you installed 1-2-3 as instructed in Section 3, type:

C:\123

If the files are saved in another directory, replace **\123** with the correct directory name.

10. Press Enter.
11. Select **Fonts-Directory**. Again, 1-2-3 prompts you to type in the directory that contains the fonts files. If you have a floppy-disk system, type:

    A:

    If you have a hard-disk system, type:

    C:\123

    If your directory's name is not **\123**, replace **\123** with the correct name.
12. Press Enter.
13. Next you need to select the printer that you will use to print graphs during this session. You can always change to another printer later on. The choices available depend on the printers that you specified during the installation procedure using **Install** in the initial Lotus Access menu. (Refer to Section 3, "Installing Lotus 1-2-3.")

    Select Printer. If the program gives you a beep with a message, you may need to reinstall 1-2-3 for graphics printers. Do that now, referring to Section 3 and then returning to this section. You will need to exit the PrintGraph program and insert the Installation disk when prompted.
14. A menu of one or more printers is displayed. Move the pointer next to the printer you want and press the Spacebar to select a printer.
15. Press Enter to leave the Printer menu and return to the Hardware menu. If you wanted to print using a serial interface such as with a Laser printer, you could select **Interface**. To change the size of the paper you are printing on, you could select **Size-Paper**. Do not perform these steps now, however.
16. Select **Quit**. 1-2-3 displays:

    Image Hardware Action Save Reset Quit
17. Select **Save** to store the directory and printer settings. After saving, 1-2-3 returns you to the initial PrintGraph menu:

    Image-Select Settings Go Align Page Exit

To select graphs

18. Select **Image-Select**. A list of graph files is displayed. In it are your two files: **BARCHART** and **STACKBAR**. See Figure 43.1.
19. Move the pointer to **BARCHART**, using the Down-Arrow key if necessary. 1-2-3 allows you to view a graph on screen by using the F10 (Graph) function key. Try this now with **BARCHART**. Press F10. Then press any key to return to the menu.
20. Press the Spacebar to select **BARCHART**. A number (#) sign appears. Press Enter to return to the main PrintGraph menu.

To print graphs

21. Be sure that paper is aligned in your printer and your printer is turned on. Select **Align** to synchronize 1-2-3 with your printer.
22. Select **Go** to print the graph. It will take a few moments for the graph to start printing.
23. Select **Page** to advance the paper when the graph is finished printing.

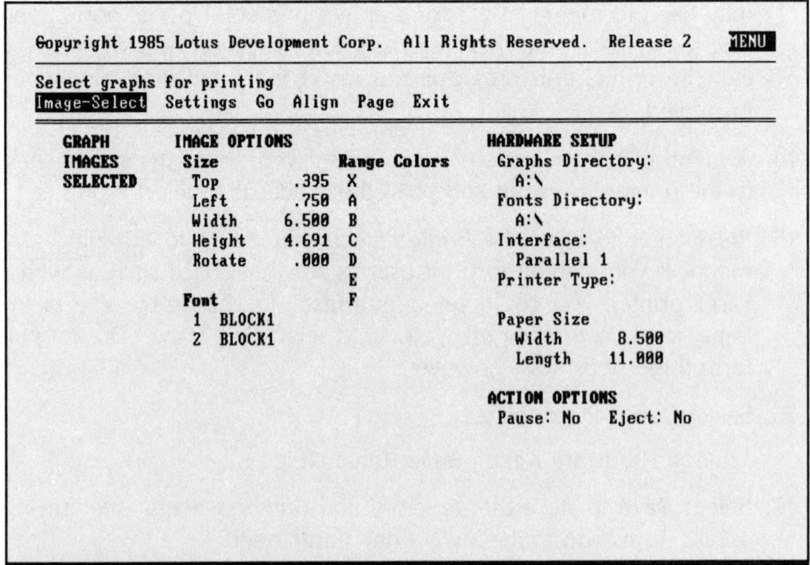

Figure 43.1: *Select Graph Menu*

To change type fonts, colors, and graph size

24. Select **Settings.**
25. Select **Image.** 1-2-3 displays:

    Size Font Range-Colors Quit

26. Select **Font.** At this point you have two choices to make for specifying type fonts: the font selected under **Font 1** will be used for the main title of the graph. The font selected under **Font 2** will be used for all other text and numbers on the graph. If you do not specify a font for **Font 2, Font 1** will be used for the entire graph.
27. Select **Font 1** to specify the font that will be used in the main title of the graph. 1-2-3 displays a list of fonts, each of which comes in two shades, one lighter, the other darker. **Block1** is lighter than **Block2,** for example.
28. Select a font by moving the pointer to one and pressing the Enter key. Generally, **Block, Bold, Forum,** and **Roman** will work on most printers; you should normally choose the darker version. The **Italic** and **Script** fonts generally are better for plotters and may not produce high-quality graphs on ordinary printers.
29. Select **Font 2** to specify the type of font that will be used for the rest of the graph. After selecting, return to the menu, which displays:

    Size Font Range-Colors Quit

30. Select **Size.** You will see these choices:

    Full Half Manual Quit

31. Select **Full.** This will rotate the graph ninety degrees. The default setting is **Half.** If you have a plotter you can use **Range-Colors** to change the pen color. Skip this step now.
32. Return to the initial menu:

    Image-Select Settings Go Align Page Exit

33. Print the graph **BARCHART** again by selecting **Go.**
34. Now experiment using the other graph **STACKBAR.** Select it with **Image-Select,** then change the type fonts and size using the Settings menu. You can **Save** any of these changes. To print a number of graphs sequentially, select **Image-Select** and press the Spacebar next to each graph you want to print. They will be printed in the order

selected. You can cause 1-2-3 to **Eject** a page after each graph. **Pause** will cause 1-2-3 to stop after each graph; until you press a key. Both of these commands are accessed using the **Settings** command.

To return to the worksheet

35. Select **Exit**. From the Access menu, select **123**. You will need to insert the System disk on a floppy-disk system.

44
Creating a Pie Chart

FEATURING:

/Graph Pie and Shading/Coloring

Version 2.0 of 1-2-3 enables you to create pie charts with "exploded" sections—one or more sections that are set apart from the rest of the pie chart. In addition, each section can be distinctively shaded or colored, depending on the monitor and printer or plotter that you have.

A 1-2-3 pie chart only requires two ranges: the X-range and the A-range. The A-range identifies the values that will be represented by the wedges of the pie. The X-range is used to identify the labels for each wedge. A third range for pie charts, the optional B-range, is new to Version 2.0. With it, you can shade and explode wedges of the pie.

The pie chart you are about to build will be shaded and it will show how much of the annual expenses is represented by each individual expense.

How to Reset a Graph's Settings to Create a Pie Chart

1. Select **/Graph Reset** to clear the graph settings associated with the previous graphs. This will *not* affect graph settings that you have named using **Graph Name.**
2. Select **Graph** to clear all settings. You also have the option here of resetting only specific ranges.
3. Now set up the pie chart. Select **Type.**
4. Specify **Pie.**
5. Select range-**A.**
6. Specify the A-range as the total expenses for each category: Overhead, Marketing, Salaries, Legal Fees. Use the range:

   F11..F14

7. Press Enter.
8. Select range-**X.**
9. Specify the X-range. Type in the range that contains the expense labels (Overhead, Marketing, Salaries, Legal Fees):

   A11..A14

10. Press Enter.
11. Select **View** to display the graph. See Figure 44.1. A basic pie chart, without shading or colors, is displayed. The percentage of the pie represented by each wedge is also calculated and displayed.
12. Press any key to return to the Graph menu.

How to Shade and Explode a Pie Chart

13. To instruct 1-2-3 to shade, color and/or explode sections of a pie chart, you need to type special codes into a range of cells, and then specify those cells as the B-range. This range can be located anywhere on the worksheet and must be the same size as the A-range. Typing in a number from 1 to 7 indicates the type of shading or color for each section. Code 0 or 8 specifies an unshaded section, as does a blank cell. If you want one or more sections exploded, add 100 to the shading code. For example, if you want a wedge shaded using code 6

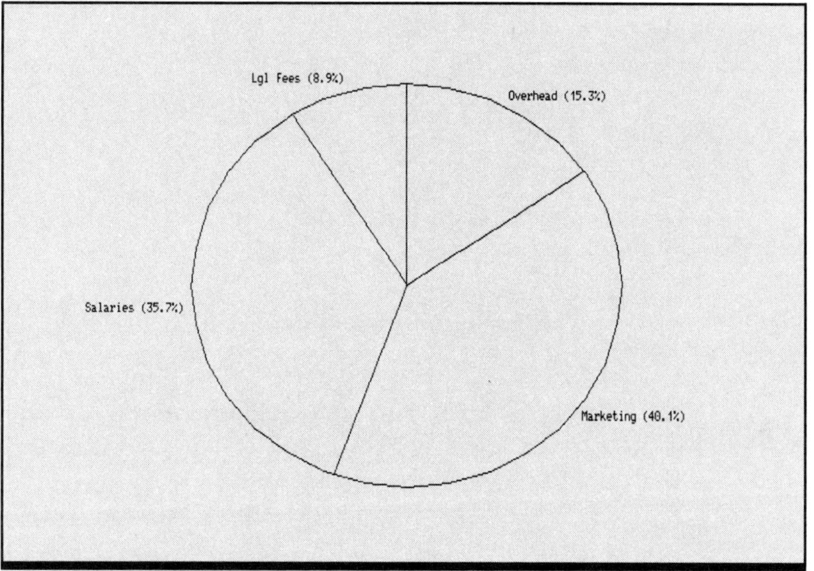

Figure 44.1: *Basic Pie Chart*

and you want it exploded, specify 106. **Quit** the **Graph** menu and return to the **READY** mode.

Type these codes in the following cells:

In cell H11, type:	**1**
In cell H12, type:	**102**
In cell H13, type:	**3**
In cell H14, type:	**4**

The number will be displayed with 2 decimals. Typing **102** in H12 will explode the Marketing section.

14. Before viewing the graph, specify the B-range as the range with the codes. Select **Graph B-range.**

15. Specify the range as **H11..H14** and press Enter.

16. Now **View** the graph. See Figure 44.2. The graph should be shaded if you have a graphics monitor, or colored if you have a color monitor, and the Marketing section should be set apart from the rest of the pie.

17. **Quit** the **Graph** menu. Experiment with changing the codes. Again, use 1 through 7 to specify different types of shading, and add 100 to any code to explode that section. Use the F10 Graph function key to display the graph again.

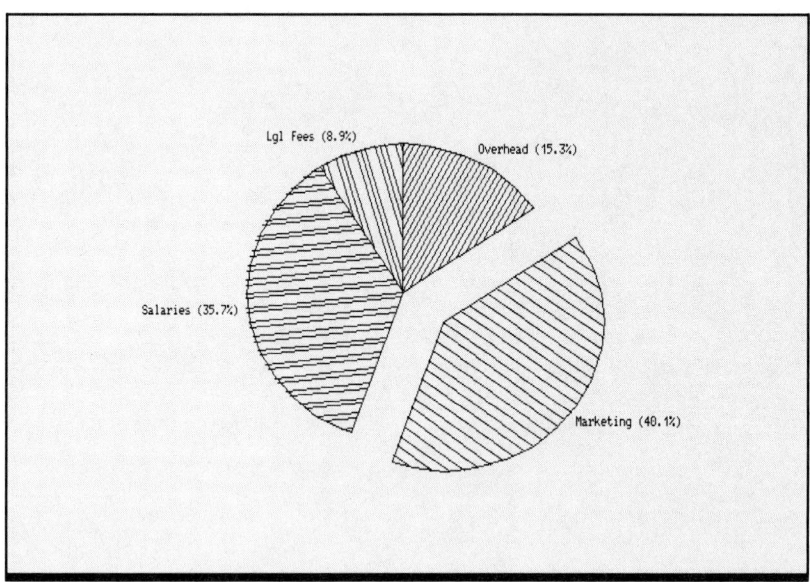

Figure 44.2: *Pie Chart with Shading and Exploded Section*

18. When you are satisfied with the pie chart, name it **Pie Chart** with the **Graph Name** command, and save it for printing with **Graph Save**. Call it **PIECHART** for the graph file name. (Remember, no spaces in file names.)

19. To print the graph, save the worksheet using **File Save, Quit** the worksheet, and use the PrintGraph program. Use the **Range-Color** settings to determine the color of each pie section, if you are using a color printer or color plotter.

123

Chapter Four

DATA-BASE MANAGEMENT

45 Creating a Data Base

To build a data base, you enter information—such as inventory, personnel, or client records—on the worksheet, just as you previously entered the numbers. All of the commands used with the worksheet are also available for the data base—and vice versa. Thus, you will print the data base, for example, the same way you printed the worksheet, using **Print** commands.

So what's new? **Data** commands, the final category of commands. By using **Data** commands in the sections that follow, you will manipulate the data you've entered.

When you build a data base, the numbers and letters no longer function as columns and rows; they function as *records* and *fields*. All the information entered across one row is a complete record, and any one part of it is a field. Thus, using your local phone book as an example, the entire entry under your name is a record; your phone number alone is a field.

How to Enter Information

1. Be sure that the screen is blank and you are in the **READY** mode.
2. Enter the following information the same way you entered labels, numbers, and formulas. However, be sure that you do not add any blank spaces after the last character in each entry. Adding a space with the spacebar causes problems when 1-2-3 reorganizes the data. Column headings A, B, C, D, and E and all of columns A, B, and C will automatically left-align without entering a label prefix. Be sure not to use a label prefix with the numbers. Since all of the entries will not fit in the columns, use **Worksheet Global Column-Width** when you are finished to widen the columns to 12. And remember to save your work. In case of any problems, this will prevent you from having to type the

data base again. Enter this information:

	A	B	C	D	E
1.	EMPLOYEE	STORE	DEPT	SALARY	SALES
2.	Esposito, S.	San Fran	Mangr	34600	111000
3.	Tanzer, H.	Atlanta	Admin	14400	0
4.	Badran, M.	New York	Sales	22600	231000
5.	Leung, L.	Atlanta	Sales	25400	260000
6.	Hoch, T.	Atlanta	Sales	23300	235000
7.	Nash, J.	New York	Admin	18600	0
8.	Raney, J.	San Fran	Admin	13000	0
9.	Temes, N.	Atlanta	Sales	19400	153000
10.	Stein, S.	Denver	Admin	13800	0
11.	Ormsby, E.	Denver	Sales	19400	187000
12.	Lehman, A.	San Fran	Sales	22900	216000
13.	Kane, L.	New York	Sales	20000	249000
14.	Gold, A.	Denver	Sales	26600	210000

3. Use **/File Save** to save with the name **EMPLOYEE**.

46

Sorting the Information

the Data Sort command

At the moment, 1-2-3 isn't anything more than a space-saving filing cabinet. But, just as 1-2-3 distinguished itself as more than a ledger pad, it will distinguish itself as more than a helpless filing cabinet with its ability to organize and reorganize information. With the **Data Sort** command, you can change the order of the records to any order that you specify.

Continuing with the personnel list you entered in the previous section, you will use **Data Sort** to sort the records by department and by amount of sales.

How to Sort the Data Base

1. Press the slash (/) key.
2. Select **Data**. 1-2-3 displays the following **Data** commands:

   Fill Table Sort Query Distribution Matrix Regression Parse

   The **Fill** command automatically assigns a sequence of numbers to a range of cells. **Table** creates statistical tables. **Sort** reorganizes the information. **Query** finds and lists subsets of information, and **Distribution** tallies the number of times an item occurs within a range.

Matrix, Regression, and **Parse** are new to version 2.0 of Lotus 1-2-3. With **Matrix,** you can easily multiply a row of numbers by a column of numbers and produce a table of the results. You can also invert a matrix, or table, of numbers. **Regression** creates statistical data based on variables. **Parse** converts a column of long labels into several columns of labels or values. This is useful when transferring data from other PC software programs or from a mainframe computer. Refer to the Lotus 1-2-3 manuals for further explanations of these three commands.

3. Select **Sort**. 1-2-3 displays another menu:

   Data-Range Primary-Key Secondary-Key Reset Go Quit

   Data-Range refers to the cells you will include in the sort. Using the **Primary-Key**, you specify the first field (formerly referred to as a column) that you will use to sort the data base by, such as by department. With the **Secondary-Key**, you can further sort the data using an additional field, such as salaries or sales. **Reset** cancels the **Data-Range** and key settings, and **Go** tells 1-2-3 to sort.

4. Since you must first tell 1-2-3 what you want it to sort, select **Data-Range**. 1-2-3 asks you to enter the range.

5. Specify all of the data except the labels at the top of each column. Just as you did on the worksheet, you can type in or point to the range: A2..E14. Use the period and arrow keys to point.

6. After pressing Enter, select **Primary-Key**. 1-2-3 asks you to enter the primary sort key address.

7. Since you will be sorting by department first, specify the department field by entering any cell in the column. Type:

   C1

8. After pressing Enter, 1-2-3 asks you if you want to sort in ascending or descending order. *Ascending* orders data from the lowest number to the highest and from the first letter of the alphabet to the last. *Descending* does the reverse.

9. Type:

   A

   Since the field is the department field, this will tell 1-2-3 to sort it by letter or alphabetically. After pressing Enter, the **Sort** menu returns to the screen.

10. Select **Secondary-Key**. To sort each department by sales, enter any cell address from the sales field.

11. Type:

    E1

    After pressing Enter, 1-2-3 again asks you if you want the information sorted in ascending or descending order.

12. This time, use descending order. Type:

    D

    Since this field is filled with sales, 1-2-3 will sort it by number, placing the highest sales first.

13. After pressing Enter, select **Go**. As shown in Figure 46.1, you now have a list of employees by department, with each department organized by sales amounts.

14. If the results shown here do not match your own, retrieve **EMPLOYEE** once more and go through the steps again.

15. **File Save** the file as **SORT**.

```
A2: 'Raney, J.                                                    READY

      A              B             C            D            E
1   EMPLOYEE       STORE         DEPT         SALARY        SALES
2   Raney, J.      San Fran      Admin         13000            0
3   Tanzer, H.     Atlanta       Admin         14400            0
4   Nash, J.       New York      Admin         18600            0
5   Stein, S.      Denver        Admin         13800            0
6   Esposito, S.   San Fran      Manag         34600       111000
7   Leung, L.      Atlanta       Sales         25400       260000
8   Kane, L.       New York      Sales         20000       249000
9   Hoch, T.       Atlanta       Sales         23300       235000
10  Badran, M.     New York      Sales         22600       231000
11  Lehman, A.     San Fran      Sales         22900       216000
12  Gold, A.       Denver        Sales         26600       210000
13  Ormsby, E.     Denver        Sales         19400       187000
14  Temes, N.      Atlanta       Sales         19400       153000
15
16
17
18
19
20
28-Sep-86  09:45 PM
```

Figure 46.1: *Reorganized Data Base*

Worksheet
Range
Name
Create

1. Input
2. Criterion } Range
3. Output

47

Assigning Numbers to the Data Base

FEATURING:

the Data Fill command

Now that you've sorted by department and sales, suppose you want to assign ratings to all of the salespeople. With the **Data Fill** command, you can add a column of numbers, used here as ratings, to the data base. Later, if you want to re-sort, the numbers remain and you can use them to return the data base to its current sort order.

How to Add a Sequence of Numbers to the Data Base

1. Press the slash (/) key.
2. Select **Data Fill**. 1-2-3 asks you to enter the fill range.
3. Since you want to assign numbers or ratings to all members of the sales force, you will need to enter numbers in the column to the right of the sales figures. Specify the range by typing or pointing:

   F7. .F14

   After pressing Enter, 1-2-3 asks you for the **Start** number.

4. Start with number one. Type:

   1

   At this point, after pressing Enter, 1-2-3 asks you for the **Step** number, or the amount of change from one number to the next. 1-2-3 suggests **1**.

5. Press Enter since you want the numbers to increase by one. 1-2-3 asks for the **Stop** number and suggests **8191** or the last record (or row) number.

6. Leave this as is; the initial Fill range of F7..Fix will stop the "fill" of numbers. After pressing Enter, the data base in Figure 47.1 appears on the screen, clearly showing the top salesperson.

7. Enter a label at the top of column F. Enter:

   RATING

To re-sort alphabetically

8. To re-sort the records in alphabetical order, the procedure is the same as that for **Sort**. Change the Data-Range.

9. Select **Data Sort**.

```
A2: 'Raney, J.                                                      READY

      A            B          C          D           E          F
1   EMPLOYEE     STORE      DEPT       SALARY      SALES
2   Raney, J.    San Fran   Admin       13000          0
3   Tanzer, H.   Atlanta    Admin       14400          0
4   Nash, J.     New York   Admin       18600          0
5   Stein, S.    Denver     Admin       13800          0
6   Esposito, S.San Fran    Manag       34600     111000
7   Leung, L.    Atlanta    Sales       25400     260000          1
8   Kane, L.     New York   Sales       20000     249000          2
9   Hoch, T.     Atlanta    Sales       23300     235000          3
10  Badran, M.   New York   Sales       22600     231000          4
11  Lehman, A.   San Fran   Sales       22900     216000          5
12  Gold, A.     Denver     Sales       26600     210000          6
13  Ormsby, E.   Denver     Sales       19400     187000          7
14  Temes, N.    Atlanta    Sales       19400     153000          8
15
16
17
18
19
20
28-Sep-86  10:35 PM
```

Figure 47.1: *Data Base with Ratings*

10. Select **Data-Range**, and specify the entire data base, including the rating field (column), but excluding the labels. Press the **Right** arrow key once to highlight **A2..G14**.
11. After pressing Enter, select **Primary-Key**.
12. Since you want to sort alphabetically by name, specify any cell in column A as the **Primary-Key** cell.
13. After pressing Enter, select **Ascending** order.
14. Select **Go**. The data base appears like the one in Figure 47.2.

To re-sort again, using the data-fill numbers

15. Select **Data Sort**.
16. Select **Primary-Key**, and specify any cell in column F. You do not have to change the Data-Range.
17. Select **Ascending** order.
18. Select **Go**. 1-2-3 re-sorts the data base using the data-fill numbers, as shown in Figure 47.3. The records without data-fill numbers are still at the top, but they are not listed in any particular order.

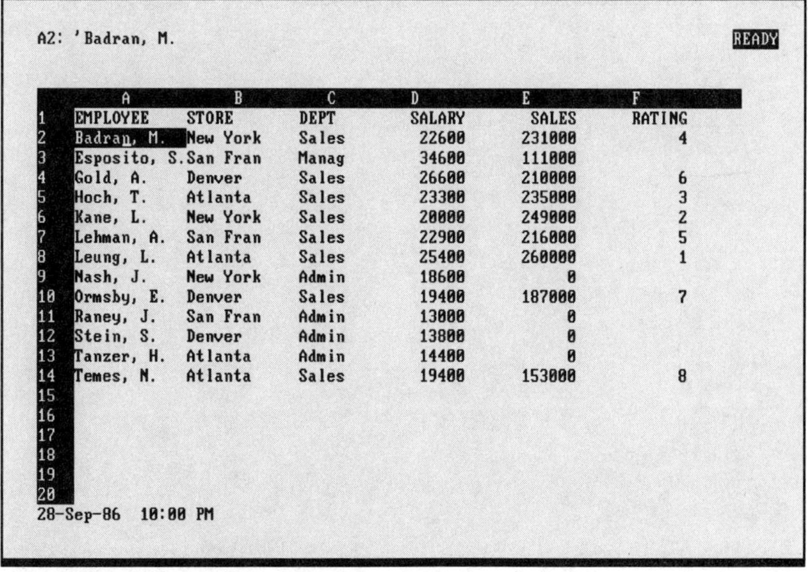

A2: 'Badran, M. READY

	A	B	C	D	E	F
1	EMPLOYEE	STORE	DEPT	SALARY	SALES	RATING
2	Badran, M.	New York	Sales	22600	231000	4
3	Esposito, S.	San Fran	Manag	34600	111000	
4	Gold, A.	Denver	Sales	26600	210000	6
5	Hoch, T.	Atlanta	Sales	23300	235000	3
6	Kane, L.	New York	Sales	20000	249000	2
7	Lehman, A.	San Fran	Sales	22900	216000	5
8	Leung, L.	Atlanta	Sales	25400	260000	1
9	Nash, J.	New York	Admin	18600	0	
10	Ormsby, E.	Denver	Sales	19400	187000	7
11	Raney, J.	San Fran	Admin	13000	0	
12	Stein, S.	Denver	Admin	13800	0	
13	Tanzer, H.	Atlanta	Admin	14400	0	
14	Temes, N.	Atlanta	Sales	19400	153000	8
15						
16						
17						
18						
19						
20						

28-Sep-86 10:00 PM

Figure 47.2: *Alphabetized Data Base*

19. If the results shown here do not match your own, retrieve the worksheet **SORT** and start with step 1.

20. **File Save** the worksheet as **RATING.**

```
A2: 'Stein, S.                                                    READY

       A           B          C          D          E          F
1   EMPLOYEE    STORE      DEPT       SALARY      SALES     RATING
2   Stein, S.   Denver     Admin      13800         0
3   Nash, J.    New York   Admin      18600         0
4   Tanzer, H.  Atlanta    Admin      14400         0
5   Esposito, S.San Fran   Manag      34600    111000
6   Raney, J.   San Fran   Admin      13000         0
7   Leung, L.   Atlanta    Sales      25400    260000          1
8   Kane, L.    New York   Sales      20000    249000          2
9   Hoch, T.    Atlanta    Sales      23300    235000          3
10  Badran, M.  New York   Sales      22600    231000          4
11  Lehman, A.  San Fran   Sales      22900    216000          5
12  Gold, A.    Denver     Sales      26600    210000          6
13  Ormsby, E.  Denver     Sales      19400    187000          7
14  Temes, N.   Atlanta    Sales      19400    153000          8
15
16
17
18
19
20
28-Sep-86  10:10 PM
```

Figure 47.3: *Data Base Sorted by Data-Fill Numbers*

48 Retrieving Information from the Data Base

FEATURING:

the Data Query commands

Once data is stored, a single piece of information or a group of related data can be retrieved. With the employee list you have entered, you can use the **Query** command to retrieve a list of all the salespeople in the Atlanta area or a list of the salespeople who have sold more than $200,000 in merchandise. Or, you could combine the two by querying for a list of the salespeople in Atlanta who have sold more than $200,000 worth of merchandise.

As with **Data Sort**, you must specify a range of cells to query or search through—called the *input range.* An input range differs from a **Data-Range** in sorting; when you query, you specify the data base *and* the column headings, referred to as *field names.*

A second range is also specified in **Query**: the *criterion range.* This range consists of field names and criteria, or the information 1-2-3 uses to determine what to select from the input range. When you query, 1-2-3 goes to the criterion range to get the criteria—actually a set of records consisting of labels, numbers, and formulas. Then 1-2-3 returns to the input range to find the records that match.

Finally, if you want 1-2-3 to make copies of the new list elsewhere on the worksheet, a third range must be specified: the *output range.* It tells

1-2-3 where to put the copy of the data it has selected. The output range must have the names of the fields you want copied in the top row.

All three ranges—input, criterion, and output—must have the same field names in the first row. This means that if one set of field names is capitalized, the others must be also.

How to Query for Subsets of Information

1. Using the **Copy** command, copy the field names twice: first, to row 17 to make a copy for the criterion range; then, to row 21 to make a copy for the output range. The data base will appear like the one in Figure 48.1.

To name the input and criterion ranges with range names

2. To assist you in working with the **Data Query** commands as well as with the Data Table in the next section, assign names to the information in the data base. Press the slash (**/**) key, and select **Range Name Create**. See Section 33 "Naming Part of the Worksheet" for reference.

```
A25:                                                              READY

        A            B           C           D           E          F
 6  Raney, J.    San Fran    Admin        13000          0
 7  Leung, L.    Atlanta     Sales        25400     260000          1
 8  Kane, L.     New York    Sales        20000     249000          2
 9  Hoch, T.     Atlanta     Sales        23300     235000          3
10  Badran, M.   New York    Sales        22600     231000          4
11  Lehman, A.   San Fran    Sales        22900     216000          5
12  Gold, A.     Denver      Sales        26600     210000          6
13  Ormsby, E.   Denver      Sales        19400     187000          7
14  Temes, N.    Atlanta     Sales        19400     153000          8
15
16
17  EMPLOYEE     STORE       DEPT        SALARY      SALES     RATING
18
19
20
21  EMPLOYEE     STORE       DEPT        SALARY      SALES     RATING
22
23
24
25
28-Sep-86  10:12 PM
```

Figure 48.1: *Data Base with Copied Field Names*

3. Type:

   DATABASE

   This is the name of the input range, or the data base.

4. After pressing Enter, specify the range beginning with the field name **EMPLOYEE** and ending with the bottom-right of the list: **A1. .G14**.

5. Press Enter.

6. Select **Range Name Create** again.

7. Type:

   CRITERION

8. After pressing Enter, specify the range beginning with the field names in row 17. Since the criterion range must include at least two rows, include row 18. Be sure to extend the range to column G: **A17. .G18**.

To prepare the query ranges

9. Press the slash (**/**) key.

10. Select **Data Query**. 1-2-3 displays the menu, shown in Figure 48.2. The first three terms have been defined. **Find** highlights the records you select from the data base one at a time. **Extract** makes copies of the query data and places them in the output range. **Unique** eliminates duplicates in the output range. **Delete** erases the records from the data base that fit the criteria and deletes the empty rows. **Reset** erases the ranges and the last query from 1-2-3's memory.

11. Select **Input**. 1-2-3 asks for the input range. Instead of entering A1..G14 as the data base, you will enter instead the predefined range name Database.

12. Press the F3 (Name) function key. A list of the range names is displayed.

13. Select **DATABASE**. The data base is now the input range. The **Data Query** menu returns.

14. Select **Criterion.**

15. Press the F3 key again.

16. Select **CRITERION**. The criterion range is now specified, and the **Data Query** menu returns.

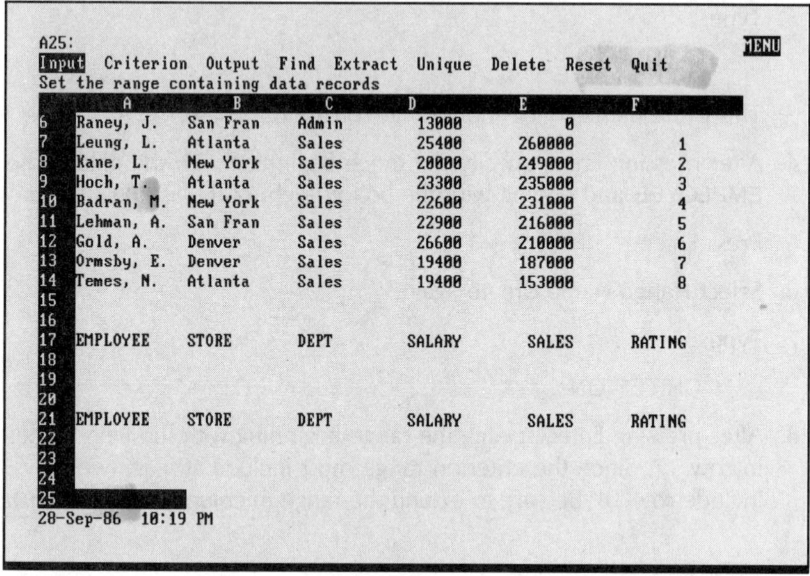

Figure 48.2: *The Data Query Command Menu*

17. Select **Output**. 1-2-3 now asks for the output range.
18. Since you didn't assign a range name to the output range, specify the range beginning with the **EMPLOYEE** cell in the bottom group of field names and ending with the last field name in the row, **RATING**: **A21. .G21**. It is only necessary to specify the field names for the output range. Not selecting rows beneath allows 1-2-3 to use as many as needed for output. After pressing Enter, the output range is specified.

To Query for all employees

19. Select **Extract** to place a copy of the query data in the output range.
20. Select **Quit**, and move down to view the results. The entire data base is copied into the output range, as shown in Figure 48.3, because no criteria were specified in the criterion range. Leaving the cells blank, rather than entering criteria in the range, pulls out the entire list of employees.

    If the results shown here differ from your own, retrieve the worksheet **RATING** and begin again with step 1.

```
A10: 'Badran, M.                                                    READY

      A           B          C            D           E          F
10  Badran, M.  New York   Sales        22600      231000          4
11  Lehman, A.  San Fran   Sales        22900      216000          5
12  Gold, A.    Denver     Sales        26600      210000          6
13  Ormsby, E.  Denver     Sales        19400      187000          7
14  Temes, N.   Atlanta    Sales        19400      153000          8
15
16
17  EMPLOYEE    STORE      DEPT         SALARY      SALES     RATING
18
19
20
21  EMPLOYEE    STORE      DEPT         SALARY      SALES     RATING
22  Stein, S.   Denver     Admin        13800           0
23  Nash, J.    New York   Admin        18600           0
24  Tanzer, H.  Atlanta    Admin        14400           0
25  Esposito, S.San Fran   Manag        34600      111000
26  Raney, J.   San Fran   Admin        13000           0
27  Leung, L.   Atlanta    Sales        25400      260000          1
28  Kane, L.    New York   Sales        20000      249000          2
29  Hoch, T.    Atlanta    Sales        23300      235000          3
28-Sep-86  10:22 PM
```

Figure 48.3: *All the Records in the Output Range*

To query for all employees in Atlanta

21. In B18, in the criterion range, type:

    Atlanta

    Remember: The criterion must be an exact match—the first letter only is capitalized.

22. After pressing Enter, try a quicker method of querying. Rather than returning to **Data Query Extract**, press the **F7** (Query) function key. This key tells 1-2-3 to perform the most recent **Query** operation—in this case, **Extract**—using the last input, criterion, and output ranges and any new criteria that are specified. All employees from Atlanta are now copied down to the output range, as shown in Figure 48.4.

To query using a second criterion: a formula

23. In E18, type the formula:

    +E2>200000

    After you press Enter, a zero is displayed. (A **0** represents a value not more than $200,000; a **1** represents a value greater than $200,000.)

```
B18: 'Atlanta                                                          READY

      A            B           C           D           E            F
10  Badran, M.   New York    Sales       22600       231000            4
11  Lehman, A.   San Fran    Sales       22900       216000            5
12  Gold, A.     Denver      Sales       26600       210000            6
13  Ormsby, E.   Denver      Sales       19400       187000            7
14  Temes, N.    Atlanta     Sales       19400       153000            8
15
16
17  EMPLOYEE     STORE       DEPT        SALARY       SALES        RATING
18               Atlanta
19
20
21  EMPLOYEE     STORE       DEPT        SALARY       SALES        RATING
22  Tanzer, H.   Atlanta     Admin       14400            0
23  Leung, L.    Atlanta     Sales       25400       260000            1
24  Hoch, T.     Atlanta     Sales       23300       235000            3
25  Temes, N.    Atlanta     Sales       19400       153000            8
26
27
28
29
28-Sep-86  10:23 PM
```

Figure 48.4: *Atlanta Employees in the Output Range*

E2 is the first cell in the data base that contains sales information. When you query, 1-2-3 begins with this cell and works down the sales column looking for values greater than $200,000. Having entered this formula, all records that you query for will now have to match two criteria: Atlanta and sales greater than $200,000.

24. Press the F7 (Query) function key. A list of employees fitting the criteria is copied to the output range, as shown in Figure 48.5.

To compile a list of Atlanta employees who sold $200,000 or less

25. In the same cell, E18, type or edit (F2) the formula:

    +E2< =200000

    1 is now displayed.

26. Press the F7 function key. A list of employees fitting the criteria is copied to the output range, as shown in Figure 48.6.

27. To display the formula, rather than the **1** or **0**, press the slash (**/**) key and select **Range Format Text**. Specify the range as **E18**. After pressing Enter, the **+E2< =200000** is displayed. The **T** in parentheses on the control panel refers to text.

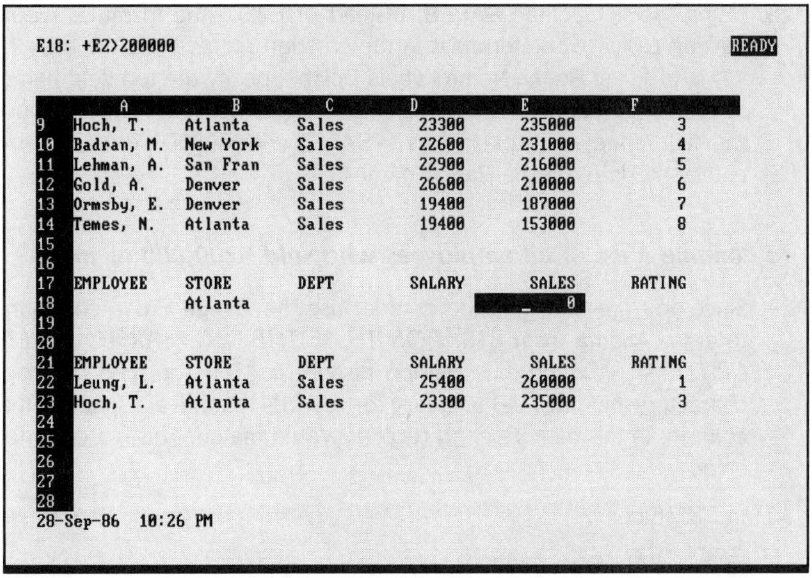

```
E18: +E2>200000                                                    READY

       A            B           C            D           E           F
 9  Hoch, T.     Atlanta     Sales        23300      235000           3
10  Badran, M.   New York    Sales        22600      231000           4
11  Lehman, A.   San Fran    Sales        22900      216000           5
12  Gold, A.     Denver      Sales        26600      210000           6
13  Ormsby, E.   Denver      Sales        19400      187000           7
14  Temes, N.    Atlanta     Sales        19400      153000           8
15
16
17  EMPLOYEE     STORE       DEPT        SALARY       SALES      RATING
18               Atlanta                                  0
19
20
21  EMPLOYEE     STORE       DEPT        SALARY       SALES      RATING
22  Leung, L.    Atlanta     Sales        25400      260000           1
23  Hoch, T.     Atlanta     Sales        23300      235000           3
24
25
26
27
28
28-Sep-86   10:26 PM
```

Figure 48.5: *Atlanta Employees Selling More Than $200,000*

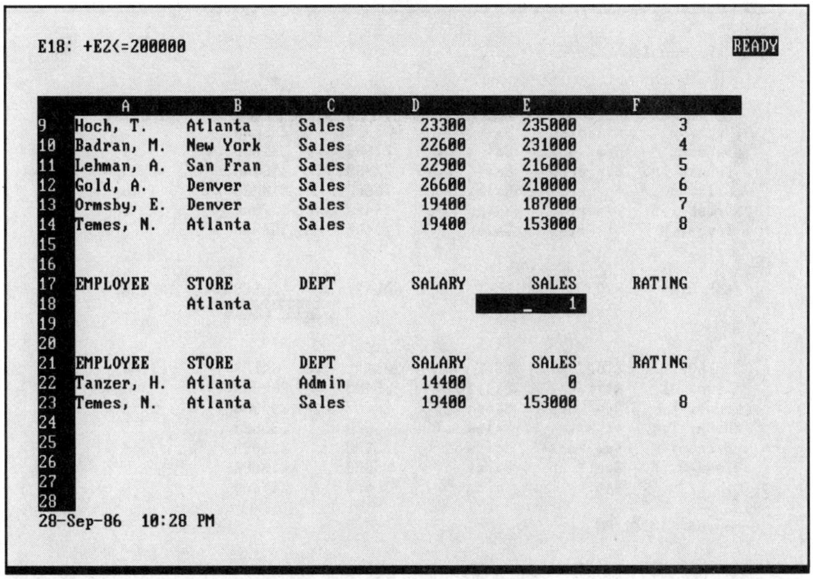

```
E18: +E2<=200000                                                   READY

       A            B           C            D           E           F
 9  Hoch, T.     Atlanta     Sales        23300      235000           3
10  Badran, M.   New York    Sales        22600      231000           4
11  Lehman, A.   San Fran    Sales        22900      216000           5
12  Gold, A.     Denver      Sales        26600      210000           6
13  Ormsby, E.   Denver      Sales        19400      187000           7
14  Temes, N.    Atlanta     Sales        19400      153000           8
15
16
17  EMPLOYEE     STORE       DEPT        SALARY       SALES      RATING
18               Atlanta                                  1
19
20
21  EMPLOYEE     STORE       DEPT        SALARY       SALES      RATING
22  Tanzer, H.   Atlanta     Admin        14400           0
23  Temes, N.    Atlanta     Sales        19400      153000           8
24
25
26
27
28
28-Sep-86   10:28 PM
```

Figure 48.6: *Atlanta Employees Selling $200,000 or Less*

28. Using the field name **SALES**, instead of **E2**, in the formulas would make it easier to use formulas in the criterion range. Press the slash (**/**) key, and select **Range Name Labels Down**. Specify the top field names as the range name: **A1. .G1**. After pressing Enter, the formula above the worksheet is displayed as **+SALES< =200000**. You can now enter criteria using the **Range** names.

To compile a list of all employees who sold $200,000 or more

29. Since you are changing the criteria, use the **Range Erase** command to erase **Atlanta** from B18. *DON'T USE THE SPACEBAR TO DELETE CRITERIA.* Although the criterion disappears, it is replaced by space characters that tell 1-2-3 to query for records that have a space in that column. In this data base, no records would match. This is a common error.

30. In E18, type:

    +SALES> =200000

31. After pressing Enter, press the F7 function key. All employees who sold more than $200,000 are copied to the output range, as shown in Figure 48.7.

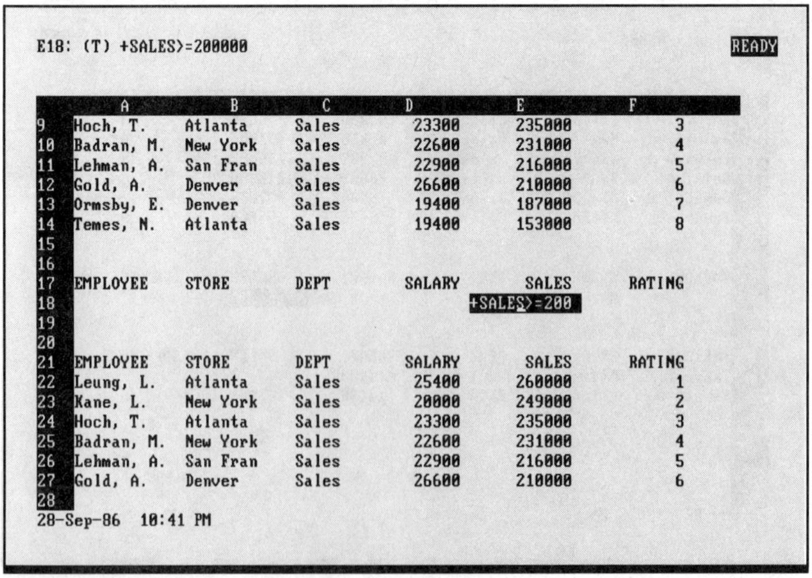

```
E18: (T) +SALES>=200000                                              READY

        A            B           C          D          E          F
9   Hoch, T.     Atlanta     Sales       23300     235000          3
10  Badran, M.   New York    Sales       22600     231000          4
11  Lehman, A.   San Fran    Sales       22900     216000          5
12  Gold, A.     Denver      Sales       26600     210000          6
13  Ormsby, E.   Denver      Sales       19400     187000          7
14  Temes, N.    Atlanta     Sales       19400     153000          8
15
16
17  EMPLOYEE     STORE       DEPT       SALARY      SALES     RATING
18                                              +SALES>=200
19
20
21  EMPLOYEE     STORE       DEPT       SALARY      SALES     RATING
22  Leung, L.    Atlanta     Sales       25400     260000          1
23  Kane, L.     New York    Sales       20000     249000          2
24  Hoch, T.     Atlanta     Sales       23300     235000          3
25  Badran, M.   New York    Sales       22600     231000          4
26  Lehman, A.   San Fran    Sales       22900     216000          5
27  Gold, A.     Denver      Sales       26600     210000          6
28
28-Sep-86  10:41 PM
```

Figure 48.7: *Employees Selling $200,000 or More*

To compile a list of employees who sold less than $200,000, but more than $150,000

32. In E18, being sure not to add any blank spaces, edit (F2) type the following:

    +SALES< =200000#AND#+SALES>150000

    The logical operator **#AND#** tells 1-2-3 to select records that satisfy both the first half of the formula and the second half. After pressing Enter, only part of the formula is displayed. This is due to the length of the formula.

33. Press the F7 key. The list of employees who fulfill the criteria is copied to the output range, as shown in Figure 48.8.

To compile a list of all employees in Atlanta and New York by using labels

34. If you want a list of employees from two cities, you must enter the labels in the same column, the **STORE** column. You cannot use #AND# or #OR# with Labels to place more than one in one cell. Therefore, you must add a row to the criterion range. Press the slash (**/**) key.

```
E18: (T) +SALES<200000#AND#SALES>150000                                   READY

      A            B            C             D            E             F
9   Hoch, T.     Atlanta      Sales         23300       235000           3
10  Badran, M.   New York     Sales         22600       231000           4
11  Lehman, A.   San Fran     Sales         22900       216000           5
12  Gold, A.     Denver       Sales         26600       210000           6
13  Ormsby, E.   Denver       Sales         19400       187000           7
14  Temes, N.    Atlanta      Sales         19400       153000           8
15
16
17  EMPLOYEE     STORE        DEPT          SALARY        SALES       RATING
18                                                   +SALES<2000
19
20
21  EMPLOYEE     STORE        DEPT          SALARY        SALES       RATING
22  Ormsby, E.   Denver       Sales         19400       187000           7
23  Temes, N.    Atlanta      Sales         19400       153000           8
24
25
26
27
28
20-Sep-86  06:02 PM
```

Figure 48.8: *Employees Selling Less Than $200,000 and More Than $150,000*

35. Select **Data Query Criterion**. The current range is displayed.
36. Press the Down-Arrow key to expand the range one row. After pressing Enter, a blank row is added to the range.
37. **Quit** the **Data Query** menu.
38. Use **Range Erase** to erase the formula beneath **SALES**.
39. In B18, type:

    Atlanta

40. After pressing Enter, in B19, type:

    New York

41. After pressing Enter, press the F7 key. A list of all employees from New York and Atlanta is copied to the output range, as shown in Figure 48.9.
42. As mentioned earlier, if you type in a full label, it must match exactly, including uppercase and lowercase. However, there is another option if, for example, you want to pull out the names of all the salespeople from Atlanta whose names begin with L. In A18 under EMPLOYEE, type:

    L*

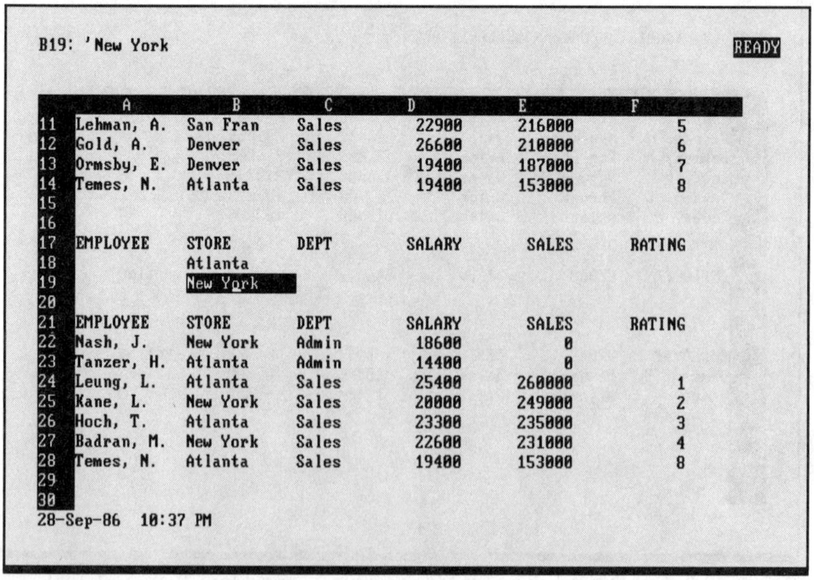

```
B19: 'New York                                                        READY

      A           B           C           D           E           F
11 Lehman, A.  San Fran    Sales        22900      216000           5
12 Gold, A.    Denver      Sales        26600      210000           6
13 Ormsby, E.  Denver      Sales        19400      187000           7
14 Temes, N.   Atlanta     Sales        19400      153000           8
15
16
17 EMPLOYEE    STORE       DEPT        SALARY       SALES      RATING
18             Atlanta
19             New York
20
21 EMPLOYEE    STORE       DEPT        SALARY       SALES      RATING
22 Nash, J.    New York    Admin        18600           0
23 Tanzer, H.  Atlanta     Admin        14400           0
24 Leung, L.   Atlanta     Sales        25400      260000           1
25 Kane, L.    New York    Sales        20000      249000           2
26 Hoch, T.    Atlanta     Sales        23300      235000           3
27 Badran, M.  New York    Sales        22600      231000           4
28 Temes, N.   Atlanta     Sales        19400      153000           8
29
30
28-Sep-86  10:37 PM
```

Figure 48.9: *Employees From New York and Atlanta*

43. Press the Query(F7) key. All people in Atlanta whose names begin with L and all New York employees are selected. A letter followed by an asterisk acts as a wild card; everything that matches the first character is selected. So, all L's from Atlanta (L* and Atlanta are in the same row) and all employees from New York are selected. Two other characters act as wild cards with labels: the ? and the ~ (tilde). The question mark is used to represent a single character. Thus, H?t selects Hot, Hat, Hit, and Hut, but not Halt or Hats. The tilde before a label tells 1-2-3 to select all records, except those matching that label.

44. Change the criterion range back to include only two rows: 17 and 18. Use **Data Query Criterion**. Stay in the **Query** menu.

To find records in the data base

45. Select **Find**. 1-2-3 searches through the data base and finds the matching records that are highlighted. The mode indicator changes to **FIND**. Only the Up- and Down-Arrow keys and the Escape key operate now.

46. Move the pointer down. 1-2-3 highlights the next record in the data base.

47. Press Escape to leave the **FIND** mode.

48. **Quit** the **Query** menu. Pressing the F7 key now instructs 1-2-3 to find, rather than extract, since it is the most recent **Data Query** operation. Press the **Right** arrow key to access different columns. To change a cell's contents, type in the change.

49. If the results shown for this section do not match your own, retrieve the worksheet **RATING** and begin again with step 1 at the beginning of the section.

50. **Quit** the Data Query menu and **File Save** the worksheet as **QUERY**.

49 Building a Statistical Table

FEATURING:

the Data Query Unique and Data Table commands,and the @DSUM and @DCOUNT data-base functions

To answer a few more questions, you can take the data base further to produce a statistical table.

Data Query Unique and **Data Table** will help you produce a table, like the one in Figure 49.1, that displays the total number of employees, the total salary amounts, and the total amount of sales for each store. You could then calculate the sales to salary and sales to number of employees ratios, based on the statistics in the table.

The first command, **Data Query Unique**, is similar to the **Data Query Extract** command that you used to place a copy of the queried data in the output range. **Data Query Unique** goes one step beyond **Query Extract**; it eliminates any duplicate records from the output range. Therefore, when you set up the new output range, the **STORE** column, each store will appear only once in the list.

```
B18:                                                                  READY

      A            B           C              D              E           F
11  Lehman, A.   San Fran    Sales          22900         216000          5
12  Gold, A.     Denver      Sales          26600         210000          6
13  Ormsby, E.   Denver      Sales          19400         187000          7
14  Temes, N.    Atlanta     Sales          19400         153000          8
15
16
17  EMPLOYEE     STORE       DEPT          SALARY          SALES     RATING
18
19
20                           EMPLOYEES     SALARY          SALES
21               STORE              13     274000        1852000
22               Denver              3      59800         397000
23               New York            3      61200         480000
24               Atlanta             4      82500         648000
25               San Fran            3      70500         327000
26
27
28
29
30
28-Sep-86   10:48 PM
```

Figure 49.1: *Statistical Table*

After entering the store names and adding more labels, you need to enter formulas to calculate the total employees, salaries, and sales. To do this, you will use a new version of the @SUM function: the data-base @DSUM. The advantage of this function is that it sums up only those cells in a range you specify with criteria. For example, if you applied the @SUM function to the data base, @SUM(D2. .D14), it would add all the salaries of all the employees. Using the data-base function @DSUM instead, you can add the salaries of all the employees in only one store.

When entering a data-base function, you must include the @ symbol, followed by the data-base function name which, in turn, is followed by the data-base range, the column of the data base that you are using for the operation, and the criterion range that specifies the records to be selected. The format is:

@Dfunction name(data base, column, criterion range)

To add all of the salaries in the data base, you specify the entire data base, **A1. .G14** (or enter the name **DATABASE** that you assigned in the last section); the **SALARY** column (3); and the criterion range, **A17. .G18** (or enter the name **CRITERION** you also assigned in the last section). (It is not necessary to invoke the **Data Query** command to specify the criterion range with data-base functions.) Thus, the formula looks like this:

@DSUM(DATABASE,3,CRITERION)

The column number is the column "offset" from the first (left) column of this data base: A=0, B=1, C=2, D=3, etc.

In addition to using @DSUM, you will use @DCOUNT to count the number of employees for each store. Just as @DSUM has a cousin in the standard function @SUM, @DCOUNT has a cousin @COUNT. @COUNT is used to count the number of items in a list, whereas @DCOUNT counts items selectively, using specified criterion. @DCOUNT is entered the same way that @DSUM is entered, except that the function name differs.

After labels and formulas are entered, you use **Data Table** to fill in the rest. **Data Table** requires you to provide some specific information before it can create a table. First, you need to specify whether you are going to use one or two cells in the criterion range to input data. You will use one cell to input store names one by one. Then you need to tell 1-2-3 where the table is by specifying its column and row boundaries. Finally, you need to tell 1-2-3 where in the criterion range the data is to be input. Since you are entering store names, you will specify the cell beneath **STORE**.

The structure of Data Table 1 is:

```
Input Cell
[        ]

             Formula 1    Formula 2   . . .
Variable 1   [results]    [results]
Variable 2   [results]    [results]
Variable 3   [results]    [results]
. . .
```

When you execute Data Table 1, the variables (Variable 1, Variable 2, etc.) are entered automatically into the input cell one at a time. Each formula (Formula 1, Formula 2, etc.) uses the input cell to calculate the results in the matrix. While the @Dfunctions are used in this section to demonstrate Data Tables, other types of formulas are also possible.

For example, the following table could be set up to calculate interest by multiplying each interest rate by a principal amount. /Data Table 1 would substitute each rate (Rate 1, Rate 2, etc.) into the Input Cell, then use that rate in the formula. Of course, to build this you would actually need to type in the different rates and the principal, and the correct cell address for the Input Cell.

```
Input Cell
[        ]
           Principal * Input cell
Rate 1     [results]
Rate 2     [results]
Rate 3     [results]
Rate 4     [results]
```

How to Build a Statistical Table

To create a list of stores using Data Query Unique

1. Use **Range Erase** to erase everything from the output range, including all headings but the **STORE** heading.
2. Use **Range Erase** again to erase all the criteria in row 18 from the criterion range. Be sure not to erase the field names.
3. Press the slash (**/**) key.
4. Select **Data Query Output**.
5. Specify the cell where **STORE** resides: **B21**. It is possible to have a partial output range.
6. After pressing Enter, select **Unique**. The list of stores in Figure 49.2 is produced. Although the data base includes more than one listing of each store, **Data Query Unique** eliminates duplicates.
7. Quit the **Data Query** menu.

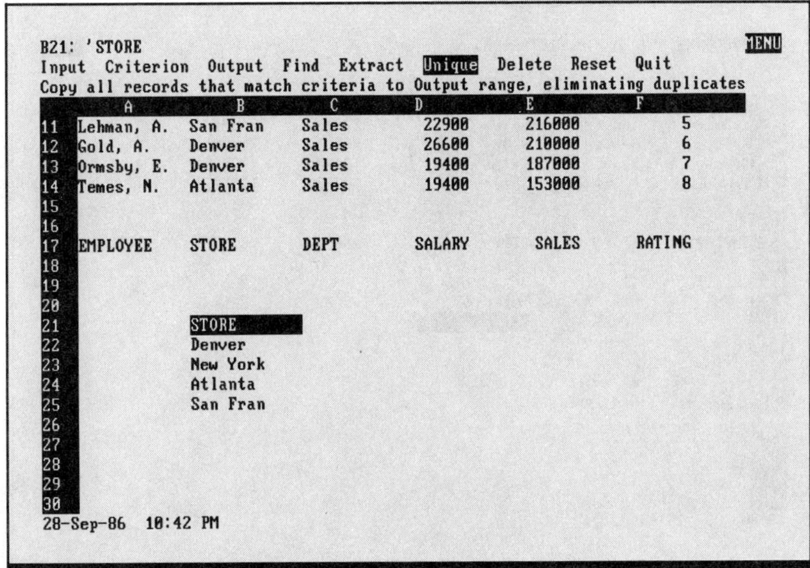

Figure 49.2: *Stores Displayed in the Data Table*

To label the table

8. Enter the following labels, not range names, in the specified cells. Along with the labels that follow, **STORE** will also serve as a label.

   in C20: **"EMPLOYEES**

   in D20: **"SALARY**

   in E20: **"SALES**

To total employees, salaries, and sales for all stores

9. Move to cell C21, below **EMPLOYEES**.
10. Type:

    @DCOUNT(DATABASE,0,CRITERION)

    In the @DCOUNT formula, columns are specified in a particular way. The **0** (zero) refers to the left column in the data base, the **EMPLOYEE** column. **1** is the first column to the right of this one; **2** is the second column to the right; and so on. After pressing Enter, the total number of employees for the company is displayed, as in Figure 49.3. 1-2-3 selected all the records in the data base because no criteria were specified in the criterion range.

```
C21: @DCOUNT(DATABASE,0,CRITERION)                                        READY

       A           B           C                D            E          F
11  Lehman, A.  San Fran    Sales             22900       216000          5
12  Gold, A.    Denver      Sales             26600       210000          6
13  Ormsby, E.  Denver      Sales             19400       187000          7
14  Temes, N.   Atlanta     Sales             19400       153000          8
15
16
17  EMPLOYEE    STORE       DEPT              SALARY        SALES     RATING
18
19
20                          EMPLOYEES         SALARY        SALES
21              STORE                 13
22              Denver
23              New York
24              Atlanta
25              San Fran
26
27
28
29
30
28-Sep-86  10:46 PM
```

Figure 49.3: *Total Number of Company Employees in the Output Range*

11. Move to D21, beneath **SALARY**.
12. Type:

    @DSUM(DATABASE,3,CRITERION)

    After pressing Enter, the total salary amount for the company will be displayed. The ranges for Database (A1..G14) and Criterion (A17..G18) could also be typed here.
13. Move to E21, beneath **SALES**.
14. Type:

    @DSUM(DATABASE,4,CRITERION)

    After pressing Enter, the total sales amount for the company is displayed. The data table, shown in Figure 49.4, now reveals the company's total number of employees, salaries, and sales. 1-2-3 has selected all the records in the data base because there are no criteria in the criterion range.
15. Move to B18, beneath **STORE** in the criterion range.
16. Type:

    San Fran

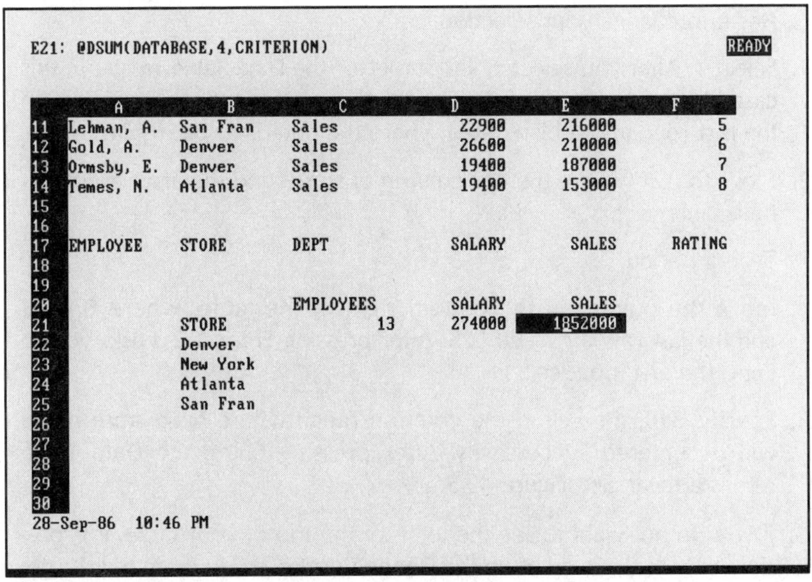

```
E21: @DSUM(DATABASE,4,CRITERION)                                        READY

        A            B            C              D            E           F
11  Lehman, A.   San Fran     Sales            22900       216000          5
12  Gold, A.     Denver       Sales            26600       210000          6
13  Ormsby, E.   Denver       Sales            19400       187000          7
14  Temes, N.    Atlanta      Sales            19400       153000          8
15
16
17  EMPLOYEE     STORE        DEPT            SALARY        SALES     RATING
18
19
20                            EMPLOYEES       SALARY        SALES
21               STORE               13       274000      1852000
22               Denver
23               New York
24               Atlanta
25               San Fran
26
27
28
29
30
28-Sep-86   10:46 PM
```

Figure 49.4: *Company Employees, Salaries, and Sales in the Data Table*

Be sure to type it exactly as it appears in the data base. After pressing Enter, the numbers for **EMPLOYEES**, **SALARY**, and **SALES** change to reflect the new criterion. You now have all the totals for the San Francisco store.

17. In B18 over **San Fran**, type:

    Atlanta

    After pressing Enter, the new numbers reflect the totals for Atlanta. You can view the totals for each store by successively typing each store's name in B18.

18. Use **Range Erase** to erase **Atlanta** from the criterion range.

To calculate the data table

19. With the **Data Table** command, you can display all the stores' totals at once, instead of one at a time. Press the slash (**/**) key.

20. Select **Data Table**. You have three choices:

    1 2 Reset

    You can enter one or two *input cells.* The input cell is the specific cell where each of the stores is to be substituted one at a time. This will be done beneath the **STORE** heading in the criterion range. (You use **Reset** to change your selection.)

21. Select **1**. After you select **1**, 1-2-3 asks for the **Data Table** range. In this case, it includes the list of stores in the first column, the formulas in the first row, and a blank area where the data is to be displayed.

22. Move to B21, where the first column of stores and the first row of formulas intersect.

23. Type a period.

24. Move the pointer to the bottom right of the table, where **SALES** and the last row intersect: E25. After pressing Enter, 1-2-3 asks you to enter the first input cell.

25. Specify **B18**, the cell in the criterion range where each store name will be entered successively. After pressing Enter, the **Data Table** results appear. See Figure 49.5.

26. If you do not want to see the totals at the top of your table, it is possible to hide them by using the **Range Format +/–** command. It produces a plus (+) or minus (–) for each integer value, i.e. + + + + +

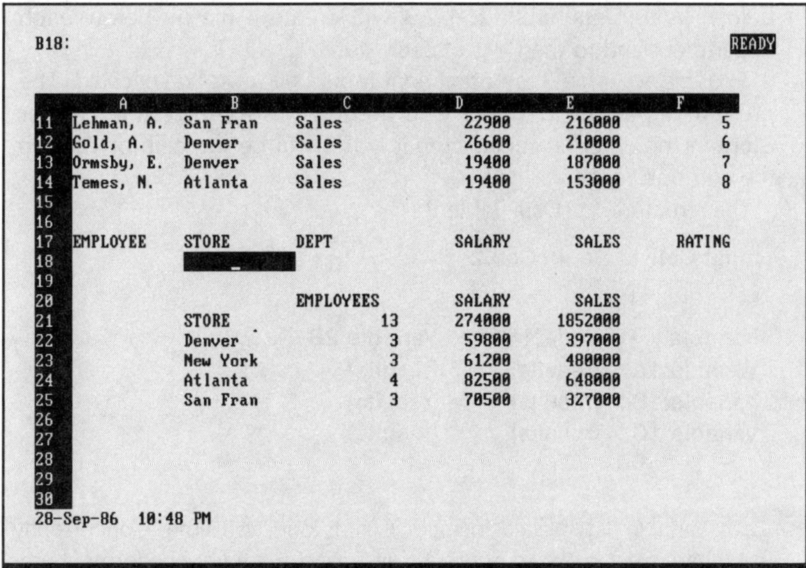

B18: READY

	A	B	C	D	E	F
11	Lehman, A.	San Fran	Sales	22900	216000	5
12	Gold, A.	Denver	Sales	26600	210000	6
13	Ormsby, E.	Denver	Sales	19400	187000	7
14	Temes, N.	Atlanta	Sales	19400	153000	8
15						
16						
17	EMPLOYEE	STORE	DEPT	SALARY	SALES	RATING
18						
19						
20			EMPLOYEES	SALARY	SALES	
21		STORE	13	274000	1852000	
22		Denver	3	59800	397000	
23		New York	3	61200	480000	
24		Atlanta	4	82500	648000	
25		San Fran	3	70500	327000	
26						
27						
28						
29						
30						

28-Sep-86 10:48 PM

Figure 49.5: *Data Table Results*

for the value 5, – – – for the negative value –3. With these you can make a simple horizontal bar graph in lieu of using the Graph commands. (This is necessary only when you do not have a color or graphics monitor.) When there are more symbols than can fit into a column, asterisks appear. Use these asterisks to hide the formulas in the data table.

To hide the numbers, select: **Range Format +/–** and specify the range **C21..E21**. Asterisks will be displayed because the column is too narrow to actually display the correct number of pluses.

27. If the results shown here differ from your own, retrieve the file **QUERY** and start this section again.

28. Save the worksheet under a new name: **TABLE1**. This will preserve the Data Table without erasing the Data Query ranges that you built in the earlier section.

To calculate the table using two variables

29. With Data Table 2 you can build a statistical table using two variables or input cells. For example, to find out what the salary amounts were for each department within each store, you will set up the table

below. With Data Table 2, 1-2-3 will create a matrix below each department and to the right of each store.

To use Data Table 2, an additional Input cell must be specified. The previous Input cell 1 will also be used in this example (the cell for **Store** in the criterion range). Input cell 2 will be the cell for **Dept** in the criterion range.

The structure for Data Table 2 is:

```
Input Cell 1   Input Cell 2
[          ]   [          ]

Formula        Variable 2A    Variable 2B   . . .
Variable 1A    [results]      [results]
Variable 1B    [results]      [results]
Variable 1C    [results]      [results]
. . .
```

Each Variable 1 is placed in Input Cell 1, one at a time. Concurrently, each Variable 2 is placed in Input Cell 2, one at a time. The formula uses both input cells to create the results in the matrix.

For the table below, Data Table 2 will begin by inserting the first store (Denver) *and* the first department (Manag) into the input cells in the criterion range. All employees who match *both* criteria will be selected. The sum of their salaries will be placed in the table, in this case beneath **Manag** and to the right of **Denver**. Then the process will repeat, using the next store in the criterion range.

In a new area of the worksheet, type:

```
             Manag   Sales   Admin
Denver
New York
Atlanta
San Fran
```

30. Data Table 2 allows you only one formula per table, unlike Data Table 1. In this case, use the same formula that you used earlier to calculate the total salaries. In the cell directly above **Denver** and directly to the left of **Manag**, type:

    @DSUM(DATABASE,3,CRITERION)

31. This formula will use the same criterion range for the Input Cells that was used in the Data Table 1 lesson. To run Data Table 2, select:

    /Data Table 2

32. Use the **Backspace** key to undo the last Table Range used in the Data Table 1 lesson above.

    Stay in the cell with the formula, above the first store and to the left of the first department.

    Anchor the range with the period key, then highlight the rest of the table, across all departments and down the rows for all stores. The blank cells below the departments will be highlighted. Then press the Enter key.

33. **Input cell 1** remains the same: the blank cell below the **Store** heading in the criterion range **(B18)**. Press Enter to select that cell.

34. **Input cell 2** should be the cell below the **Dept** heading in the criterion range: cell **C18**. Move the pointer to that cell, or type it in, and press Enter. The new Data Table will be created. See Figure 49.6. Use **Range Format +/−** to hide the @dsum formula.

35. If the results here do not match your results, retrieve the worksheet **TABLE1** and begin again with step 29.

36. **Quit** the Data menu. Save this worksheet under: **TABLE2**. As we have demonstrated, more than one Data Table, Query, or Sort can refer to the same ranges—in this case the ranges named DATABASE and CRITERION.

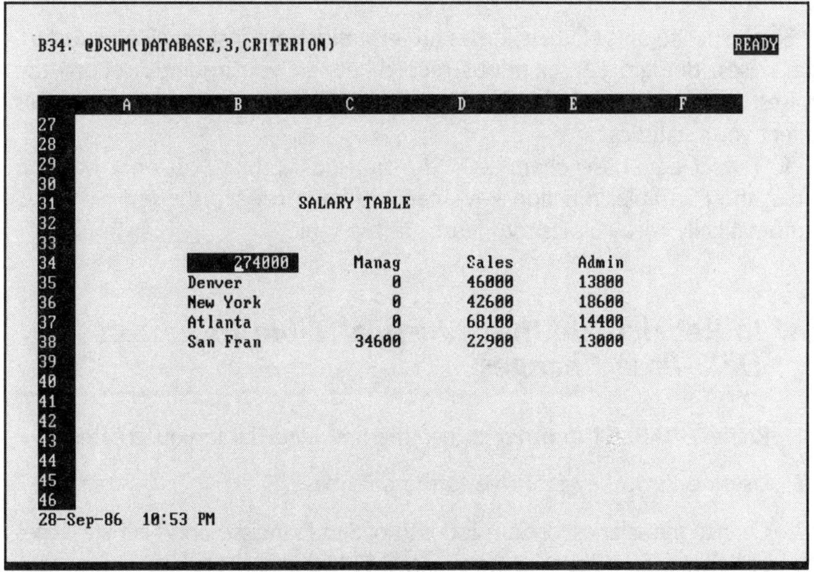

Figure 49.6: *The New Data Table*

50 Playing "What if": Reflecting Data-Base Changes in the Statistical Table

FEATURING:

the F8 (Table) function key

Sam Esposito and Nathan Temes are ecstatic. Both just received substantial raises. Being a conscientious record-keeper, you instantly record the raises in the personnel file. You would also like to know how their raises affect your statistics.

To reflect data-base changes in the statistical table, you only have to press the F8 (Table) function key after you have revised the entries. 1-2-3 automatically recalculates the figures in the table.

How to Recalculate the Statistical Table to Reflect Data-Base Changes

1. Retrieve **TABLE1** in order to use the first Data Table you created.
2. Use the PgUp key to move to the data base.
3. Change the salaries for Sam Esposito of San Francisco and Nathan Temes of Atlanta. Sam Esposito now earns $54,600, and Nathan Temes now earns $39,400. Don't type $ or commas.

4. Move the pointer to any cell in row 26 to view the table.
5. Press the F8 (Table) function key. 1-2-3 recalculates the totals for the two stores. Data tables must be recalculated with either the F8 function key or the **Data Table** command. They are not automatically recalculated in the same way that worksheets are.

51 Playing "What if" Again: Reflecting Data-Base and Statistical Changes on a Graph

Not only did Sam Esposito and Nathan Temes cause some excitement at home when they announced their raises, they made some significant changes in the salary totals for the cities of San Francisco and Atlanta. To view these changes graphically, you create a graph that reflects the stores' totals before the raises, then enter the new salaries.

How to Reflect Data-Base and Statistical Changes on a Graph

1. Using the worksheet retrieved in the last section, return Sam Esposito's salary to $34,600 and Nathan Temes' salary to $19,400.
2. Press the F8 function key to recalculate the table.
3. Using the **Graph** command, create a bar graph. Specify the store names as the **X** range B22..B25, the total salaries for the four stores as the **A** range D22..D25, and the total sales amounts as the **B** range E22..E25, as in Figure 51.1.
4. **View** the graph.
5. **Quit** the **Graph** menu.
6. Return to the data base and enter the following new salaries:

   Sam Esposito **$54,600**

   Nathan Temes **$39,400**
7. Move down to view the data table.
8. Press the F8 function key to reflect the data-base changes in the statistical table.

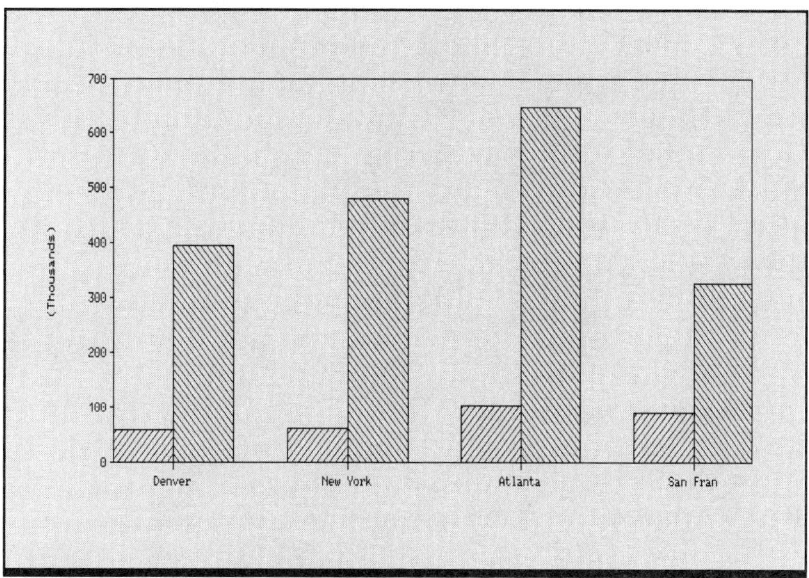

Figure 51.1: *Graph with Specified Ranges*

9. Press the F10 (Graph) function key. The changes in the salary totals for San Francisco and Atlanta are reflected in the graph.

10. **Save** the worksheet as **TABLE1** again. **Replace** the old version with the new.

123

Chapter Five

MACROS

52 Building a Simple Macro

FEATURING:

Macro names, special keys, macro commands, and custom menus

Keyboard macros enable you to program 1-2-3 to accomplish tasks automatically. Simply stated, programming can be considered as writing a series of instructions that are automatically initiated one after the other. Once these instructions are stored in a macro, you can use them any time.

In 1-2-3, these instructions accomplish anything that you can accomplish by typing instructions at the keyboard. You might use a macro to copy ranges of cells, to erase numbers, or to save a file. Because they save keystrokes, macros are also called the *typing alternative.*

In addition to completing tasks normally completed by typing, you can create a macro to do special commands. For example, macros can make decisions based on whether or not certain criteria are fulfilled. Or, you could create a macro that displays your own customized command menu that would appear each time you retrieve a worksheet and would guide you and others in using the worksheet for specific needs, leaving no room for error. Your own menu might include entering data, viewing a graph, printing a report, and querying for information—and might look like the one in Figure 52.1.

```
A1: 'EMPLOYEE                                                        MENU
DATA ENTRY  GRAPH  PRINT  QUERY  QUIT
Enter data into Database
      A            B           C            D            E          F
1   EMPLOYEE     STORE       DEPT        SALARY        SALES     RATING
2   Stein, S.    Denver      Admin        13800            0
3   Nash, J.     New York    Admin        18600            0
4   Tanzer, H.   Atlanta     Admin        14400            0
5   Esposito, S.San Fran     Manag        34600       111000
6   Raney, J.    San Fran    Admin        13000            0
7   Leung, L.    Atlanta     Sales        25400       260000          1
8   Kane, L.     New York    Sales        20000       249000          2
9   Hoch, T.     Atlanta     Sales        23300       235000          3
10  Badran, M.   New York    Sales        22600       231000          4
11  Lehman, A.   San Fran    Sales        22900       216000          5
12  Gold, A.     Denver      Sales        26600       210000          6
13  Ormsby, E.   Denver      Sales        19400       187000          7
14  Temes, N.    Atlanta     Sales        19400       153000          8
15
16
17  EMPLOYEE     STORE       DEPT        SALARY        SALES     RATING
18               Atlanta
19               New York
20
28-Sep-86  04:18 PM                  CMD
```

Figure 52.1: *Customized 1-2-3 Menu*

Whenever there is a series of frequently used instructions, you can create a macro. However, you might also want to create one if the instructions aren't frequently used, but are many and complicated.

Three steps are necessary to set up and use a macro: entering the macro as a label on the worksheet, assigning a name to the first cell of the macro, and initiating the macro—or putting it into action. It is also a good idea to document macros for future reference.

Macros are stored in cells on the worksheet. For example, to use a macro that would erase one cell, you would enter the following on the worksheet:

'/R E~

The label prefix is necessary because the macro is a label beginning with a slash. Whenever macros begin with a slash or a number, they must be preceded by a label prefix. The slash is the symbol for command, and **RE** represents the **Range Erase** command. The tilde (~) represents the Enter key. Thus, all of the characters after the label prefix represent what you would type at the keyboard to erase a cell.

All the function and pointer-movement keys can be used when creating macros. All you have to do is enclose them in brackets. This is covered in Section 53.

Long macros are entered one instruction after the other down a column. Even if a macro is not long, you can break it up at any point and continue entering it in the next cell down. Blank cells signify the end of a macro. The preceding macro could also be entered as:

'/R
E~

Once a macro is entered on the worksheet, it should be documented. This way, when you refer to the worksheet at a later date, you will know what the macro is called and what it accomplishes. Comments can be placed to the right or left of each macro.

Name the macro with a backslash (\) followed by a single letter, one that relates to the function, such as **E** for **Erase**. There are 27 possible macros on a worksheet: the letters of the alphabet, plus the zero. When you name a macro, use the **Range Name Create** command, then the left slash (\) followed by a single letter or a zero.

Even if a macro takes up more than one cell, only the first cell needs to be named. Once named, you initiate the macro by holding down the Alt key on the left side of the keyboard and tapping the macro's letter name. The backslash (\) in the macro's name represents the Alt key.

To interrupt a macro once it has been executed, hold down the **Ctrl** key and tap the **Break** key located at the top right of the keyboard. This will return you to the **READY** mode.

How to Use Macros

To erase a cell using a simple macro

1. Retrieve the file **87BUDGET**. If you've forgotten what it looks like, refer to section 25 for a complete picture of the worksheet.
2. Move to column AB, row 1. This is the 28th column after the end of A-Z. It's wise to place your macros outside the worksheet area. Column AB is a common area; it is not so far away that it will take up a lot of memory in your computer, nor is it so close that it will prevent you from expanding your worksheet. You can move macros later if you need to.
3. In AB1, type:

   '/RE~

   Remember the label-prefix.
4. Press Enter.

5. To name the macro, press the slash (**/**) key and select **Range Name Create.**
6. Specify the name as **E**, press Enter, then the range as **AB1**.
7. To initiate the macro, move to any cell with information in it. Try B5.
8. Hold down the Alt key, and tap the letter E. The number in B5 is erased.
9. The following steps are not necessary for your macro to operate properly, however they are suggested in order to document your work. They will help to remind you of the macro's name later, especially if you have many.

   In a cell to the left of the macro, type in the name '**E**. Use the apostrophe as a label-prefix. See Figure 52.2.

Building additional macros

10. Try a few more macros. Type in the list below, the macros in column AB, the names in column AA. Use **/Range Name Create** to assign the name on the left to the cell containing the commands on the right. Remember to precede macros that start with a slash with a label-prefix character. Refer to steps 4–7 to enter and name the following macros.

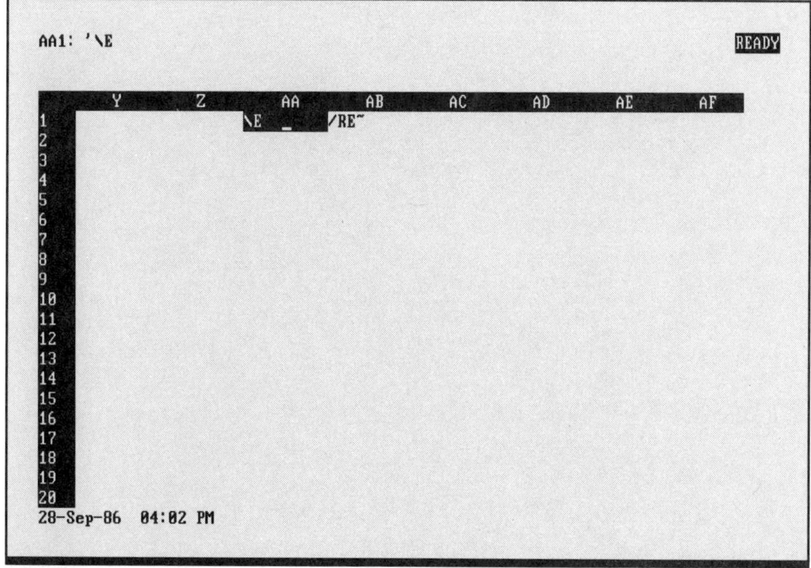

Figure 52.2: *Simple Macro*

To format a cell for **Currency**, with no decimals:

Assign this name	*To this macro*
\F	'/RFC0~~

To change the column width:

\C	'/WCS15~~

To name-stamp a cell:

\N	'General American Consolidated, Inc.~

Use the Alt key with the F, C, or N keys to execute the macros once you have used **/Range Name Create** to name each one.

53 Using Special Keys in Macros

FEATURING:

@Now,
CALC Key,
Repeating Macros

Lotus allows you to use special keys from the keyboard in macros. This includes all the function keys and the pointer-movement keys. These keys (shown in Figure 53.1) are included in brackets when used in a macro. The macro that follows makes use of some of these.

In version 2.0 of Lotus, to cause a special key macro to repeat, include the number of repetitions in the brackets, i.e. {RIGHT 4}, {PGDN 10}.

How To Build a Date-Stamp Macro Using Special Keys

With a macro you can set up an automatic date-stamp for your worksheets. This is useful for keeping a history of changes to a worksheet. For instance, you can automate a daily log of transactions (phone calls, sales) by creating a macro to automatically stamp today's date next to each transaction entry.

The following macro will stamp the "last update" date on the top of the worksheet into an update cell. Use it to record the current date for future

Type Macro	For Key	Type Macro	For Key
~	Enter	{ESC}	Escape
{DOWN}	Down Arrow	{EDIT}	F2
{UP}	Up Arrow	{NAME}	F3
{LEFT}	Left Arrow	{ABS}	F4
{RIGHT}	Right Arrow	{GOTO}	F5
{PGDN}	Page Down	{WINDOW}	F6
{PGUP}	Page Up	{QUERY}	F7
{END}	End	{TABLE}	F8
{HOME}	Home	{CALC}	F9
{DEL}	Delete	{GRAPH}	F10
{BIGRIGHT}	Ctrl-Right Arrow	{BIGLEFT}	Ctrl-Left Arrow
{BS}	Backspace		

Figure 53.1: *Special Keys for Macros*

reference. It can be separated into several parts. First, a special date function will be used which calculates the current date: **@NOW**. (Use **@TODAY** if you are using Lotus version 1A.) Then the **CALC** key [F9] will be used to change that calculation into a number which will be entered into the worksheet. This will prevent the **@NOW** function (which always displays the current date) from changing the update date when you next retrieve the worksheet. To stamp a new date into the update cell you will need to execute the date-stamp macro. The **Format** command will be used to display the five-digit number as a date.

(Refer to the sections on "Formatting the Entire Worksheet," Section 18, and "Formatting Part of the Worksheet," Section 20, for a further explanation of the Date Format.)

1. When building macros it is best to try it manually first. So . . .

   Move the pointer to cell E1, and type: **@NOW**. Do not press the Enter key yet.

   Note: If you are using Lotus version 1A, type **@TODAY**.

2. Press the **CALC** key [F9]. The number changes into a five-digit number. This number represents today's date: the number of days since January 1, 1900.

3. Press Enter to place the number on the worksheet.

4. Format the number so it will display as today's date. Select **/Range Format Date 1**. The **Range Format Date** commands translate the number created by the date function **@NOW** into a date.

5. If asterisks appear, the column is too narrow. If this happens, select:

   /Worksheet Column Set-width 12

6. Now that you've gone through the procedure manually, use the same keystrokes to build the macro. In a cell in column AB, and below the other macros, type:

   ```
   {HOME}{RIGHT 4}
   '@NOW
   {CALC}~
   '/RFD1~
   '/WCS12~
   ```

   The **{HOME}** and **{RIGHT 4}** will move the pointer first to A1 (with the Home key), then right 4 cells. This will guarantee that the date is always entered in the same cell each time. This is an example of using pointer-movement keys within macros.

   Note: Lotus version 1A does not allow you to specify how many times a pointer-movement command is to repeat, as in: **{RIGHT 4}**. To repeat a macro in version 1A, you must type it in the number of times you want, for instance, **{RIGHT}{RIGHT}{RIGHT}{RIGHT}**.

   The rest of the commands mimic what you typed above. The **@NOW** function is typed and calculated (with the **{CALC}** key), then entered on the worksheet as a number. That number is then translated into a date with the Range Format Date command. Finally the column is widened using Worksheet Column. **{CALC}** is an example of using function keys within macros.

7. Use **/Range Name Create** to name the first cell, containing **{HOME}{RIGHT 4}**, as **\D**. Move the pointer to the cell with **{HOME}{RIGHT 4}**:

   - Select **/Range Name Create.**
   - Type **\D.**

- Press Enter.
- Press Enter again to specify the range.

8. Erase any numbers in cell E1. Execute the macro by pressing Alt D. In the future, pressing Alt D will stamp the worksheet with the last update date.

Obviously, you do not need to format this cell and widen this column each time. In situations where a different cell is to be date-stamped each time—a log or a new worksheet—this is more useful.

54 Using Macro Commands

FEATURING:

Ctrl-Break,
Looping Macros

Lotus 1-2-3's macro capability constitutes an entire programming language in itself. Lotus macros include commands found in programming languages such as Pascal, BASIC and C. Some of the more commonly used commands are listed in Figure 54.1.

In the following steps use the appropriate version of the listed macro command for the version of Lotus 1-2-3 you are working with.

How to Build a "Numeric Keyboard" Macro Using Macro Commands

A common complaint about many PC keyboards is the lack of a numeric keypad that is separate from the pointer-movement keys. The macro that follows solves this problem. It allows you to enter a column of numbers using the more efficient numeric keypad, while the macro automatically moves the pointer down to the next cell after each entry. It also demonstrates a macro that loops or repeats itself, a common procedure in programming.

Version 2.0	Version 1A	Function
{IF}	/XI	If-then-else
{BRANCH ***position***}	/XG	Go to *position*
{QUIT}	/XQ	Quit macro
{MENUBRANCH ***menu***}	/XM	Execute custom menu
{?}	{?}	Halt macro (temporarily)

Figure 54.1: *Commonly used macro commands*

1. Move below the macros you have already created in column AB. Type the following macro:

   {?}
   {DOWN}
   {BRANCH \K}

   When you execute the macro, the first thing it will do (with {?}) is allow you to enter the first number. Use the numeric keypad. (The NumLock key should be locked beforehand.) After you enter the number, the macro will take over by moving down one cell. At that point, the macro loops or starts over with the {BRANCH} command, allowing you to type in the next number. The {BRANCH} command instructs the macro to continue at location \K. Since this is the starting cell of the macro, it repeats. This will continue until you stop the macro with a Ctrl-Break.

   Note: For Lotus 1A, type:

   '/XG\K~ instead of {BRANCH \K}

2. Name the macro. Move to the first cell (containing {?}) and select **/Range Name Create.** Name it as \K.

3. Document the macro by typing the macro name ('\K) in a cell to the left of the first cell. Precede the macro name with a label-prefix.
4. To use the macro, move to a blank range of cells in order to type in a column of numbers starting at the position of the pointer.
5. Turn on the numeric keypad by pressing the NumLock key once. **NUM** will be displayed at the bottom of the screen. This will allow you to use the numeric keypad rather than the numbers along the top of the keyboard.
6. Execute the macro by typing **Alt-K**. The only visible change is the **CMD** displayed on the screen. The macro is in execution waiting for you to type in the first number.
7. Type in **123**, and press Enter. The pointer moves down to the next cell, ready for the next number. You can see that the macro is still in execution by the **CMD** on the screen. Enter several more numbers.
8. To end the macro, hold down the Ctrl key and press Break on the top right of the keyboard.
9. Turn off the NumLock key.

Whenever you are ready to enter a column of numbers, turn on the NumLock key and execute this macro. To build a macro for filling in a row, instead of a column of numbers substitute {**RIGHT**} for {**DOWN**} in the macro.

55 Creating Customized Menus with Macros

Lotus macros allow you to create your own custom menus. Custom menus work similarly to the 1-2-3 menus: they are displayed above the worksheet, and you select choices by moving the pointer or by typing in the first letter of the choice. With your own menus you can further automate your worksheet. For a view of customized menus built with macros, refer to Figure 52.1 and 55.1.

How to Create a Print Menu

You will be creating a menu that allows you to print different parts of the **87BUDGET** worksheet without changing the print range manually. The following steps will also demonstrate the use of **Range Names** in macros.

1. Make sure you are in the **87BUDGET** file. In order to print out different areas of this worksheet, it is best first to assign names to each print range.
   Select **/Range Name Create.**
2. Name the range **MARGIN**. Press Enter.
3. Highlight, or type, cells **A5..F8.**
4. Press Enter to complete the process.
5. Repeat steps 1–3, but this time use the name **EXPENSES** to name the range **A10..F16.**
6. Repeat steps 1–3 again, naming the cell range **A1..G18** as **TOTAL.**
7. Move the pointer two cells below any macros created previously. Type in the following macro in a single cell:

   {MENUBRANCH menu}

   Note: With Lotus 1A, type: **'/XMmenu~**.

{MENUBRANCH menu} instructs 1-2-3 to go to the menu named "menu" and display it above the worksheet. You can then move the pointer to a selection or press the first letter of a selection.

8. In the same cell, use **/Range Name Create** to name the cell containing **{MENUBARNCH menu}** as \P. This is the macro that will call up the print menu.

9. Customized menus are composed of up to eight selections. Each is entered in a separate cell and all are entered in the same row. It is a good idea to start each selection in a menu with a different letter in order to be able to select a choice using the first letter. Refer to Figure 55.1.

   Below each menu selection is a description. Below the description are the actual commands that are executed when that menu selection is chosen.

   Move the pointer two cells down, in order to leave at least one blank cell between the **{MENUBRANCH}** command above and the menu you will create. The blank cell marks the end of the preceding macro. Type the macro in columns, as shown in Figure 55.1

   Note: With Lotus 1A, type:

   '/XG\P~ instead of **{BRANCH \P}**
   '/XQ~ instead of **{QUIT}**

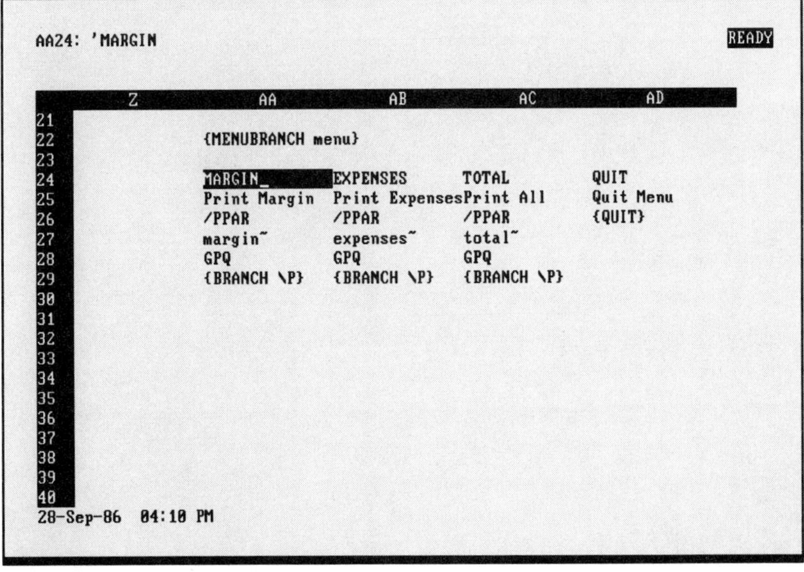

Figure 55.1: *A Print Menu Macro*

10. Use **/Range Name Create** to name the first cell in the menu as **MENU**. The first cell is the first menu item—the cell containing **MARGIN**. When the {**MENUBRANCH**} macro is executed with Alt-P (because it was named **P**), it will, in turn, call up the menu called MENU. After a selection is made, the menu will display itself again; the {**BRANCH \P**} causes it to loop. Selecting **Quit** from the menu will end it. (Ctrl-Break will also end a macro.)
11. Turn on your printer before executing the macro. Then hold down **Alt** and press **P**. The menu is displayed in the Control Panel above the worksheet. Select one of the reports to print. After the report prints, the menu will be displayed again. To stop, select Quit.
12. Save the worksheet under **87BUDGET**.

56 Creating an Automatic Macro

FEATURING:

AUTO123, \0

It is possible to create a macro that will execute automatically whenever you retrieve a worksheet—you don't have to press the Alt key with a letter. For example, in the last exercise you created a macro for a print menu. It might be useful to have this print menu displayed automatically whenever the **87BUDGET** worksheet is retrieved. A special macro name is used for this: **\0**. This is the only time when a number, not a letter, is used for a macro name.

It is also possible to instruct Lotus to retrieve an entire worksheet automatically. Selecting **123** from the Access menu would retrieve the worksheet without using the **File Retrieve** command. This is done by naming a worksheet with a special file name: **AUTO123**. Normally this procedure is most useful in setting up "turnkey" or "fool-proof" systems in Lotus that direct computer users to perform various tasks without the need for extensive knowledge of how to use the program as a whole. These turnkey systems usually consist of extensive custom menus created with macro commands.

In the following steps, you will use both the automatically executed macro (**\0**) and the automatically retrieved file (**AUTO123**).

1. Move the pointer to the cell containing {**MENUBRANCH menu**}.
2. Use **/Range Name Create** to name the print macro as **0**. This is the number zero, not the letter O. This creates the automatically executed macro. The macro has already been named as \P, but it is possible to assign two or more range names to the same macro, or cells. Whenever this worksheet is retrieved the print macro will execute.
3. Now, save the worksheet under a new name: **AUTO123**. Use **/File Save**.
   Whenever you start Lotus 1-2-3 this worksheet will be retrieved automatically. In addition, the print macro will be executed automatically because of the **0** macro name.
4. Try this by selecting **/Quit** to return to the Access menu.
5. Now, from the Access menu, return to the worksheet by selecting **123**. AUTO123 will be retrieved and the print menu will be displayed.
6. When you have completed the previous steps and are satisfied with your knowledge of automating Lotus 1-2-3 macros, erase **AUTO123** using **/File Erase Worksheet**. This will prevent it from being retrieved the next time you start up Lotus 1-2-3.
   (Don't worry, the worksheet is still saved as **87BUDGET**.)

Chapter Six

FUNCTIONS

57

Applying Commonly Used Functions

FEATURING:

@SUM, @AVG, @HLOOKUP, @IF, and @DATE functions

The function @SUM was introduced earlier. However, it is only one of many 1-2-3 formulas that perform specialized calculations. Using @SUM, you were able to save keystrokes by entering @SUM(A1..A6) rather than the entire range of numbers: +A1+A2+A3+A4+A5+A6.

Lotus 1-2-3 functions provide shortcuts when calculating numbers and manipulating labels. In addition to the @SUM function, you can average ranges of numbers with @AVG, do statistics such as standard deviation with @STD, do mathematical functions with @SIN, make decisions with @IF. With Lotus version 2.0, you can now perform "string" manipulation of labels as well. For instance, you can find a label from a list, and you can join two labels from different cells into a third cell.

Below is a list of some of the most commonly used functions: @SUM, @AVG, @HLOOKUP, @IF, and @DATE. In this chapter you will use them to build a worksheet.

@SUM	adds a range of numbers
@AVG	averages a range of numbers

@HLOOKUP	finds a label or value from a table
@IF	makes a choice between two options
@DATE	translates a date to a five-digit number for use in calculations

To learn about other 1-2-3 functions refer to the Lotus User Manual or the Help screens [F1].

How to Use the @HLOOKUP and @AVG Functions

1. Save the current worksheet. Then clear the screen with **Worksheet Erase**. Enter the Monthly Salary Report shown in Figure 57.1.

   The RATING TABLE is necessary in order to calculate the BONUS amounts later. The Bonus Pct figures should be typed in either as **.05** or as **5%**. To display these figures with percent signs, use **Range Format Percent** with 2 decimal places.

2. In cell C15, type the following formula for total salaries:

   @SUM(C9..C13)

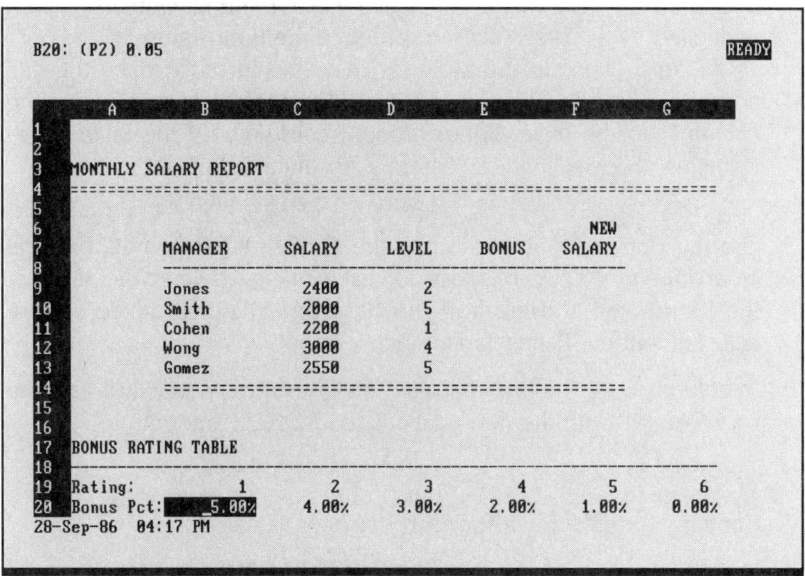

```
B20: (P2) 0.05                                                      READY

     A         B         C         D         E         F         G
1
2
3  MONTHLY SALARY REPORT
4  ==================================================================
5
6                                                      NEW
7            MANAGER      SALARY     LEVEL     BONUS   SALARY
8            ----------------------------------------------
9            Jones          2400        2
10           Smith          2000        5
11           Cohen          2200        1
12           Wong           3000        4
13           Gomez          2550        5
14           ==============================================
15
16
17 BONUS RATING TABLE
18 ------------------------------------------------------------------
19 Rating:           1         2         3         4         5         6
20 Bonus Pct:     5.00%     4.00%     3.00%     2.00%     1.00%     0.00%
28-Sep-86  04:17 PM
```

Figure 57.1: *The Monthly Salary Report*

3. In cell D15, calculate the average of all RATINGS using the following formula:

   @AVG(D9..D13)

4. In the following formula you will use the @HLOOKUP function to search through a table and find the correct Bonus Pct value based on an employee's base salary. The format of this function is:

   @HLOOKUP(*search value,table range,table row*)

   where the *search value* is a manager's salary, the *table range* is the Rating Table below, and the *table row* is the number of rows to search down in the Rating Table. The formula will take the search value (number or label) and scan along the numbers in the first row of the lookup table. When it finds a match, it drops down the designated number of rows and selects the correct value or label. The value or label selected is then used in further calculations above or displayed in the cell of the @HLOOKUP formula.

   In cell E9, type:

   @HLOOKUP(D9,$B$19..$G$20,1)*C9

   In this formula, @HLOOKUP compares the rating located in cell D9 with the Ratings in the first row of the Rating Table located in B19 through G20. When it finds a match, it drops down one row and selects the Bonus Percent for that rating. The Bonus Percent is then multiplied by the base Salary to produce the Bonus amount.

   The dollar signs in the table range in the formula make the cell addresses absolute. This is necessary in order to copy them down the column into the other Bonus amount cells without the table range changing. (See Section 23, "Entering Absolute Formulas.")

   The @VLOOKUP function is used for vertical tables.

5. Use the **Copy** command to copy the @HLOOKUP formula into the other four BONUS cells, once for each manager. Check to see that the Rating cell address and the base SALARY cell address were adjusted, but the Rating Table range was not.

6. In column F for the first manager, enter a formula that will add the base SALARY with the newly calculated BONUS amount.

   +C9+E9

7. Copy the formula down for each manager as well.

8. Use @SUM to build two formulas that will add Bonuses together and New Salaries together. Refer to Figure 57.2.

```
E9: @HLOOKUP(D9,$B$19..$G$20,1)*C9                                    READY

      A          B          C          D          E          F          G
1
2
3   MONTHLY SALARY REPORT
4   ====================================================================
5
6                                                              NEW
7            MANAGER       SALARY      LEVEL      BONUS      SALARY
8            ----------------------------------------------------
9            Jones          2400          2         96         2496
10           Smith          2000          5         20         2020
11           Cohen          2200          1        110         2310
12           Wong           3000          4         60         3060
13           Gomez          2550          5       25.5       2575.5
14           ====================================================
15                         12150        3.4      311.5      12461.5
16
17  BONUS RATING TABLE
18  --------------------------------------------------------------------
19  Rating:              1          2          3          4          5          6
20  Bonus Pct:       5.00%      4.00%      3.00%      2.00%      1.00%      0.00%
28-Sep-86  04:07 PM
```

Figure 57.2: *Worksheet with Lookup Formula*

How to Use the @DATE and @NOW Functions

Date and time functions allow you to perform calculations based on dates and times. With date and time functions you can subtract one date from another, average among dates, add dates, and so on.

Date and time functions generate numbers based on the number of days since the turn of the century (January 1, 1900), or the fraction of the day since midnight. For example, 31697 represents October 12, 1986, and .5 represents noon. These numbers are then displayed in a date or time format with the **Global** or **Range Format** commands, or they are used to calculate differences in days, etc.

To use the @DATE function, follow it with the year, month, and day: **@DATE(87,1,10)**. To use the @TIME function, follow it with the hour, minute, and second: **@TIME(10:10:10)**. @NOW does not require any date or time elements; it generates the current date and time: **@NOW**.

In the following steps you will enter the date-of-hire for each manager, then use it to determine whether a manager is eligible for a bonus. Assuming that a manager must work for two months, or 60 days, before becoming eligible for a bonus, the formula must subtract the hire date from today's date. If a manager has worked more than 60 days, he is included in the lookup operation to calculate his bonus.

9. Move to column A, and widen it with **Worksheet Column** to **12**. This will allow for the date format.
10. In cell A5, type: **@NOW** (**@TODAY** for Lotus 1A). Press Enter. A five-digit number will be displayed representing today's date.
11. Display the number in a date format. Type:

    /Range Format Date

12. Select the **1** date format, then highlight the range from **A5..A13** for the rest of the hire dates. The number will be displayed as a date in the format of DD-MM-YY.

    (If today's date is not displayed, you probably did not enter the correct date when you started your computer. Use the **System** command to exit to DOS. At the DOS prompt, type **DATE** and press Enter. DOS will prompt you for the date. Type the correct date and press Enter. At the DOS prompt type **EXIT** followed by the Enter key to return to 1-2-3.)

13. Now that the column is formatted for dates, enter the hire dates for each manager.

in A9	**@DATE(84,7,12)**
in A10	**@DATE(84,2,11)**
in A11	use the **@DATE** function to type in the date for one month ago, using the format above
in A12	type in the date for one week ago
in A13	type in the date for yesterday

Refer to Figure 57.3.

How to Use the @IF Function

The @IF function allows you to make decisions within formulas. If a condition is true, then do option 1, otherwise do option 2. The format of the @IF function is:

@IF(condition, option 1, option 2)

Use the @IF function in this worksheet to determine whether a manager is eligible for a bonus based on whether his date of hire is 60 days or more from today's date. If a manager's date of hire is fewer than 60 days

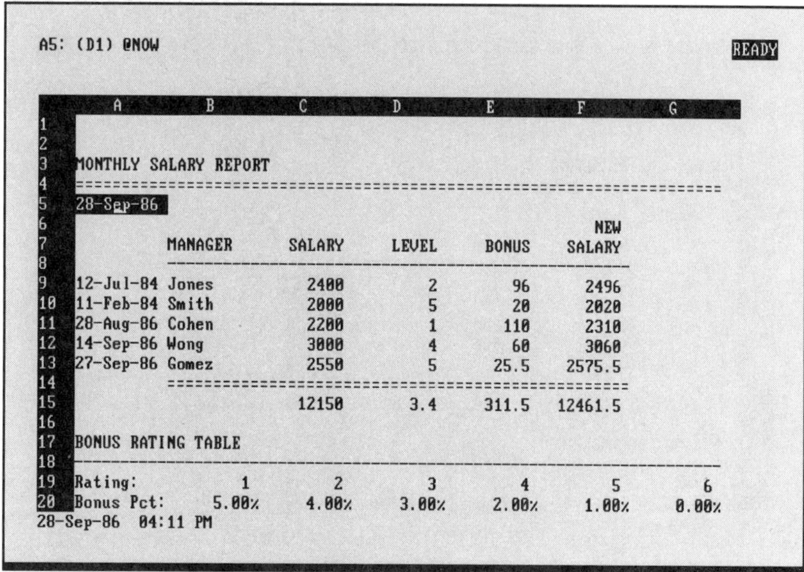

Figure 57.3: *Worksheet with Dates*

from today, then there is no Bonus, otherwise use the @HLOOKUP function to calculate the bonus, as earlier.

14. Use the Edit key, F2, to edit the formula in E9, the first Bonus formula, to read as follows:

    @IF($A$5-A9<60,0,@HLOOKUP(D9,$B$19..$G$20,1)*C9)

    This formula states: If today's date (A5) minus the hire date (A9) is less than 60 days, then the bonus amount is 0, otherwise calculate the Bonus amount by using the @HLOOKUP formula.

    Again, the dollar signs designate today's date as an absolute value. Cell A5, today's date, will not adjust when you copy the formula into the cells below.

15. Copy the formula down into the other manager's bonus cells. The first two managers should have bonuses. The last three have no bonuses since they have not worked more than 60 days. (See Figure 57.4.)

16. Experiment with several other functions:

@MAX(range)	Maximum value in a range
@MIN(range)	Minimum value in a range
@COUNT(range)	Number of non-blank cells in a range

```
E9: @IF($A$5-A9<60,0,@HLOOKUP(D9,$B$19..$G$20,1)*C9)                    READY

        A          B          C          D          E          F          G
1
2
3   MONTHLY SALARY REPORT
4   ======================================================================
5   28-Sep-86
6                                                              NEW
7              MANAGER      SALARY     LEVEL      BONUS      SALARY
8              ----------------------------------------------------
9   12-Jul-84 Jones          2400          2         96        2496
10  11-Feb-84 Smith          2000          5         20        2020
11  28-Aug-86 Cohen          2200          1          0        2200
12  14-Sep-86 Wong           3000          4          0        3000
13  27-Sep-86 Gomez          2550          5          0        2550
14             ====================================================
15                          12150        3.4        116       12266
16
17  BONUS RATING TABLE
18  ----------------------------------------------------------------------
19  Rating:            1          2          3          4          5          6
20  Bonus Pct:     5.00%      4.00%      3.00%      2.00%      1.00%      0.00%
28-Sep-86  04:12 PM
```

Figure 57.4: *Worksheet with @If Formula*

Calculate the maximum and minimum Bonus amounts, and the total count of managers. All three functions are used like @SUM(range).

Using 1-2-3 on Hard-Disk Systems

Because you can store thousands of files on a hard disk, the operating system (DOS 2.0 and higher) for hard-disk computers allows you to divide the disk into *subdirectories.* Subdirectories are separate storage areas on the hard disk, each with its own directory of files, each with its own name.

DOS (2.0 and higher) creates tree structured subdirectories, with the main or root directory branching out into any number of subdirectories, as shown in Figure A.1.

In many ways subdirectories function as separate disks; you transfer files between subdirectories in much the same way that you transfer files from one disk to another.

How do you know if you need a subdirectory? If, for example, you are using more than one program, such as 1-2-3 and a word-processing program, it is a good idea to place each program in a subdirectory. You might also consider doing it if there are a number of people in your office who will be using the computer for different tasks. You could call each subdirectory the name of the person or department responsible for it. Still another reason to create subdirectories might be if there is critical work that needs to be protected. You could place it in a subdirectory to separate it from other users and files.

If you create a subdirectory for the 1-2-3 files, you will need to change the default settings in the program that determine where the worksheet and graph files are stored. This is covered in Section 12 on saving files and Section 43 on printing graphs.

In addition, it is often helpful to create "batch files" to simplify the use of directories, as explained below.

How to Create a Batch File

The following steps will create a batch file named lotus.bat that will switch you automatically to the 123 subdirectory and start 1-2-3 when you type: **Lotus**. Then it will return to the root directory when you **Quit** Lotus. This is especially useful when using 1-2-3 with other programs, to ensure that you always have access to programs from the root directory.

1. Make sure you are in the main, or root, directory of your hard disk. Do this by typing **CD ** at the **C>** prompt.
2. At the **C>** prompt, type:

   COPY CON LOTUS.BAT

3. Press Enter. You will not get a **C>** at this point.
4. Type: **CD \\123**.
5. Press Enter.
6. Type: **Lotus**.
   (To skip the Access menu and go directly to the Lotus 1-2-3 worksheet each time, type **123**. You may do this even without a batch command.)
7. Press Enter.
8. Type: **CD **.
   This will return you to the root directory when you **Quit** Lotus.
9. Press Enter. You should see:

```
C>COPY CON LOTUS.BAT
CD \123
LOTUS
CD \
```

10. Press the F6 function key and press Enter. The Lotus.bat batch file is saved on the hard disk.
11. To execute the batch file, type Lotus.

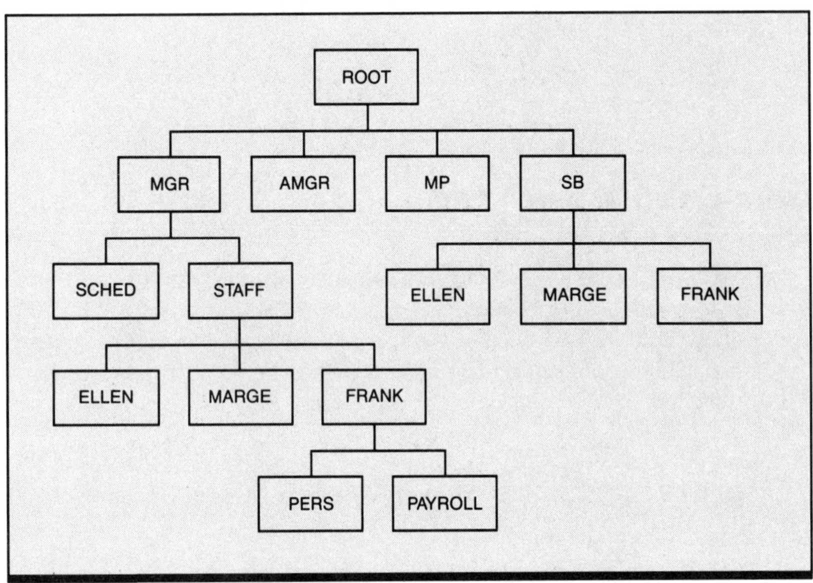

Figure A.1: *Structure of Subdirectories*

INDEX

Selections from The SYBEX Library

Introduction to Computers

THE SYBEX PERSONAL COMPUTER DICTIONARY

120 pp. Ref. 199-3

All the definitions and acronyms of micro computer jargon defined in a handy pocket-sized edition. Includes translations of the most popular terms into ten languages.

FROM CHIPS TO SYSTEMS: AN INTRODUCTION TO MICROPROCESSORS

by Rodnay Zaks

552 pp., 400 illustr., Ref. 063-6

A simple and comprehensive introduction to microprocessors from both a hardware and software standpoint: what they are, how they operate, how to assemble them into a complete system.

Software Specific

SPREADSHEETS

MASTERING SUPERCALC 3

by Greg Harvey

300 pp., illustr., Ref. 312-0

Featuring Version 2.1, this title offers full coverage of all the sophisticated features of this third generation spreadsheet, including spreadsheet, graphics, database and advanced techniques.

DOING BUSINESS WITH MULTIPLAN

by Richard Allen King and Stanley R. Trost

250 pp., illustr., Ref. 148-9

This book will show you how using Multiplan can be nearly as easy as learning to use a pocket calculator. It presents a collection of templates for business applications.

MULTIPLAN ON THE COMMODORE 64

by Richard Allen King

250 pp., illustr. Ref. 231-0

This clear, straightforward guide will give you a firm grasp on Multiplan's function, as well as provide a collection of useful template programs.

WORD PROCESSING

PRACTICAL WORDSTAR USES

by Julie Anne Arca

303 pp., illustr. Ref. 107-1

Pick your most time-consuming office tasks and this book will show you how to streamline them with WordStar.

THE COMPLETE GUIDE TO MULTIMATE

by Carol Holcomb Dreger

250 pp., illustr. Ref. 229-9

A concise introduction to the many practical applications of this powerful word processing program.

THE THINKTANK BOOK

by Jonathan Kamin

200 pp., illustr., Ref. 224-8

Learn how the ThinkTank program can help you organize your thoughts, plans and activities.

PRACTICAL MULTIMATE USES
by Chris Gilbert
275 pp., illustr., Ref. 276-0
Includes an overview followed by practical business techniques, this covers documentation, formatting, tables, and Key Procedures.

MASTERING WORDSTAR ON THE IBM PC
by Arthur Naiman
200 pp., illustr., Ref. 250-7
The classic Introduction to WordStar is now specially presented for the IBM PC, complete with margin-flagged keys and other valuable quick-reference tools.

MASTERING MS WORD
by Mathew Holtz
365 pp., illustr., Ref. 285-X
This clearly-written guide to MS WORD begins by teaching fundamentals quickly and then putting them to use right away. Covers material useful to new and experienced word processors.

PRACTICAL TECHNIQUES IN MS WORD
by Alan R. Neibauer
300 pp., illustr., Ref. 316-3
This book expands into the full power of MS WORD, stressing techniques and procedures to streamline document preparation, including specialized uses such as financial documents and even graphics.

INTRODUCTION TO WORDSTAR 2000
by David Kolodnay and Thomas Blackadar
292 pp., illustr., Ref. 270-1
This book covers all the essential features of WordStar 2000 for both beginners and former WordStar users.

PRACTICAL TECHNIQUES IN WORDSTAR 2000
by John Donovan
250 pp., illustr., Ref. 272-8
Featuring WordStar 2000 Release 2, this book presents task-oriented tutorials that get to the heart of practical business solutions.

MASTERING THINKTANK ON THE 512K MACINTOSH
by Jonathan Kamin
264 pp., illustr., Ref. 305-8
Idea-processing at your fingertips: from basic to advanced applications, including answers to the technical question most frequently asked by users.

DATABASE MANAGEMENT SYSTEMS

UNDERSTANDING dBASE III PLUS
by Alan Simpson
415 pp., illustr., Ref. 349-X
Emphasizing the new PLUS features, this extensive volume gives the database terminology, program management, techniques, and applications. There are hints on file-handling, debugging, avoiding syntax errors.

UNDERSTANDING dBASE III
by Alan Simpson
250 pp., illustr., Ref. 267-1
The basics and more, for beginners and intermediate users of dBASEIII. This presents mailing label systems, bookkeeping and data management at your fingertips.

ADVANCED TECHNIQUES IN dBASE III
by Alan Simpson
505 pp., illustr., Ref. 282-5
Intermediate to experienced users are given the best database design techniques, the primary focus being the development of user-friendly, customized programs.

MASTERING dBASE III: A STRUCTURED APPROACH
by Carl Townsend
338 pp., illustr., Ref. 301-5
Emphasized throughout is the highly successful structured design technique for constructing reliable and flexible applications, from getting started to advanced techniques. A general ledger program is used as the primary illustration for the examples.

UNDERSTANDING dBASE II

by Alan Simpson

260 pp., illustr., Ref. 147-0

Learn programming techniques for mailing label systems, bookkeeping, and data management, as well as ways to interface dBASE II with other software systems.

ADVANCED TECHNIQUES IN dBASE II

by Alan Simpson

395 pp., illustr. Ref., 228-0

Learn to use dBASE II for accounts receivable, recording business income and expenses, keeping personal records and mailing lists, and much more.

INTEGRATED SOFTWARE

MASTERING 1-2-3

by Carolyn Jorgensen

420 pp., illustr., Ref. 337-6

This book goes way beyond using 1-2-3, adding powerful business examples and tutorials to thorough explanations of the program's complex features. Detailing multiple functions, powerful commands, graphics and database capabilities, macros, and add-on product support from Report Writer, Spotlight, and The Cambridge Spread-sheet Analyst. Includes Release 2.

SIMPSON'S 1-2-3 MACRO LIBRARY

by Alan Simpson

300 pp., illustr., Ref. 314-7

This book provides many programming techniques, macro examples, and entire menu-driven systems that demonstrate the full potential of macros. The full power of 1-2-3 version 2 is laid out in powerful, time-saving business solutions developed by bestselling author Alan Simpson.

ADVANCED BUSINESS MODELS WITH 1-2-3

by Stanley R. Trost

250 pp., illustr., Ref. 159-4

If you are a business professional using the 1-2-3 software package, you will find the spreadsheet and graphics models provided in this book easy to use "as is" in everyday business situations.

MASTERING SYMPHONY

by Douglas Cobb (2nd Ed)

763 pp., illustr., Ref. 224-8

This bestselling book has been heralded as the Symphony bible, and provides all the information you will need to put Symphony to work for you right away. Packed with practical models for the business user. Includes Version 1.1.

ANDERSEN'S SYMPHONY TIPS & TRICKS

by Dick Andersen and Janet McBeen

325 pp., illustr. Ref. 342-2

Organized as a reference tool, this book gives shortcuts for using Symphony commands and functions, with troubleshooting advice.

BETTER SYMPHONY SPREADSHEETS

by Carl Townsend

287 pp., illustr., Ref. 339-2

For Symphony users who want to gain real expertise in the use of the spreadsheet features, this has hundreds of tips and techniques. There are also instructions on how to implement some of the special features of Excel on Symphony.

MASTERING FRAMEWORK

by Doug Hergert

450 pp., illustr. Ref. 248-5

This tutorial guides the beginning user through all the functions and features of this integrated software package, geared to the business environment.

ADVANCED TECHNIQUES IN FRAMEWORK

by Alan Simpson

250 pp., illustr. Ref. 257-4

In order to begin customizing your own models with Framework, you'll need a thorough knowledge of Fred programming language, and this book provides this information in a complete, well-organized form.